# PANZERS
# IN NORMANDY

# The Stackpole Military History Series

**THE AMERICAN
CIVIL WAR**
Cavalry Raids of the
   Civil War
Ghost, Thunderbolt, and
   Wizard
Pickett's Charge
Witness to Gettysburg

**WORLD WAR I**
Doughboy War

**WORLD WAR II**
Armor Battles of the
   Waffen-SS, 1943–45
Armoured Guardsmen
Army of the West
Australian Commandos
The B-24 in China
Backwater War
The Battle of Sicily
Beyond the Beachhead
The Brandenburger
   Commandos
The Brigade
Bringing the Thunder
Coast Watching in
   World War II
Colossal Cracks
A Dangerous Assignment
D-Day Deception
D-Day to Berlin
Destination Normandy
Dive Bomber!
A Drop Too Many
Eagles of the Third Reich
Eastern Front Combat
Exit Rommel
Fist from the Sky
Flying American Combat
   Aircraft of World War II
Forging the Thunderbolt
Fortress France
The German Defeat in the
   East, 1944–45
German Order of Battle, Vol. 1
German Order of Battle, Vol. 2
German Order of Battle, Vol. 3
The Germans in Normandy
Germany's Panzer Arm in
   World War II
GI Ingenuity

Goodwood
The Great Ships
Grenadiers
Hitler's Nemesis
Infantry Aces
Iron Arm
Iron Knights
Kampfgruppe Peiper at the
   Battle of the Bulge
Kursk
Luftwaffe Aces
Massacre at Tobruk
Mechanized Juggernaut or
   Military Anachronism?
Messerschmitts over Sicily
Michael Wittmann, Vol. 1
Michael Wittmann, Vol. 2
Mountain Warriors
The Nazi Rocketeers
On the Canal
Operation Mercury
Packs On!
Panzer Aces
Panzer Aces II
Panzer Commanders of the
   Western Front
The Panzer Legions
Panzers in Normandy
Panzers in Winter
The Path to Blitzkrieg
Penalty Strike
Red Star under the Baltic
Retreat to the Reich
Rommel's Desert Commanders
Rommel's Desert War
Rommel's Lieutenants
The Savage Sky
A Soldier in the Cockpit
Soviet Blitzkrieg
Stalin's Keys to Victory
Surviving Bataan and
   Beyond
T-34 in Action
Tank Tactics
Tigers in the Mud
Triumphant Fox
The 12th SS, Vol. 1
The 12th SS, Vol. 2
The War against Rommel's
   Supply Lines
War in the Aegean
Wolfpack Warriors

**THE COLD WAR /
VIETNAM**
Cyclops in the Jungle
Expendable Warriors
Flying American Combat
   Aircraft: The Cold War
Here There Are Tigers
Land with No Sun
Phantom Reflections
Street without Joy
Through the Valley

**WARS OF THE MIDDLE
EAST**
Never-Ending Conflict

**GENERAL MILITARY
HISTORY**
Carriers in Combat
Desert Battles
Guerrilla Warfare

# PANZERS IN NORMANDY

General Hans Eberbach and the German
Defense of France, July–August 1944

Samuel W. Mitcham, Jr.

STACKPOLE
BOOKS

Published by
STACKPOLE BOOKS
5067 Ritter Road
Mechanicsburg, PA 17055
www.stackpolebooks.com

*Cover design by Tracy Patterson*

Printed in the United States of America

10  9  8  7  6  5  4  3  2  1

FIRST EDITION

**Library of Congress Cataloging-in-Publication Data**

Mitcham, Samuel W.
Panzers in Normandy : General Hans Eberbach and the German defense of France, July–August 1944 / Samuel W. Mitcham, Jr.
    p. cm. — (Stackpole military history series)
Includes bibliographical references and index.
ISBN 978-0-8117-3553-7
1. World War, 1939–1945—Campaigns—France—Normandy. 2. Eberbach, Heinrich, 1895–1992. 3. World War, 1939–1945—Tank warfare. 4. Germany. Heer—Armored troops—History—20th century. I. Title.
D756.N6M58 2009
940.54'21421—dc22
                                              2008025754

# Contents

# Introduction

The earth shakes under the impact of thousands of tons of bombs, dropped by swarms of Allied bombers and fighter-bombers. In the distance is the roar of a thousand artillery pieces, mortars, and even naval gunfire—all Anglo-Canadian. The German front is pounded again and again. The great British offensive is about to begin.

At the edge of the hedgerows, hidden in the bushes and under the camouflaged netting, are a handful of worn-out tanks, backed by a few hundred army and SS infantrymen—all Germany has left to check the vast Allied attack.

Outnumbered three to one in men, five to one in tanks, six to one in guns, and by an infinite number in the air, the German *Wehrmacht* would seem to have no chance against the overwhelming Allied might—and it wouldn't, either, were it not for the incredibly efficient and self-confident commander, barking his final orders to his leaders from his forward command post.

Hans Eberbach, commander in chief of the 5th Panzer Army and *die General der Panzertruppen*, the general of panzer troops, was the embodiment of the only two categories in which the Germans outshone the enemy: brains and experience. He would even have been handsome, except that he had no nose, the result of an encounter he lost with a French rifleman in 1915. Even this he turned into a victory of sorts, however, because he married his nurse and became a devoted husband and father for decades.

Chief lieutenant of the Desert Fox in Normandy, almost a son to "father of the *blitzkrieg*," Heinz Guderian, and better trained than anyone else, Eberbach was a pioneer in the employment of motorized formations as early as 1920—fifteen years before the creation of the *Panzer-waffe*, the armored branch. He fought in most campaigns of the war. He helped crush Poland in five weeks and overran France in six, assisted in the destruction of the Belgian Army, and helped push the British Expeditionary Force back into the sea in 1940. Along with a few others, he built the 4th Panzer Division, and then led it on the Eastern Front, where it became the most decorated unit in the German Army. Eberbach led a panzer corps after the Stalingrad debacle, and he was largely responsible for stabilizing the Eastern Front after Germany lost a quarter of a million men on the Volga. Recalled to Berlin, he became deputy chief of the Panzer Inspectorate, technical adviser, and chief troubleshooter for General Guderian at a time when Germany was producing some of the best tanks of World War II, including the Tiger and the Panther. Finally, in 1944, he was sent to Normandy, where the dam seemed about to break. With a single understrength army, he was given the task of checking Montgomery's entire army group and preventing it from breaking out into the interior of France.

Though highly respected by friends, foes, SS men, and anti-Hitler conspirators during World War II, he has been almost forgotten by historians today, but in 1944, all eyes turned to him to check the British and Canadian armies in the *bocage* country of Normandy and the plains south of the invasion beaches. And in spite of their material superiority, he did beat back the great Allied offensive—just as he had done the time before that, and the time before that, and the time before that.

This is the story of a panzer general. The main source for this book is Eberbach's own unpublished papers, written when he was a prisoner of war. Unfortunately, this officer and gentleman did not choose to write his memoirs after the war, opting instead to devote the rest of his life to evangelical Christian charities. He was ninety-six years old when he died in bed.

✠

In addition to General Eberbach, I wish to thank the usual people for helping me write this book: my wife, Donna, and my son and daughter, Gavin and Lacy. Thanks also to Melinda Mathews, the chief interlibrary loan librarian at the University of Louisiana at Monroe, which is known throughout the world as "Cambridge on the Bayou." I am also grateful to Theodor-Friedrich von Stauffenberg, cousin of the leader of the anti-Hitler conspiracy, who sent me his papers shortly before he died in 1989. They provided many insights into the career and character of Hans Eberbach. Any mistakes found herein are mine alone.

# CHAPTER 1

# The Making of a Panzer General

Heinrich Karl Alfons Willy "Hans" Eberbach was born in Stuttgart, Germany, in the old kingdom of Wuerttemberg, on November 24, 1895. His father, also named Heinrich Eberbach, was a prominent businessman. After the senior Eberbach died of pneumonia on April 14, 1905, Hans's widowed mother, Frieda, remarried one of the partners in her husband's firm, Karl Hoehne, the following year. Both were killed in an accident on November 10, 1907, leaving the twelve-year-old Hans a ward of the firm, which speedily placed him in a senior boarding school.

As the nation drifted toward war in the summer of 1914, the nineteen-year-old orphan was filled with patriotic enthusiasm. He enlisted in the Royal Wuerttemberg 10th Guards Regiment (the 180th Infantry Regiment of the Imperial Army) as a *Fahnenjunker* (officer-cadet) on July 1, 1914.[1] Initially, he was assigned to the 3rd Company, where he began his training. On August 3, he was transferred to the 180th Replacement Battalion, where he finished his short basic training and then was shipped to the front. He first saw action in Belgium on August 28 as a member of the 180th Infantry Regiment. He was promoted to *Fahnenjunker-Gefreiter* (equivalent in rank to a corporal) on October 8 and was advanced to *Fahnenjunker-Unteroffizier* (sergeant) nine days later. He was patented as a *Leutnant* (second lieutenant) on February 25, 1915, retroactive to June 23, 1913. (See Appendix A for a Table of Comparative Ranks.) The spirited young officer was given command of a platoon in the 8th Company of the 122nd Reserve Infantry Regiment (8./122nd Reserve) on May 15, 1915.

In action during the summer and early fall of 1915, Eberbach earned the Iron Cross, 2nd Class. On September 25, however, he was severely wounded in the face, when an enemy rifleman shot his nose off, and was captured by the French. Partially because of his wound, he was repatriated to a hospital in Constance, Switzerland, in December 1916 and remained there until he returned to Germany during a prisoner exchange on September 4, 1917. The terrible conditions of the prison camps had badly undermined his health, and he was unable to resume duty right away. He was sent to a convalescent home in Tuebingen, where his nose was partially rebuilt. It never was right again, however, and he avoided having photographs taken of his profile whenever possible.

In Tuebingen, he was cared for by nursing sister Anna Lempp, a girlfriend from his youth, whom he later married. Meanwhile, he was assigned to the replacement battalion of the 122nd Infantry Regiment.[2] On January 11, 1918, he resumed field duty as a platoon leader in 10th Company of the 116th Infantry Regiment, part of the German Army in Macedonia.

Eberbach was transferred to Turkey that summer and appointed a liaison officer to the Turkish 8th Army in Palestine on June 1. He fought in the battles in Palestine later that year and about this same time was awarded the Iron Cross, 1st Class. On September 20, he was given command of the rear guard of the Turkish Army during the retreat from Palestine but was captured by the British three days later. On October 18, his promotion to *Oberleutnant* (first lieutenant) came through, although he did not learn of it for some time.[3]

Eberbach spent the next year languishing in POW camps. He was finally released on November 16, 1919, and returned to Stuttgart, where he was sent to the processing office of the skeleton 180th Infantry Regiment. He promptly proceeded to volunteer for the Wuerttemberg government's defense forces but was quickly informed that despite his solid record, he would not be selected for the peacetime army, which was called the *Reichsheer*. (Under the terms of the Treaty of Versailles, which ended World War I, Germany was allowed an army of only 100,000 men, of which only 4,000 could be officers. It had more than 32,000 officers when the war ended.) Instead, Eberbach was encouraged to enter the Wuerttemberger State Police force, which he did on December 13. He was posted to the state police headquarters at Esslingen, where on January 30, 1920, he was confirmed as a first lieutenant of police and officially discharged from the army.

On March 11, 1920, he married Anna Lempp, and the couple moved into a house on the main highway between Esslingen and Stuttgart. His abilities in the law enforcement service during the tense series of crises in the early days of the republic were rewarded on March 1, 1921, when he was promoted to captain of police. Like another young ex-army officer who had also transferred to the state police service in Silesia, Willibald Borowietz, Captain Eberbach undertook to equip his units with motor vehicles and motorcycles.[4] Between February 28 and March 16, he took a strenuous course in athletic fitness, and he now put his men through rigorous paramilitary training, with special emphasis on crowd and riot control.

Eberbach's first son, Heinz, was born at the Stuttgart Gynoceum on July 2, 1921, an event which elated him. He was to have two more sons: Wolfram, born on February 28, 1924, and Gottfried, born on January 10, 1930. The year after Heinz's birth, on June 13, 1922, Eberbach was sent to the Police Training Academy. He completed a course in command on July 19, whereupon he took over the duties of adjutant to the commander at Esslingen, an assignment he held until 1925. By this time, his abilities had attracted the attention of the Central Police Command of the Weimar Republic,[5] and he was ordered to take over the police academy itself, a post he assumed on May 8, 1925. He thus became the man most responsible for training police officials for a wide area and, in particular, for proficiency in the use of motor vehicles—cars, armored cars, and motorcycles.

With the rise of the National Socialist state in 1933, the police forces of Germany were centralized under the police president of Prussia, Hermann Goering. In appreciation of his work, Eberbach was promoted to major of *Schutzpolizei* (state police) on June 1 of that year and continued in his training command. As the new regime began to expand the *Reichswehr*, however, Hans began to look longingly at his former career. Police work did not hold the potential he began to see in the armed forces. He therefore wrote several letters to the *Reichswehrministerium* (Reich Defense Ministry) in Berlin, to people he had known during the war. Meanwhile, on April 1, 1935, he was named chief of the Organizational Department of the Reich *Landespolizei* Staff in the Ministry of Interior in Berlin. That summer, however, his efforts to rejoin the military bore fruit. The Army Personnel Office resurrected his service record and restored him to the active list on August 1, with the rank of major, retroactive to January 1.

Eberbach was initially posted to Motorized Battalion "Doeberitz" at the Infantry School at Doeberitz, near Berlin. On September 20, he was detached to Motorized Battalion "Schwerin," in Mecklenburg, and on October 15, he was named as commander of the 12th Anti-Tank Battalion (*Panzer Abwehr Abteilung 12*), which was also stationed at Schwerin in Pomerania, in the II Military District (*Wehrkreis II*).[6] It was part of the newly formed 12th Infantry Division, then commanded by Maj. Gen. Alexander Ulex.[7]

Eberbach had had only negligible association with artillery of any sort, but he was keenly interested in the towed field pieces of this unit and rapidly mastered the art of gunnery. He continued to improve his military education by taking the signals course for commanders of motorized combat troops at the Signals School at Halle/Saale in late 1935. He also attended the brief sports course for staff officers at the Army Sports School at Wuensdorf in October 1936 and did a period of detached duty with the 6th Panzer Regiment of the 3rd Panzer Division that fall, in order to learn more about armored operations.

In Berlin, meanwhile, the staff of the recently created Panzer Inspectorate had been meticulously searching for officers with some mechanized background, and Eberbach's name surfaced in mid-1937. On October 1, he was routinely promoted to lieutenant colonel and was summoned to the Bendlerstrasse by Col. Heinz Guderian.[8] Needless to say, Hans was delighted at the opportunity to don the pink *Waffenfarbe* of the panzers and resume service with motorized troops. His year and a half with antitank guns was also to stand him in good stead. Eberbach spent the first eight months of 1938 alternately with the Panzer Inspectorate and on liaison duty with the three active panzer divisions. He accompanied the 2nd Panzer Division in its triumphant, if accident-ridden, march into Austria in March.

On October 1, Eberbach's fondest wish came true: The War Ministry authorized the creation of a new panzer division, the 4th, to be headquartered at the old garrison city of Wuerzburg, the former base of the 2nd Panzer Division. On October 10, the lieutenant colonel reported to Maj. Gen. Georg Reinhardt, the divisional commander,[9] and Maj. Gen. Max von Hartlieb genannt Walsporn, the commander of the 5th Panzer Brigade.[10] He was to command the 35th Panzer Regiment, which, with the 36th, made up the armored fist of this powerful formation.

The next six months were some of the busiest and most exacting of his life. Training and equipping the units constituting the regiment (within the divisional and brigade framework) were hurried along by the omnipresent threat of the coming war. During this time, Eberbach became close personal friends with Capt. Meinrad von Lauchert, who came to regard him as a father figure.[11] Their wives also developed a special friendship and worked closely together in the wives' club of the 35th Panzer Regiment. Both of the Laucherts called Eberbach "der Schnulch," a playful, nonsensical nickname with no real meaning.[12] Lauchert later gained fame as the commander of the 2nd Panzer Division during the Battle of the Bulge.

Meanwhile, on February 4, 1938, Hitler had established what essentially became the German command structure for the next war. He dismissed Col. Gen. Werner von Fritsch, the commander in chief of the army; forced the war minister, Field Marshal Werner von Blomberg, into retirement; named himself supreme commander of the armed forces; and abolished the War Ministry, replacing it with *Oberkommando der Wehrmacht* (OKW), the High Command of the *Wehrmacht*, under Col. Gen. (later Field Marshal) Wilhelm Keitel.[13] Theoretically, OKW also directed the *Luftwaffe* (air force) and navy, but Hermann Goering, commander in chief of the *Luftwaffe*, quickly informed Keitel that the *Luftwaffe* would be independent of OKW, and there was nothing Keitel could do about it. The navy also maintained its corporate independence, although its commander in chief expressed himself in more diplomatic terms than Goering. Also established on February 4 was *Oberkommando des Heeres* (OKH), the High Command of the Army, under Col. Gen. Walter von Brauchitsch. By 1944, OKH would be responsible for the Eastern Front and OKW would have hegemony over all other sectors, but this is getting ahead of the story.

On June 1, 1939, Eberbach was promoted to colonel. Although his good friend Hermann Breith, commander of the 36th Panzer Regiment, was longer in service, Breith was not promoted until September 1.[14]

The division was activated in July and moved toward the Polish frontier. It was part of Gen. of Cavalry Erich Hoepner's XVI Motorized Corps under Col. Gen. Walter von Reichenau's 10th Army (Map 1.1).[15] On September 1, the German armies rolled into Poland, and the 4th Panzer moved rapidly across southern Poland, spearheading the drive.

The Poles fought doggedly but were terribly overmatched, and by September 12, the campaign was basically over. Though the 4th Panzer Division as a whole had performed well, the officers were not too well pleased with the numerous errors and mix-ups that had occurred.

On September 23, Eberbach received the clasp to his Iron Cross, 2nd Class, and on October 2, he also got the clasp to the Iron Cross, 1st Class, as did his friend Hermann Breith. The division now returned to Wurzburg for refitting. Eberbach at this point wrote a quick note to General Guderian in Berlin, praising the general's oldest son, Heinz, a lieutenant and Eberbach's regimental adjutant, whose bravery in the campaign had earned him the Iron Cross, 2nd and 1st Classes.

After a quiet Christmas with his family in Esslingen, the colonel led his regiment in its move to the Western Front opposite the Belgian-Dutch frontier at Maastricht. Again the 4th Panzer was under the command of Hoepner's XVI Corps, but General Reinhardt had been replaced in April 1940 by Maj. Gen. Hajo Stever, an old-time panzer man but unfortunately afflicted with a recurring illness.[16]

During the early spring of 1940, while continuous exercises were carried out to prepare for the upcoming campaign. Col. Hermann Breith had been promoted to the command of the panzer brigade. So close were he and Eberbach that the issue of seniority was not even raised, and Hans loyally supported his friend in his new post. In fact, to justify Breith's assignment, the Army Pesonnel Office made his promotion to colonel retroactive to August 1, 1937.

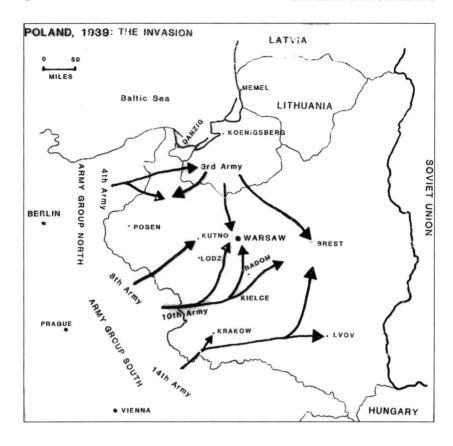

POLAND, 1939: THE INVASION

On May 10, the XVI Corps crashed across the Dutch frontier and seized the critical Dutch frontier city of Maastricht on the very first day. On May 11 and 12, the corps fought the battle of Hannut, defeating the French forces of General Prioux and forcing them to fall back to the line of the Dyle River. The 3rd and 4th Panzer Divisions swept southwest toward Valenciennes, effectively isolating the Netherlands and bypassing some major Allied formations. By the twenty-third, both were lined up to assault the encircled seaport of Dunkirk—an assault that never took place. Instead, the corps was pulled back to Amiens for refitting. Regrettably, Breith had been wounded on May 22, and the acting command of the brigade devolved on Eberbach.

All in all, the 5th Panzer Brigade had suffered negligible losses. Its three senior officers—Breith, Eberbach, and Colonel Jesser of the 36th Panzer Regiment—had handled it perfectly, but with lifesaving caution as well.[17] All three were subsequently awarded the Panzer Battle Badge in silver for their exploits, receiving this decoration on June 20.

Still under Hoepner's XVI Corps, the divisions were moved up to the Meuse as part of Ewald von Kleist's panzer group.[18] The renewed attack on the French "Weygand" line along the Meuse was temporarily checked by the French in the Peronne sector. The German forces, which attempted to seize a bridgehead with infantry, had their armor badly mauled by the French artillery. General Stever was ailing, though staying at his post, and much of the responsibility of command devolved on Col. Baron Hans von Boineburg-Lengsfeld, the commander of the divisional rifle brigade, and on Eberbach. They attempted to suggest to Kleist a more intelligent method of attack, but the confusion was so great that nothing could be accomplished.

At length, the XVI Corps was ordered to Chateau Porcien, to avail itself of the crossings already made by the divisions of Guderian's group. Once into open country, the panzers charged southward, reaching Dijon by June 20—the day the badges arrived for the three colonels. By June 24, France had sued for an armistice, and the division settled down to a short rest in the sunny countryside.

Orders arrived on July 1 for the 4th Panzer to move up into Belgium for semipermanent cantonment in the Pas de Calais. It was to be part of the force preparing for the invasion of England known as Operation Sealion. On July 4, General Hoepner arrived to confer the Knight's Cross on both of the brigade commanders. Later in the month, Stever's health grew even worse, and he had to be relieved. Senior Colonel von Boineburg took over temporary command, pending the hoped-for recovery of the commanding general.

The rest of the summer and fall was spent in the rigorous training of the newer recruits and exercises in mixed-arms combat groups. In early September, when the medical authorities definitely vetoed any chance of Stever's return to active duty, Maj. Gen. Baron Willibald von Langermann und Erlenkamp arrived to take permanent command of the division.[19] The baron had served in the Panzer Branch in Berlin, then had taken over the 20th Motorized Division for the French campaign, in which he had distinguished himself. He worked closely with the brigade commanders. The division was also fortunate enough to acquire Maj. Otto Heidkaemper as its new operations officer (I-a).[20] He had served with Erwin Rommel in the 7th Panzer.[21]

In November, the division was ordered back to Wuerzburg. The proposed invasion had been canceled, and unbeknownst to the officers, Hitler was already planning on a war with Russia and was ruthlessly expanding the number of panzer divisions—by cutting their armored strength in half. Col. Kurt von Jesser's 36th Panzer Regiment was packed off to the new 14th Panzer Division's headquarters at Dresden under considerable protest from both Langermann and Eberbach. This resulted in a stiff remonstrance from the High Command in Berlin, but later led to the acquisition of a third artillery battalion for its regiment. In addition, Guderian, whose son had been wounded in Belgium but had now resumed his post as Eberbach's adjutant, arranged for a trainload of new Panzer Mark IV Ausf E models, twenty in number, to be delivered to the division in January 1941.

Eberbach was able to spend his Christmas at Esslingen again, but he also sought out Hermann Breith in Berlin, where his friend, now a major general, had been attached to the advisory staff of Field Marshal Walter von Brauchitsch, the commander in chief of the army (*Oberbefehlshaber des Heeres*).[22] The two friends passed a pleasant evening together reminiscing before each went his own way.

In February, the 4th Panzer was again shipped back to France for large-scale maneuvers on the coastal plains around Calais and Dunkirk— also as a decoy for the enemy. The invasion of England was still being predicted. The panzer staffs worked diligently at getting their units into fighting shape. By the time they were loaded aboard trains for the rapid transit across half of Europe to the plains of Poland, the 4th was a truly elite formation.

The 4th Panzer was now under the XXIV Panzer Corps, under Gen. Leo Geyr von Schweppenburg, called "von Geyr."[23] The corps formed a part of 2nd Panzer Group, under the excellent Col. Gen. Heinz Guderian.[24] This was to be a great offensive. The men gladly put their leader's initial "G" on their equipment, for it was an honor to serve under "Fast Heinz," the victor of France.

On June 22, 1941, the great advance began, and on July 1, after only nine days, Eberbach was told to take command of the 5th Panzer Brigade, comprising his own 35th Panzer Regiment, the 4th Panzer Reconnaissance Battalion, and a motorized infantry battalion from the 12th Motorized Regiment. As part of Guderian's 2nd Panzer Group, it fought in the battle of encirclement at Minsk in June and early July, where 324,000 prisoners were captured, along with 3,332 tanks and 1,809 guns; at Smolensk in July, where Stalin lost 310,000 men, 3,205 tanks, and 3,120 guns; at Gomel in August, where 84,000 Russians were captured and 144 tanks and 848 guns destroyed; at Kiev in September, in the largest battle of encirclement in history, where 667,000 Soviets were captured and 3,718 guns and 884 armored vehicles captured or destroyed; and in the double battle of Vyazma-Bryansk from September 30 to October 17, where the

Red Army lost another 663,000 men captured and 1,242 tanks and 5,412 guns captured or destroyed. (Map 1.2 shows the Eastern Front.)

Eberbach was respected by Guderian, whose trust was amply demonstrated in a conversation between them following the colonel's capture of Orel on October 5. Resupply was already becoming difficult because of the long distances involved, and a few of the divisional and brigade commanders were claiming an inability to advance farther due to lack of petrol. Near Sevsk, Guderian sought out Colonel Eberbach to get a better picture of circumstances.

"I hear you're forced to halt, Eberbach," Guderian observed.

The colonel stared at him in amazement. "Halt, *Herr Generaloberst?* Why? We're just going nicely, and in my opinion, it would be a mistake to stop now."

"But what about your go-juice, Eberbach? I'm told you're running on empty tanks."

The colonel grinned slyly at his commander; some of his officers chuckled. "Ah? Well, you see—we're running on the petrol that we've forgotten to mention at corps headquarters."

Everyone now joined in the laughter. Between Guderian and Eberbach, much was tacitly understood. The fraternity of the panzer *Jaegers* was a close association. This was again indicated very clearly in November—just six weeks before Guderian was summarily dismissed from his command.

The desperate, too-long-delayed drive on Moscow had floundered and frozen to a halt within sight of the city's skyline. Eberbach's brigade had hacked and bled its way yard by grueling yard among the townships southeast of the Soviet capital, and the toll had been staggering. Guderian—as always concerned about his men and their equipment—visited Eberbach's depleted forces around Dedilovo overnight on November 14–15: "Eberbach's fine brigade had only some fifty tanks left and that was all we had available. . . . Ice was causing a lot of trouble . . . the cold made the telescopic sights useless. . . . In order to start the engines . . . fires had to be lit beneath them. Fuel was freezing on occasions and the oil became viscous."[25]

The 5th Panzer Brigade (and the 4th Panzer Division) had now lost about two-thirds of its original strength since the campaign began in June. Most of the surviving tanks were worn out—as were the men. Guderian recalled: "For the first time during this exacting campaign Colonel Eberbach gave the impression of being exhausted, and the exhaustion that was now noticeable was less physical than spiritual. It was indeed startling to see how deeply our best officers had been affected by the latest battles."[26]

On December 25, Hitler sacked Guderian for ordering an unauthorized retreat, in defiance of one of the Fuehrer's irrational "hold at all costs" orders. He was replaced by Gen. of Panzer Troops Rudolf Schmidt, who was promoted to colonel general on January 1, 1942. That same day, Eberbach was belatedly awarded the Oak Leaves to his Knight's Cross for his capture of Orel and other brilliant exploits during the terrible Soviet offensive, which continued until March. On January 6, as a result of the rapid burn out of so many senior officers, Eberbach succeeded Col. Dietrich von Saucken as acting commander of the 4th Panzer.[27] Langermann, after a short rest leave, had assumed command of the XXIV Panzer Corps, under which the battered 4th was still serving.

The situation was indeed critical. The *Wehrmacht* had been pushed back as far as Orel, and the Soviets were penetrating deeply between the isolated German units, holding out in towns such as Yukhnov and Sukhinichi. Eberbach was constantly on the defensive throughout the month. In fact, he had to give up his 12th Rifle Regiment during the latter part of January to rescue a garrison at Sukhinichi.

On February 2, Colonel Eberbach was wounded in the shoulder and arm while directing a counterattack at Utsensk on the Aka. He was rushed back to a base hospital at Smolensk. Lieutenant Colonel Heidkaemper, the I-a, took over the acting command of the division and led it for more than a month. On February 16, Eberbach was put on Fuehrer Reserve and sent to a specialist back in Wuerzburg. The physician removed a jagged slab of shrapnel lodged in his shoulder. The colonel was up and about within a week and petitioning to return to duty. On March 2, after much controversy, he rejoined his men, who were in the process of being relieved by infantry. The 4th Panzer withdrew to the Smolensk area for rest and reinforcement. Losses in both men and equipment had been terrible, and the division required a full month for the refitting of its decimated units.

On April 1, 1942, Eberbach was promoted to major general. He was thirty-seventh in seniority that day, when fifty-two colonels were jumped up to make up for losses due to illness, wounds, death, and early retirement or dismissal of senior officers. He was also confirmed as the permanent commander of the 4th Panzer, which was now ready to resume active duty on the Orel front.

The XXIV Panzer had already been sent southward for the proposed summer drive to the Volga and into the Caucasus, so the 4th came under LVI Panzer Corps, commanded by Gen. of Panzer Troops Ferdinand Schaal. It was assigned to the Liudinovo area, south of Kirov and northeast of Bryansk, as its area of defense.[28] Throughout the summer and early fall, the division took part in a couple of preventive strikes against Soviet forces around Kirov, but it was forced into antipartisan warfare against tremendous enemy guerrilla formations, which were playing hob with the German lines of communications.

On August 14, while engaged in one of these retaliatory attacks near Dorogobush, Eberbach received his *Ostmedaille*, awarded for continuity of service in Russia. Meanwhile, he constantly worked with his troops, keeping up their morale and improving their efficiency. It took a considerable toll on his health, as he still suffered from the results of his operation. In addition, he had lost most of his veteran officers, mostly through promotion, and by the onset of the second winter, in late October 1942, only Col. Dr. Erich Schneider, the former artillery commander now in charge of the 4th Panzer Brigade,[29] and Col. Oskar Shaub of the 12th Rifle Regiment remained of the divisional veterans.

Eberbach was ordered back to Germany on November 20 for a less demanding assignment and to undergo further treatment for his health. He remained at divisional headquarters for three more days, familiarizing Dr. Schneider with the routine of command, and then was forced into a completely new situation.[30]

On November 19, the huge Soviet counterattack in the south had overrun the 3rd and 4th Romanian Armies and within four days had cut off the German 6th Army in Stalingrad, on the Volga (Map 1.3). A panzer corps, assigned to the Romanians as a support, had been engulfed in the onslaught and virtually destroyed. Lt. Gen. Ferdinand Heim, the commander of the XXXXVIII Panzer, had done his best with an understrength 22nd Panzer Division and the Romanian 1st Armored Division.[31] The latter had been surrounded and slaughtered, almost to the last man; the former, with defective tanks, had been scattered and was lucky to make a precipitous *sauve qui peut* (roughly "every man for himself") retreat across the Don. Heim was summarily recalled, court-martialed for dereliction of duty, and thrown in prison. His battered corps headquarters had been assigned to Maj. Gen. Hans Cramer, sent posthaste from Berlin's panzer headquarters.[32]

Cramer arrived on November 20, to find that Heim's chief of staff had also been recalled. He made a valiant effort to pull together the survivors of his single division, plus some rear area personnel from the trapped forces and a regiment of the 16th Panzer Division, which had been en route to the rear for a rest. Cramer experienced little success in his efforts. By November 22, his reports were so pessimistic that OKH realized he was not up to the assignment. Otto von Knobelsdorff, a veteran lieutenant general, was chosen next to take the command, but he had gone on leave in October, and his whereabouts were unknown. An officer at the *Panzertruppenamt* (Panzer Troop Office) recommended that Eberbach be rushed in to take up the slack. Orders were immediately cut; Eberbach was bundled aboard a Fieseler Storch two-seat reconnaissance airplane and flown directly to the banks of the Don, relieving Cramer on November 26.

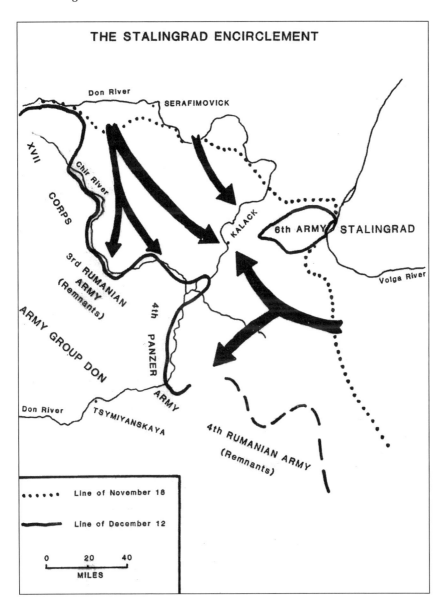

### THE STALINGRAD ENCIRCLEMENT

Already weary and ill, Eberbach nevertheless took charge of the deteriorating situation. He conferred with Maj. Gen. Eberhard Rodt[33] and Lt. Col. Hermann von Oppeln-Bronikowski of the 22nd Panzer, and with Col. Rudolf Siekenius and Maj. Bernhard Sauvant of the 16th Panzer's isolated battle group. A counterattack without much reinforcement was an impossibility. Even to hold the precarious positions they were in would be a risky business.

In keeping with his orders and his inclination to hold firm, Eberbach dug in his few tanks as pillboxes and deployed every soldier he could lay his hands on—even the headquarters bakery and signal personnel. A Russian probe against his unsecured southern flank on November 27 was repulsed by the general himself, leading a flying squad of motorcyclists and a quartet of half-tracks.

At noon on November 30, Lieutenant General Knobelsdorff arrived on the perimeter, having been flown almost nonstop from his vacation at Garmisch-Partenkirchen. He toured the makeshift defenses with Eberbach and commended him on his forethought. Now relieved, and already under orders to return to Germany, Eberbach nevertheless volunteered to remain at the front and assist in any way he could to hold the position. Knobelsdorff and his new chief of staff, Lt. Col. Friedrich Wilhelm von Mellenthin, did not feel the need of a general without troops, however. Eberbach took a plane for Kharkov late on December 1 and reached Wuerzburg on the third. Here, after reporting to the *Wehrkreis* commander's deputy, Eberbach checked into the military hospital for a three-week series of tests and cures.

Discharged for limited duty just after Christmas, he was able to get a leave to home at Esslingen, where he received the news that he had been promoted to lieutenant general on January 1, 1943. He also was apprised that glowing letters of commendation for his work on the Chir in November had been received from the officers who had worked with him.

He returned to Wuerzburg on February 4 for a final checkup from the medical authorities and had just been granted a clean bill of health when a special call came through from Berlin. Maj. Gen. Viktor Linnarz, a panzer staff officer currently acting as deputy to General Schmundt of the Army Personnel Office, wished him to come at once to Vinnitza, where Supreme Headquarters of the Army was currently located.[34]

Eberbach reported to Linnarz on February 9. The personnel man had a bit of top secret news: The Fuehrer was again employing Guderian, with the rank of inspector general of panzer troops; Guderian was asking for almost unlimited authority over the armor and its production, and it was highly likely that Hitler would agree.

General Linnarz wanted Eberbach to head up a special panzer staff to be ready to give the new inspector whatever assistance might be needed. The general readily agreed and set out again for Berlin with the new title *Kommander der Sonderstabes Panzer*. He was provided an office in the Home Army Building on the Bendlerstrasse on February 11 and at once summoned several recuperating panzer officers to be prepared to stand by for assignments.

On February 26, Guderian and Hitler formalized the agreement on the post of inspector general, and upon his return to Berlin on February 28, Guderian appointed Lieutenant General Eberbach as his deputy, with the responsibility of the Home Army's panzer units, including training, inspection, doctrine, production, and development. Eberbach, in turn, appointed as his chief of staff the former Afrika Korps tanker, Col. Dr. Ernst Bolbrinker, who also now occupied the post of In6 in the OKH Inspectorate Command, with responsibility for production and development.[35]

During the summer of 1943, Eberbach made exhaustive tours of training facilities, reserve divisional headquarters, and production centers, making copious notes and suggesting shortcuts, improvements, and refinements. By the beginning of autumn, however, he called upon Guderian and pointed out that too much time had been spent in desk jobs; he was ready for a couple months' duty at the front to get firsthand information about the panzer formations.

After a conference with people at OKH, permission was granted. On October 15, Eberbach, who had been promoted to *General der Panzertruppen* on August 1, relieved the veteran Gen. of Panzer Troops Joachim Lemelsen in temporary command of the XXXXVII Panzer Corps on the southern sector of the Russian Front.[36] The corps was short of tanks, self-propelled guns, and other armored vehicles.

On October 22, General Lemelsen returned from his conference in Berlin to arrange the handing over of command of the XXXXVII to its permanent holder, Gen. of Panzer Troops Erhard Raus. General Eberbach motored southward toward the disintegrating front around threatened Kiev. He had received an urgent call from his old commander, Col. Gen. Hermann Hoth, and reached his headquarters at Makarovka, despite Soviet air attacks.[37]

Hoth was deeply concerned. Huge Soviet forces were breaking irresistibly into the Kiev salient, and the city would fall without some miracle taking place. What was worse, however, was that the commander of the powerful XXXXVIII Panzer Corps, Gen. of Panzer Troops Otto von Knobelsdorff, was cracking up.[38]

"According to reliable people at the XXXXVIII's Headquarters near Pervomaysk," Hoth recounted, "this normally capable general is tormented by our losses. He envisions hordes of Russians closing in upon us like giant ocean waves. All our efforts to halt them will be shattered and they will roar on and on until they eventually submerge Germany itself. He has even begged permission to see the Fuehrer himself and tell him the effects of this unequal struggle and how untenable the situation is here on the front."

The colonel general shrugged helplessly.

"Of course he is partially right, but we can't have that sort of attitude in a commander if we plan to be able to do anything at all to reverse the situation. So I am giving him permission to go to Rastenburg—for what little good it will do him–and I want you to take temporary command of the corps," he said to Eberbach. "I understand that you are on detached loan from *Panzertruppe,* so I have asked them to assign a full-time commander as soon as possible."[39]

Eberbach hurried off to the corps headquarters, just missing the departing general who was already airborne to East Prussia. He conferred with the capable, if opinionated, chief of staff, Friedrich von Mellenthin, who corroborated Hoth's report. Then he set out on a flying tour of his divisional positions to see for himself how critical the situation was.

It was every bit as bad as he had been led to believe. The 19th Panzer Division was under almost unceasing assault by waves of Soviet infantry, supported by huge concentrations of artillery. The 1st Infantry Division was down to battle group strength, while the newly committed 3rd Panzer was struggling helplessly to stabilize the situation. Eberbach promptly assembled a mixed battle group of as much available armor as he could round up and began a series of rushes to the most threatened positions, as a fire brigade. By October 25, he had managed to stall the Soviet assault.

Though this area had been temporarily secured, this was not so on other fronts. That very day, Dnepropetrovsk was captured, and despite a counterattack at Krivoy Rog on November 2, to the north, the Soviet armies smashed across the Dnieper to the right and left of Kiev, and on November 6, that vital city was captured.

In desperation, the XXXXVIII Panzer Corps was rushed to this threatened area and a temporary headquarters was set up at Belaya Tserkov on November 7. A proposed defensive line, enclosed on the supply hub of Fastov, was ruined when Soviet armor seized that town late on the seventh. A series of desperate counterattacks launched by the green 25th Panzer Division on the eighth and ninth not only decimated the division, but was unable to liberate Fastov. Colonel General Hoth was held responsible and was summarily relieved by Fuehrer order, and Gen. of Panzer Troops Erhard Raus was sent to take over command. The actual change, however, did not take place until November 26.

Eberbach began the assemblage of as many panzer units as were readily available southwest of Kiev, meanwhile importuning the Inspectorate through Field Marshal Manstein's army group headquarters for a certain general who would be ideally suited for the leadership of the proposed counterattack. On November 14, therefore, Eberbach shook hands with his handpicked successor, Gen. of Panzer Troops Hermann Balck, at Belaya Tserkov, and hurried out to the aircraft that had flown him in.

The little Fieseler Storch took off amid rain squalls and flew due south to the Nikopol area, from which Balck had just been called and where Eberbach was to hold charge over the besieged XXXX Panzer Corps in the bridgehead. Soviet forces had all but encircled the collection of German troops in the loop of the lower Dnieper. Theoretically under Col. Gen. Karl Adolf Hollidt's 6th Army on the west bank, the heavily engaged forces on the east bank at Nikopol, Apostolovo, and Grusehevka consisted of the XXXX Panzer, XXIX Infantry (Gen. of Panzer Troops Erich Brandenburger) and IV Infantry (Gen. of Infantry Friedrich Mieth), to which the XVII Corps (Gen. of Mountain Troops Hans Kreysing) was later added.

Eberbach toured his decimated units—the 13th Panzer and 16th Panzer Grenadier Divisions—and conferred with his fellow officers. He then flew out of the pocket to confer with Manstein and Kleist, the army group commanders. His appreciation of the situation was sent on to Fuehrer Headquarters in East Prussia. If the Nikopol pocket had to be held, then a suitable senior general should be placed in overall command—one who also had skill and tenacity in defense.

Guderian recalled Eberbach on November 25—the same day that the tough Gen. of Mountain Troops Ferdinand Schoerner was flown in to take command of "Group Schoerner," which included the XXXX Panzer Corps. On November 27, Eberbach reported back to the Bendlerstrasse with a sheaf of recommendations on reorganization, tank development, and commendations for certain officers. A series of conferences resulted, lasting until December 2, at which gathered such prominent personages as Albert Speer; Ferdinand Porsche; Gen. of Artillery Eduard Wagner, the quartermaster general of the army; Col. Gen. Fritz Fromm, the commander in chief of the Replacement Army and chief of army equipment; Gen. of Infantry Kurt Zeitzler, the chief of the general staff; and Guderian. Many ideas were dropped as unfeasible, but numbers of others were to be put into effect.

Hans Eberbach went home to Esslingen to spend his last Christmas for several years to come. His middle son, Wolfram—now twenty-two and a panzer noncom—was also on leave, so the family was all together.

The year 1944 began with the general busily engaged in prodding the armaments industry into producing more and better tanks, in driving the panzer reserve headquarters into revising its training schedules, and in touring the *Panzertruppenschulen* (the panzer troops schools), lecturing on strategy and tactics.

In April, he began a month's circuit of the fighting fronts, this time not as an acting commander, but as an observer—well qualified and with the full authority of the Inspectorate and OKH to make changes in command if needed. He spent two weeks in Russia, touring from north to south, then flew to the Italian battlefront, where he particularly sought out the capable Gen. Frido von Senger und Etterlin for a report on the difficulties of using armor in mountainous terrain.[40]

His last week was spent in France, where badly damaged panzer units were being sent to rebuild and rest before returning to the east. After conversations with Field Marshals Gerd von Rundstedt and Erwin Rommel and with Gen. of Panzer Troops Baron Leo Geyr von Schweppenburg, the commander of the amorphous Panzer Group West, he became involved in the controversy then raging in France about the disposition of the panzer units and the D-Day invasion.

The "eastern generals," by far the majority, recommended the posting of the mobile forces in central locations from which they could be rushed to any threatened area—a vital collection of force that could launch viable counterattacks at any invasion beach. This seems eminently sensible and in Russia doubtless would have been extremely effective. At this point, the Soviet Air Force was not a major factor. In the west, however—as Rommel was intensely aware—the Allied air forces would immediately establish aerial domination and smash any major armored concentrations in their assembly areas. Only by greatly reducing the distance from the panzers to their intended victims could the Germans realistically hope to defeat the Anglo-Americans on or near the beaches and throw them back into the sea.

From concrete air-raid shelters up and down the French coast that week in April 1944, Eberbach watched the waves of Allied bombers and fighters sweeping with impunity across the French skies. Always openminded, he made his position known as favoring Rommel's solution: put the panzers as close to the coast as possible, which would reduce the length of time that they would be exposed to Allied fighter-bombers.

Back in Berlin, his opinions created no little consternation: Guderian shared Geyr von Schweppenburg's reserve theory and had so informed Hitler. As a result, for the first time, a certain coolness entered the relationship between Eberbach and his superior. Because of this, during May, Eberbach suggested that it would be best to let him return permanently to active field duty.

There is an old adage that states, "One should be careful what one wishes for . . ." Eberbach's request was not acted on for several weeks. Then, on July 2, he was given command of Panzer Group West in Normandy, where the Allies had landed hundreds of thousands of men and the floodgates were creaking.

## NOTES

1. Like the Bavarian Army, the Royal Wuerttemberg Army functioned independently of Berlin in peacetime. In time of war, it was absorbed by the Imperial (Prussian) Army.
2. Papers of Friedrich von Stauffenberg. Unpublished papers in the possession of the author. Hereafter referred to as Stauffenberg Papers.
3. www.islandfarm.fsnet.co.uk, accessed November 24, 2006.
4. Samuel W. Mitcham, Jr., *Rommel's Desert Commanders* (Westport, CT: Praeger, 2007).
5. The Second Reich (Empire) existed from 1871 until November 1918, when Kaiser Wilhelm II abdicated. It was replaced by the democratic Weimar Republic (1918–1933), which in turn was replaced by the Third Reich under Adolf Hitler.
6. Georg Tessin, *Verbaende und Truppen der deutschen Wehrmacht und Waffen-SS im Zweiten Weltkrieg, 1939–1945*. Vol. 1 (Osnabrueck, Germany: Biblio-Verlag, 1979–86), 234–35.
7. Alexander Ulex was born in Bremerhaven in 1880. He joined the army as an officer-cadet in the 24th Field Artillery Regiment in 1899 and earned his commission in 1901. He fought in World War I, served in the *Reichsheer*, and commanded a battalion in the 6th Artillery Regiment. During the Nazi era, he commanded the 2nd Artillery Regiment (1931–33), was artillery commander VI at Muenster (1933–34), and was briefly Infantry Commander II at Schwerin (1935). He then commanded the 12th Infantry Division at Schwerin (1935–36) and *Wehrkreis XI* and XI Corps at Hanover (1936–39), before retiring on March 31, 1939. Recalled to active duty when World War II began, Ulex commanded Wehrkreis X in Hamburg (September–October, 1939), Frontier Guard Sector South in Poland (October 1939–June, 1940) and *Wehrkreis I* (June 1940–April 30, 1941). Meanwhile, he was promoted to first lieutenant (1909), captain (1913), major (1922), lieutenant colonel (1928), colonel (1931), major general (October 1, 1933), lieutenant general (August 1, 1935), and general of artillery (October 1, 1936). Together with Blaskowitz, Curt Liebmann (the commander of the 5th Army, 1939–40), and future Field Marshal Georg von Kuechler, Ulex protested against the SS atrocities in Poland, in 1939–40. He retired for the second and final time in 1941 and died in Bremen in 1959.
8. The Bendlerstrasse was the street on which the huge complex of the German War Ministry (mostly an army operation) was located. Later, just days before World War II began, the High Command of the Army (OKH), which included the general staff, moved to Zossen, about thirty miles south of Berlin, and the Bendlerstrasse became the headquarters of the Home (or Replacement) Army. It remained so until the end of the Third Reich.

9. Georg-Hans Reinhardt was born in Bautzen, Saxony, eastern Germany, in
   1887 and joined the army as an infantry *Fahnenjunker* in 1907. Commissioned in 1908, he fought in World War I, served in the *Reichsheer*, and was
   promoted to major general in 1937. A very capable commander, he was promoted to lieutenant general (1939), general of panzer troops (1940), and
   colonel general (January 1, 1942). He commanded the 1st Rifle Division
   (1937–38), 4th Panzer Division (1939–40), XXXXI Panzer Corps
   (1940–41), and 3rd Panzer Group (later Army) (October 5, 1941–August
   16, 1944). Reinhardt commanded Army Group Center from August 16,
   1944, to January 25, 1945, when he was relieved of his command for dis-
   obeying a senseless Fuehrer order. He would have had to be replaced in any
   case, as a Russian bullet had struck him in the head a few hours before,
   though word had not yet reached Berlin. He recovered from his wound several months later. General Reinhardt died in Munich on November 24,
   1963. He held the Knight's Cross with Oak Leaves and Swords.
10. Max von Hartlieb genannt Walsporn was born in 1883 in Hienheim, not far
    from Essing in Bavaria. He joined the army as a volunteer in 1904 and
    received his commission in the 127th Infantry Regiment in 1906. He fought
    in World War I, served in the *Reichsheer*, and was a colonel commanding the
    2nd Rifle Regiment in 1934. He assumed command of the 2nd Panzer
    Brigade in 1935 and took charge of the 5th Panzer Brigade in 1938. Pro-
    moted to major general on April 1, 1937, and lieutenant general on August
    1, 1939, he replaced General Vietinghoff as commander of the 5th Panzer
    Division on October 18, 1939. He was relieved of his command by General
    Hermann Hoth, the commander of the XV Motorized Corps, on May 29,
    1940, a move that effectively ended his chances for further advancement.
    He later commanded the 179th Replacement Division (1940–42) and 585th
    Rear Area Command (1942), but he never received another promotion or
    field command. He was wounded, apparently by partisans, on May 19, 1942
    and was in the hospital until September. In Fuehrer Reserve until February
    1943, he then served as commander of the 226th Field Administrative Com-
    mand in Krakau, Poland (1943–44), and the 601st Special Purposes Division
    (1944–45). He retired in April 1945, just before his division was captured by
    the Red Army in Czechoslovakia. General Walsporn died in Starnberg,
    Upper Bavaria, in 1959.
11. Meinrad von Lauchert was born in Potsdam, Brandenburg, in 1905. He
    joined the army as a *Fahnenjunker* in 1924 and became a second lieutenant
    in the 5th Cavalry Regiment in 1931 and became a company commander in
    the 35th Panzer Regiment in late 1938. During World War II, he com-
    manded the I Battalion, 35th Panzer Regiment (1939–43), Panzer Regi-
    ment "Grafenwoehr" (1943), and 15th Panzer Regiment (1943–44).
    Apparently he was wounded on August 1, 1944. In any case, on the eve of
    the battle of the Bulge, he was an excess officer on the staff of the 5th
    Panzer Army when Gen. Heinrich von Luettwitz, the commander of the
    XXXXVII Panzer Corps, decided to sack the commander of the 2nd Panzer
    Division. Luettwitz and the army commander, Gen. of Panzer Troops Baron
    Hasso von Manteuffel, quickly decided that Lauchert was the best available
    replacement. He assumed command of the 2nd Panzer on December 15—
    the day before the offensive began. Lauchert did not even have time to

meet some of his principal subordinates before the battle started. The 2nd Panzer nevertheless pushed farther forward than any other German division, although its casualties were very heavy. Promoted to major general on March 1, 1945, Lauchert had by now acquired a reputation as a brilliant divisional commander, although he was disgusted by Hitler's conduct of the war and the unnecessary slaughter of his division that month. Because the Nazi dictator would not allow a timely retreat, the 2nd Panzer was pushed back against the Rhine with no bridge in its sector. Most of its men—including Lauchert—were forced to swim for it on March 20. The wet general then "quit the war," deserting and walking to Bamberg, the peacetime home of the 35th Panzer Regiment, apparently assuming the Nazis would conclude that he had been killed or captured and would not look for him. This assumption proved to be correct. After the war, General Lauchert lived in a number of locations. He died at Stuttgart-Moehringen in late 1987, at the age of eighty-two.

12. Frederick L. Clemens, Axis History Forum, www.forum.axishistory.com, accessed May 27, 2005.

13. Wilhelm Keitel was born on the family estate of Helmscherode in 1882. Although he would have preferred to have spent his life as a farmer, his family's farm was not large enough to support both his and his father's families, so he joined the army as an artillery *Fahnenjunker* in 1901. As a battery commander, he was severely wounded by a shell splinter on the Western Front during World War I. On recovery, he was posted to the general staff as a captain in 1915. Although later known as "Lakeitel" (*Lakei* means lackey in German), he definitely had organizational talents. Except for a brief tour as commander of the 6th Artillery Regiment, he served in the Defense Ministry from 1925 to 1933, rising to the head of the Organizations Office. After briefly commanding the 22nd Infantry Division in Bremen, Keitel returned to Berlin in October 1935, as head of the General Office of the War Ministry. When the war minister, Field Marshal Blomberg, fell from power in February 1938, the position of war minister was abolished, and Keitel became commander in chief of the High Command of the Armed Forces (OKW), although he was largely a figurehead and the real power lay with Hitler. Keitel was hanged at Nuremberg as a war criminal on October 16, 1946.

14. Hermann Breith was born in Pirmasens in the Rhineland in 1892. He joined the Imperial Army as an officer-cadet in 1910, fought in World War I as an infantry officer, and joined the *Reichswehr* in 1919. He assumed command of the 36th Panzer Regiment in late 1938. Breith was promoted rapidly during the Nazi years, to lieutenant colonel (1936), colonel (1938), major general (1941), lieutenant general (1942), and general of panzer troops (March 1, 1943). He led the 36th Panzer until February 1940, then commanded the 5th Panzer Brigade until May 22, when he was severely wounded during the battle of France. He resumed command after he recovered. In July 1941, he became the general of mobile troops at OKH, but on October 2, he returned to the front as commander of the 3rd Panzer Division. He assumed command of the III Panzer Corps on January 3, 1943 and led it for the rest of the war. He was considered a capable and solid commander but not a brilliant one. Breith, however, was felt to be an exceptionally brave man. He held the Knight's Cross with Oak Leaves and Swords. He

managed to surrender to the Western Allies at the end of the war. A POW until May 1947, he settled in Pech, near Godesberg in his native Rhineland, and died there in 1964.

15. Erich Hoepner was a member of the anti-Hitler conspiracy before the war began. He later led the 3rd Panzer Army on the Eastern Front but was sacked by Hitler for ordering an unauthorized retreat. He was arrested the day after the unsuccessful attempt to assassinate Adolf Hitler on July 20, 1944, and was hanged on August 8. Walter von Reichenau, who was strongly pro-Nazi and one of Hitler's most brutal generals, later commanded the 6th Army in Belgium and France. He also commanded Army Group South on the Eastern Front (1941–42). He suffered a massive heart attack after completing a six-mile run in Russia in January 1942 and died a few days later.

16. Johann Joachim "Hajo" Stever was born in Berlin on April 27, 1889. He joined the Imperial Prussian Army as a *Fahnenjunker* in 1908 and became a second lieutenant in the infantry the following year. He fought in World War I, served in the *Reichsheer*, and was a colonel by 1935. From 1938 to 1940, he was chief of staff of the XV Motorized Corps. Not a huge success as commander of the 4th Panzer Division, at least partially because of his illness, he was given command of the Saxon 336th Infantry Division in late 1940—a serious demotion. He led his new unit on the Eastern Front until March 1942, when he apparently fell ill again. When he returned to duty that summer, he was put in charge of *Oberfeldkommandantur 399* (OFK 399), a military territorial command. Apparently this also was too much for his health. He was unemployed as of late 1943 and retired the following year. A lieutenant general as of June 1, 1941, he was picked up by the Soviets shortly after they captured Berlin in May 1945. He was never seen or heard from since and was almost certainly murdered by the Communists.

17. Stauffenberg Papers. Despite his performance in France, Jesser, who was an Austrian, apparently was not highly thought of as a panzer leader. Born in Poland in 1890, he joined the Austro-Hungarian Army in 1910 as an officer-cadet in the infantry. After fighting in World War I, he joined the Austrian Army in 1919 and was commander of the 3rd Motorcycle Battalion in 1938, when Austria was annexed by the Third Reich. Jesser was immediately inducted into the Panzer Branch (*Panzerwaffe*), initially as a staff officer in the 2nd Panzer Regiment. Later he commanded the 36th Panzer Regiment in France and Russia (1940–42), commanded the XIII School for Mobile Troops (1942), and briefly led the mediocre 386th Motorized Infantry Division from December 1942 until it was absorbed by the 3rd Panzer Grenadier Division on March 1, 1943. He was promoted to major general on December 1, 1942. Next, he reportedly commanded a security brigade in France. After briefly commanding the 155th Reserve Panzer Division in northern France (August 24–September 6, 1943), Jesser was unemployed for more than a year. He was then placed in charge of a fortified sector of Steiermark. Captured by the Soviets, he was soon released because he was an Austrian. He died in Vienna in 1950.

18. Ewald von Kleist was born in the province of Hessen in 1881, the descendent of a long line of Prussian generals. Three other field marshals came from his family besides Ewald, who reached that rank on February 1, 1942. Although not considered a great panzer commander, he was a gentleman of

the old school who treated the people of occupied territories with humanity. Kleist joined the army in 1900 and was commissioned second lieutenant in the 3rd Royal Field Artillery Regiment in 1901. He was promoted to first lieutenant in 1910 and posted to the War Academy in Berlin, where he underwent general staff training. In 1914, he transferred to the cavalry and, during World War I, spent more than three years on the Eastern Front, commanding a cavalry squadron and serving in general staff positions, including chief of operations of the Guards Cavalry Division. He served on the Western Front in 1918. After the armistice, Kleist briefly joined the *Freikorps* before being accepted into the *Reichsheer*. He rose rapidly in the Weimar Republic era and, by 1928, was chief of staff of *Wehrkreis III* in Berlin. In 1931, he was named commander of the elite 9th Infantry Regiment in Potsdam and the next year was promoted to major general and named commander of the 2nd Cavalry Division at Breslau, replacing Gerd von Rundstedt. In 1936, he became commander of *Wehrkreis VIII* in Breslau, Silesia, until Hitler forced him into retirement in February 1938. Recalled in 1939, Kleist led the XXII Corps in Poland and Panzer Group von Kleist in Belgium and France (1940). This command later became the 1st Panzer Group, then 1st Panzer Army, which Kleist led in the Balkans and Russia (1941–42). He commanded Army Group A on the Eastern Front from late 1942 to March 30, 1944, when Hitler sent him into retirement again. He was captured by the Americans but turned over to the Yugoslavs, who handed him over to the Russians. He died in a Soviet prison in 1954.

19. Maj. Gen. Baron Willibald von Langermann und Erlenkamp was born in Karlsruhe, Baden-Wuerttemberg, on March 29, 1890. He was a cavalry officer who became a capable armored officer. Commissioned in the 5th Dragoon Regiment in 1910, he fought in World War I, where he was adjutant of the 7th Reserve Dragoons (1914) and a company commander in the 21st Reserve Division (1915). He became a general staff officer in 1916 and served with the X Reserve Corps and 22nd Reserve Division. He spent the *Reichswehr* era in cavalry and school units and became commander of the 4th Cavalry Regiment in late 1935. The baron was named Higher Cavalry Officer I in 1938, and then became inspector of cavalry and transport troops in late. In late 1939, he was named commander of Special Administrative Division Staff 410—a real backwater post. Three days before the invasion of France began, he was given command of the elite 29th Motorized Infantry Division—a surprising appointment, given Langermann's background and the fact that he had been promoted to major general less than three months before. He nevertheless proved to be a skillful commander of mobile formations in the conquests of Belgium and France and was rewarded for his success by being given command of the 4th Panzer Division. On January 8, 1942, he was named commander of the XXIV Panzer Corps on the Eastern Front, followed a week later by a promotion to lieutenant general. He became a general of panzer troops on June 1, 1942. Langermann was killed in action during the battle of Stalingrad on October 3, 1942.

20. Otto Heidkaemper was born in Lauenhagen, Lower Saxony, in 1901. He joined the army in July 1918 and spent the last weeks of World War I at the front with the 10th Engineer Battalion. He was still a lieutenant in 1933, when the was selected for general staff training. He graduated from the War

Academy in 1937 and spent virtually all of the next eight years in general staff positions, serving as I-a of the 2nd Light/7th Panzer Division (1938–40), I-a of the 4th Panzer Division (1940–42), chief of staff of the XXIV Panzer Corps (1942–43), chief of staff of the 3rd Panzer Army (1943–44), and chief of staff of Army Group Center. He was sacked by Col. Gen. Ferdinand Schoerner because of his lack of enthusiasm for National Socialism and involvement in an unauthorized retreat ordered by General Reinhardt. Heidkaemper ended the war as commander of the 464th Infantry Division in Saxony. He had also served as acting commander of the 4th Panzer Division in March 1942 (as a lieutenant colonel!) and acting commander of the XXIV Panzer Corps in early 1943 (as a colonel), both highly unusual votes of confidence for the young Heidkaemper. He managed to surrender to the Americans, who kept him only two weeks. He settled in Bueckeburg, Lower Saxony, formerly Schaumburg-Lippe, where he died in 1969.

21. At this point in his career, Erwin Rommel was particularly distrustful of general staff officers. Difficult to work with in any case, Rommel clashed with Heidkaemper on more than one occasion.

22. Walter von Brauchitsch was born in Berlin in 1881 and served as commander in chief of the army from February 4, 1938, to December 19, 1941, when he was fired by Hitler because of his failure to take Moscow. He was never reemployed. He had been promoted to field marshal on July 19, 1940. Brauchitsch was arrested by the Allies at his estate in Rachut, Holstein, and died in a British prison hospital in Hamburg in 1948.

23. The son of an old military family, Baron Leo Geyr von Schweppenburg, who was called "von Geyr," was born in Potsdam on February 2, 1886. He entered the service as a *Fahnenjunker* in 1904 and was commissioned in the family regiment, the 26th Light Dragoons (2nd Wuerttemberg Dragoons), in 1905. He was appointed to the War Academy in 1911 and spent most of World War I in general staff positions, although he did briefly command a battalion in 1917. Sophisticated and urbane, bright, articulate, and well educated, and possessing great social skills, von Geyr represented Germany as military attaché in London, Brussels, and The Hague in the 1930s and was an excellent military diplomat. Seeing that the future belonged to the panzer branch, he befriended Heinz Guderian, and then transferred to the tank arm in 1937. He commanded the 3rd Panzer Division (1937–40), XXIV Panzer Corps (1940–42), XXXX Panzer Corps (1942), and LVIII Reserve Panzer Corps (late 1942–43), before being assigned to OB West in July 1943 as commander designate of Panzer Group West, which was formed in October 1943. An aristocratic snob, he found it difficult to get along with Erwin Rommel, the Desert Fox, who was the son and grandson of schoolteachers.

24. Heinz Wilhelm Guderian, who came to be known as the "father of the *blitzkrieg*"—was born in Kulm, West Prussia, in 1888. Both his father and son became German generals. Heinz became Germany's leading advocate of mobile, armored warfare before World War II and greatly influenced Hitler in that direction. He was promoted to major general on August 1, 1936, and lieutenant general on February 1, 1938. Shortly thereafter, he was given command of the XVI Motorized Corps and, in 1939, the XIX Motorized (later Panzer) Corps. He distinguished himself in Poland (1939), France

(1940), and the early stages of the Russian campaign (1941), where he commanded the 2nd Panzer Group (later Army). Promoted to general of panzer troops in late 1938 and colonel general on July 19, 1940, he was relieved by Hitler for ordering an unauthorized retreat in December 1941 and held no further commands, but was inspector general of panzer troops (1943–44) and acting chief of the general staff of the army (July 21, 1944–March 1945), a job for which he was intellectually and temperamentally unsuited. The outspoken Guderian was again relieved by Hitler after a bitter argument in March 1945 and surrendered to the Western Allies in northern Italy the next month. Later he wrote a book, *Panzer Leader*, which has been translated into many languages. Although a highly valuable historic document, it should be read very carefully, and not every word should be accepted at face value—especially Guderian's alleged opposition to Hitler and the Nazis. As chief of the general staff, for example, he did nothing to prevent the spread of Nazi doctrine within the army—in fact, quite the opposite is true. Guderian's first order as chief of the General Staff, for example, was to outlaw the traditional army salute and order the adoption of the Nazi (Hitler) salute in its place. He also acted to expel anti-Hitler conspirators from the army so that they could be tried (and usually hanged) by civilian authorities. Despite this, Guderian was an outstanding field commander and brilliant tactician. He died in Schwangau, Bavaria, in 1954.

25. Heinz Guderian, *Panzer Leader* (New York: Ballantine, 1957), 235 and 248.
26. Ibid.
27. Dietrich von Saucken was born in Fischhausen in 1892. He was an East Prussian cavalry officer who possessed incredible courage and the skill to match. As late as March 1945, he categorically (and rudely) refused to obey one of Hitler's orders to the dictator's face—and got away with it. Saucken joined the army as an infantry cadet in 1912 but soon transferred to the mounted branch. He led the 2nd Cavalry Regiment (1937–late 1940), 4th Rifle Brigade (1940–December 1941), and 4th Panzer Division (December 27, 1941–January 2, 1942). Seriously wounded, he did not return to active duty until August 24, 1942, as commander of the School for Mobile Troops. Reassuming command of the division on May 31, 1943, shortly after his promotion to lieutenant general, he became deputy commander of the III Panzer Corps (May 1944), and commander of the XXXIX Panzer Corps (June 1944), Grossdeutschland Panzer Corps (December 1944), and 2nd Army in East Prussia (March 1945). Saucken was the last man to receive the Knight's Cross with Oak Leaves and Swords. Promoted to general of panzer troops on August 1, 1944, he surrendered his army to the Soviets in May 1945 and spent the next ten years in Communist prison camps. He died in Munich, Bavaria in 1980.
28. Ferdinand Schaal was born in 1881 in Freiburg/Breisgau, on the southern edge of the Black Forest. He joined the 22nd Dragoons as a *Fahnenjunker* in 1908. A veteran cavalry officer, he commanded the 1st Panzer Brigade (1935–39) and 10th Panzer Division (1939–41) and was promoted to lieutenant general on April 1, 1939. Promoted to general of panzer troops effective October 1, 1941, Schaal reportedly briefly commanded the Afrika Korps that autumn. He was acting commander of the XXXIV Corps (1941) and LVI Panzer Corps in Russia (late 1941–43), during which his health was

severely strained. He returned to Germany in August 1943, where he was
named military plenipotentiary and commander of *Wehrkreis Bohemia und
Moravia* (1943–44). He was arrested on July 21, 1944, for his part in the
attempt to assassinate Adolf Hitler and spent the rest of the war in prison.
General Schaal died in Allensbach, Konstanz, near the Swiss border, in 1962.

29.  Erich Schneider was born in Biedenkopf in 1894. A Hessian artillery officer
with an advanced engineering degree, he was a ballistics expert and spent
much of his career in the Ballistics Branch. He commanded the 103rd
Panzer Artillery Regiment of the 4th Panzer Division (June 1940–early
1942), before assuming command of the division. Promoted to major general on January 1, 1943, he returned to the Weapons Office on June 1 and
was promoted to lieutenant general a month later. In 1944, he was the head
of the Experimental and Testing Group of the Army Ordnance Office. His
last post was as commander of the 14th Panzer Grenadier Division on the
Eastern Front and in East Prussia (December 28, 1944–March 20, 1945). He
was without an assignment at the end of the war. Schneider held the
Knight's Cross with Oak Leaves. He died in Wiesbaden in 1980.

30.  The 4th Panzer Division later fought in the Kursk and Dnieper campaigns
(1943–early 1944) and unsuccessfully opposed the Russian summer offensive near Bobruisk in 1944. It was isolated in the Courland pocket in
November 1944 but was evacuated by sea to East Prussia in early 1945. Now
in remnants, it underwent a partial refitting at Danzig but could not be
completely rebuilt. It was isolated on the Frischen Nehrung, along with the
rest of the 2nd Army, and surrendered to the Soviets on May 9, 1945. A
superior unit, even by German standards, it was the most heavily decorated
of the German panzer divisions.

31.  Ferdinand Heim was born in Reutlingen, in the Swabian district of south
Wuerttemberg, in 1895. He entered the Imperial Army as an officer-cadet in
1914. An artilleryman by trade, he served as chief of staff of XVI Motorized
Corps (1939–40), a branch chief at OKW (1940), and chief of staff of the
6th Army (1940–42) before taking over 14th Panzer Division on July 1,
1942. He was named commander of the XXXXVIII Panzer Corps on
November 1. The corps, ordered to prevent the encirclement of Stalingrad,
was a technical disaster. Most of Heim's tanks broke down almost immediately, and the corps barely escaped encirclement. An enraged Hitler
ordered Heim arrested on November 26. He was subsequently court-martialed and imprisoned. Eventually released, Heim was named commandant
of Boulogne and surrendered it to the Canadians in September 1944. He
lived in Ulm after the war and died there in 1977.

32.  Hans Cramer was a native of Minden, Westphalia. Born in 1896, he was educated in cadet schools and joined the army as a *Fahnenjunker* when World
War I began. Commissioned in December 1914, he served as a company
commander, battalion adjutant, and machine gun company commander.
He was also wounded at least three times. In August 1918, he was captured
by the British. Cramer was selected for the *Reichswehr* and in 1923 was transferred to the cavalry. He was commander of the 13th Cavalry Regiment
from 1930 to 1933. Later, he commanded the Panzer Reconnaissance Lehr
(Demonstration) Battalion (1939–40) and 8th Panzer Regiment of the
Afrika Korps (1941). Seriously wounded in the summer of 1941, he

returned to duty in 1942 as chief of staff to the general of mobile troops at OKH. He was promoted to major general on November 1, 1942, and lieutenant general on January 22, 1943. He was acting commander of the XXXXVIII Panzer Corps (November 20–26, 1942) and then deputy corps commander. He was sent back to Africa as commander of the Afrika Korps in February 1943. After the German supply lines to Tunisia collapsed, Cramer surrendered his command to the British. He was subsequently promoted to general of panzer troops. Exchanged in 1944 because he was suffering from severe asthma, Cramer was a special adviser to Panzer Group West. After Rommel's involvement in the plot to overthrow Hitler became known, Cramer, who was close to Rommel, was involuntarily retired on August 17, 1944, retroactive to July 20, 1944. He lived in Minden after the war and died at Hausberge on October 28, 1968.

33. Eberhard Rodt, born in 1895, was a native of Munich. He joined the Bavarian 2nd Ulam Regiment as a war volunteer in 1914 and was commissioned the following year. He served in the *Reichsheer* and later commanded the I/18th Cavalry Regiment (1936–39), 7th Cavalry Regiment (1939), 25th Reconnaissance Battalion (1939–40), 66th Panzer Grenadier Regiment (1942), and 22nd Panzer Division (November 8, 1942–March 1943). Sent to Italy to recuperate with the remnants of his staff, Rodt was promoted to major general on March 1, 1943. Although he had basically failed as a panzer division commander in Russia, Rodt was charged with forming the 15th Panzer Grenadier Division in Sicily out of the survivors of the 15th Panzer Division of the Afrika Korps plus assorted miscellaneous units; he was thus, in effect, given a second chance professionally. Rodt took full advantage of this opportunity by performing brilliantly as a divisional commander in Sicily, Italy, and on the Western Front, fully justifying the confidence his superiors had in him, despite his previous failure in the east. He was promoted to lieutenant general in 1944 and led the 15th Panzer Grenadier until mid-January 1945, when the was wounded by an Allied fighter-bomber. He was still recovering at the end of the war. He retired in Hinterstein and died in the city of his birth in 1979, just after his eighty-fourth birthday.

34. Viktor Linnarz was born in the beautiful ancient town of Alfeld, Lower Saxony, in 1894. A signals officer, he was a lieutenant in the 2nd Telegraph Battalion when World War I began. He served in the *Reichswehr* and was in motorized units throughout the 1920s. He worked at the Kasan Panzer School, on the Volga in Russia, in 1929 and 1930, and later commanded a company in the 3rd Reconnaissance Battalion (1932–34) and a battalion in the 6th Panzer Regiment (1934–36). He was a major in the Army Personnel Office when the next war began. Promoted to a branch chief's job in 1940, he first saw field service as a commander of the 5th Panzer Brigade (June 3–August 31, 1941). Almost certainly wounded in action, he did not return to active duty for more than a year. In late 1942, he became an office group chief (P1) at HPA and then deputy chief of HPA (1943–45). He was promoted to major general on January 1, 1943, and lieutenant general on April 1, 1945. He commanded the 26th Panzer Division from March 1, 1945, to the end of the war. A POW until 1946, he resided in Hanover after the war and died there in 1979.

35. Ernst Bolbrinker was born in Graz, Austria, in 1898. He enlisted in the German Army as a private in 1916 but earned a commission as a second lieutenant of reserves in 1917. He emerged from the war with both grades of the Iron Cross and a determination to get a superior education. This he accomplished by earning a graduate degree in engineering, followed by a doctorate in engineering with a specialization in motor vehicles. He was recalled to the service in 1936 as a first lieutenant of reserves and was soon transferred to the mobile branch for obvious reasons. Promoted to captain in 1939, he served on the staff of the 1st Panzer Regiment in Poland, before being transferred to the staff of Hoepner's XVI Panzer Corps. Promoted to major in 1940, he was a battalion commander in the 5th Panzer Regiment (3rd Panzer Division) in the Netherlands, Belgium, and France. The following year, his battalion was transferred to the 5th Light (later 21st Panzer) Division of the Afrika Korps, where Bolbrinker won the Knight's Cross in the battle of Mechili. Shortly thereafter, during the drive on Tobruk, he was seriously wounded, with his face permanently disfigured. After he recovered, he served on the staffs of the Panzer School and then the Tropical (Desert) Warfare School. He was promoted to colonel in 1942 and the next year became a department head in the Panzer Inspectorate. He was promoted to major general on July 1, 1944. After being released from the American POW camps, he moved to Bielefeld, where he died in 1962.

36. Joachim Lemelsen was born in Berlin in 1888. He entered the service as an artillery *Fahnenjunker* in 1907. Commissioned the following year, he served in World War I as a general staff officer in infantry and artillery units. He was commander of the Artillery Lehr (Demonstration) Regiment (1934), a course commandant at the Infantry School at Dresden (1935–38), and commander of the 29th Motorized Infantry Division (1938–40). Named commander of the 5th Panzer Division in the last days of the French campaign, in part because he was close at hand, he was promoted to general of artillery on August 1, 1940. Later, on June 4, 1941, he changed his branch affiliation and became a general of panzer troops. Lemelsen commanded the 5th Panzer for only two weeks. He led the XXXXVI Panzer Corps (1940–43) in Russia, was acting commander of the 10th Army in Italy (October–December 1943), and commanded the 1st Army in France (May–June 5, 1944) and 14th Army in Italy (1944). He was demoted to deputy army commander in Italy in December 1944. Lemelsen held the Knight's Cross with Oak Leaves. A pro-Nazi, he was an excellent motorized divisional commander and did well leading panzers in Russia. He was less successful as an army commander in Italy. A British prisoner of war until 1948, he died in Goettingen in 1954.

37. Hermann Hoth was born in Neuruppen, northern Brandenburg, in 1885. He attended a number of cadet schools, entered the army as a *Faehnrich* in 1904, and was commissioned in the infantry in 1905. Although an infantryman by trade, he proved to be an excellent commander of motorized and armored forces. During World War II, he commanded the XV Motorized Corps (1938–40), 3rd Panzer Group (later Army) (1940–41), 17th Army (1941–42), and 4th Panzer Army (1942–43). He was promoted to general of infantry in 1938 and colonel general on July 19, 1940. Hitler did not appreciate his opinions on the deteriorating situation on the Eastern Front and forced him into retirement on November 30, 1943. He was never reem-

ployed. Hoth was captured by the Americans, tried as a war criminal, and sentenced to fifteen years in Landsberg Prison in late 1948. He was released in April 1954 and retired to Goslar am Harz, where he died on January 25, 1971.
38. Stauffenberg Papers.
39. Ibid.
40. Fridolin von Senger und Etterlin was born in 1891 in the medieval town of Waldshut, Baden, on the Upper Rhine. He grew up in an aristocratic family of wealth and prestige and was very well educated. During World War I, he served mainly with the 76th Field Artillery Regiment. After the war, he transferred to the cavalry and spent much of his career (1920–33) with the 18th Cavalry Regiment at Stuttgart-Cannstatt. He also served in the 1st Cavalry Division, about which he later wrote a book. After leaving the 18th Cavalry, he was chief of staff of the Cavalry Inspectorate (1934–38) and commanded the 3rd Cavalry Regiment (1938–39), 22nd Cavalry Regiment (1939–40), and 2nd Rifle Brigade (1940), before becoming a German delegate to the Italian-French Armistice Commission (1941–42). He commanded the 10th Panzer Grenadier Regiment in occupied France briefly (July–September,1942), then the 17th Panzer Division (October 10, 1942–June 1943). After leaving the 17th Panzer, Senger—who possessed considerable diplomatic ability—was briefly *Wehrmacht* commander in Sicily (1943) and German liaison officer to the Italian 6th Army before taking over the XIV Panzer Corps on October 23, 1943, which he led on the Italian Front for the rest of the war. He was promoted to lieutenant general on May 1, 1943, and general of panzer troops effective January 1, 1944. He also briefly commanded the 14th Army in Italy in October 1944. An American POW until May 1948, he became the headmaster of a private school near Lake Constance, a writer, and a military journalist after the war. He died at Freiburg in Breisgau in January 1963.

# CHAPTER 2

# The Normandy Campaign before July 3, 1944

Adolf Hitler became chancellor of Germany on January 30, 1933. Over the next six years, he established and consolidated his dictatorship; began a campaign of persecution against minority groups, most notably the Jews; and pursued an aggressive foreign policy. The Saar, Austria, the Sudetenland, the Czech Republic, Movaria, and Memel were all annexed by more or less peaceful means. On September 1, 1939, however, Hitler went one step too far: He invaded Poland and began World War II in Europe. To his surprise, Great Britain and France declared war on the Third Reich within days.

At first there were only victories. Poland was conquered in less than six weeks. Denmark, Norway, Luxembourg, the Netherlands, Belgium, and even France were overrun with the next year. Although the *Luftwaffe* was checked in the battle of Britain, it was not decisively defeated, and the *Wehrmacht* (the German armed forces) soon had other fish to fry. It overran the Balkans, destroyed Yugoslavia, conquered Greece, and even captured the island of Crete in a daring airborne operation. Meanwhile, the Afrika Korps, under the dashing "Desert Fox," Gen. of Panzer Troops Erwin Rommel, saved the Italian empire of Fascist dictator Benito Mussolini in North Africa, overrunning almost all of Libya in the process and pushing to the frontiers of Egypt. Meanwhile, Slovakia, Hungary, Romania, and Bulgaria all became more or less puppet states of the Third Reich. But once again Hitler went too far. On June 22, 1941, he invaded the Soviet Union.

It was one of the turning points of the war.

Hitler's armies won massive victories in Russia in 1941 but were stopped at the gates of Moscow. Stalin began a massive counteroffensive all along the Eastern Front on December 6. The next day, the Japanese bombed the American naval base at Pearl Harbor, Hawaii. True to his ally, Hitler quickly declared war on the United States—a country whose potential he vastly underestimated.

From that moment, it was no longer possible for Germany to win the war by conventional means.

Germany achieved more victories, but not on the scale of those of 1939–41. Then, in November 1942, the German 6th Army was surrounded at Stalingrad. Hitler stubbornly refused to allow it to break out, so the 6th Army died. By February 2, 1943, it was all over. Some 240,000 Germans (including a few allied troops) were in the Stalingrad pocket when it was encircled. Only 90,000 surrendered. Of these, only about 6,000 ever saw the lights of home again.

From that point on, generally speaking, all roads led backward for Nazi Germany.

In 1943, the supply lines of Army Group Afrika collapsed, and the 5th Panzer Army and Italian-German 1st Panzer Army were forced to surrender in May 1943. The Axis lost another 130,000 men, including some of Germany's best soldiers. The German civilians called this defeat "Tunisgrad." More defeats followed. The wolf packs of the German Navy were defeated in the North Atlantic, the Allies conquered Sicily, Mussolini was overthrown, and the Anglo-Americans invaded Italy.

In the east, in the largest armored battle of all time, the German armies were decisively defeated in the battle of Kursk. The *Wehrmacht* could now no longer defeat the Red Army, even in the summer. By late 1943, Stalin's armies were pushing toward the borders of Europe and the Reich, and Germany's allies were becoming increasingly nervous.

Meanwhile, aided by the United States, the United Kingdom recovered. By late 1943, the U.S. and Royal Air Forces were pounding Germany around the clock, and the Anglo-Saxon allies were planning to reenter northwestern Europe. Everyone knew that this cross-channel invasion—the greatest amphibious operation in history—would take place in the spring or summer of 1944. It represented a great threat to the existence of Nazi Germany, but also perhaps its greatest remaining opportunity. If the invasion could be repelled, the Allies would not be able to make another attempt for a year. This would free dozens of divisions, including several elite panzer and SS units, for use on the Russian Front. With these men, it might be possible to stabilize the Eastern Front and perhaps even throw the Soviets back. If Germany could not regain its military superiority, it could at least restore the balance of power and perhaps force the Allies to accept a negotiated peace. Even if this failed, it would give German scientists another year to perfect their "miracle weapons," including new and more dangerous panzers and U-boats, jet airplanes, rockets, remote-controlled tanks, and perhaps even an atomic bomb. On the other hand, if the invasion succeeded, Germany's chances became slim indeed.

The prinicipal German command in western Europe was OB West, the German abbreviation for the *Oberbefehlshaber West*, the commander in chief, west, or his headquarters. Since the spring of 1942, it had been led by Field Marshal Gerd von Rundstedt, a distinguished but aging and energy-deficient veteran of fifty years' service.[1] Even his good friend, General von Geyr, told his interrogators: "Of all the German generals, Field Marshal von Rundstedt knew the least of panzer tactics. He was an infantryman of the last generation. He and his staff were armchair strategists who didn't like dirt, noise and tanks in general—as far as I know, Field Marshal von Rundstedt was never in a tank. Do not misunderstand me, however," he added quickly. "I have the greatest respect for von Rundstedt, but he was too old for this war."[2]

OB West was further handicapped by its chief of staff, Lt. Gen. Guenther von Blumentritt. General von Geyr recalled that he was "unsuitable [for the post] in ability or character."[3] Blumentritt, in fact, thought that the entire Allied invasion might be a giant bluff that might not take place at all.[4]

Rundstedt decided that if the Allies did invade, the decisive battle for western Europe should be fought somewhere in the interior of France, out of range of the big guns of the U.S. and Royal Navies. As he basically thought that the beaches should be conceded, he neglected the coastal defenses, which were dubbed the Atlantic Wall. In October 1943, he established Panzer Group West under Gen. of Panzer Troops Baron Leo Geyr von Schweppenburg. Its mission was to defeat the Anglo-American armies and push them back into the sea. To accomplish this task, Rundstedt gave von Geyr all of his tank and motorized divisions. By the end of 1943, von Geyr controlled the I SS Panzer Corps with five divisions, all north of the River Loire: 1st SS Panzer "Leibstandarte Adolf Hitler," 12th SS Panzer "Hitler Youth," 2nd Panzer, 21st Panzer, and 116th Panzer. South of the Loire lay the LXIII Panzer Corps with the 9th and 11th Panzer Divisions. The 2nd SS Panzer Division "Das Reich" and the 17th SS Panzer Grenadier Division "Goetz von Berlichingen" were in panzer group reserve, south of the Loire.

The mission of OB West's other commands—15th, 7th, 1st, and 19th Armies and the Armed Forces Netherlands—was to delay the Allies, inflict casualties on them, and channelize their advance until von Geyr could deal them the decisive blow.

Everything changed when Field Marshal Erwin Rommel, the Desert Fox, arrived to inspect the German coastal defenses. Although the German propaganda machine had boasted of its almost invincible strength, Rommel saw through the curtain of deception immediately. He quickly dubbed it a farce—the figment of what he called Hitler's *Wolkenkuckucks-heim* ("cloud cuckoo land").[5] He denounced it as an "enormous bluff . . . more for the German people than for the enemy"[6] and derisively dubbed it the "Propaganda Wall."

On December 30, Rommel's headquarters, Army Group B, assumed command of the coastal defenses of the Netherlands, Belgium, and northern France. It controlled (north to south) the Armed Forces Netherlands, the 15th Army, and the 7th Army. To counter Rommel, Rundstedt established Army Group G under Col. Gen. Johannes Blaskowitz. He controlled the 1st and 19th Armies in southern France.

Just as he quickly saw through the fiction of the Atlantic Wall, the Desert Fox immediately identified the flaw in the Rundstedt–von Geyr strategic plan: It did not take into account Allied air supremacy. Whereas he had witnessed the devastating effects of Allied aerial domination first-hand in North Africa, the "eastern generals," such as von Geyr, Guderian, and Rundstedt, had not. Rommel knew that it would be impossible to defeat the Allies in an armored battle once they established themselves on the continent. His plan called for checking the Allies on the beaches, and then hurling them back into the sea via an immediate counterattack by the panzer divisions. The first forty-eight hours of the invasion, he said, would be decisive, one way or the other. Unfortunately for Rommel, his army group did not have a single tank division. This led to a battle of influence at Fuehrer Headquarters—a place where Rommel had few allies, for both Keitel and his chief of operations, Col. Gen. Alfred Jodl, had little use for him.

Hitler should have chosen between Rommel's concept of operations and that of Rundstedt and von Geyr, but he did not. Instead, he compromised. The 2nd, 21st, and 116th Panzer Divisions were assigned to Army Group B, but even then their areas of operations were dictated by OKW. The 2nd SS, 9th, and 11th Panzer Divisions were assigned to Army Group G in southern France. Panzer Group West was allowed to keep only four of its original ten divisions: the 1st SS Panzer, the 12th SS Panzer, the 17th SS Panzer Grenadier, and the Panzer Lehr. The compromise pleased no one. It did not give Rommel enough panzers to carry out his plan, and deprived von Geyr of the tanks necessary to try his. The argument continued until D-Day.

One reason for all of the opposition to Rommel's concept of operations was that no one on the German side had any real idea where the Allies would land. The *Abwehr* (OKW's military intelligence bureau) had been a failure from the beginning. Allied air supremacy over the United Kingdom prevented the *Luftwaffe* from instituting a successful aerial reconnaissance program and the *Abwehr*'s network of spies in Great Britain—never strong to begin with—had virtually ceased to exist by the fifth year of the war. By 1944, all of Germany's best agents had been killed, captured, or forced to hurriedly flee the country. German military intelligence therefore had to rely on signal communications. That meant they were also subject to signal deception, at which the British were the masters. By early 1944, the *Abwehr* was convinced that the British 4th Army had twelve combat divisions concentrated around the Firth of Forth, ready to invade Norway, when in fact it had none. As a result, Hitler kept thirty coastal U-boats in the Bergen sector to help meet the threatened invasion. Obviously they were in no position to disrupt the Allied invasion, which came across the Bight of the Seine. Hitler also refused to transfer divisions from Norway to the mainland because of this supposed threat.

Another British army—Force Anderson under Lt. Gen. Kenneth Anderson, who had commanded the British 1st Army in Tunisia—was believed to be in Essex and Suffolk, preparing to invade the Netherlands. Finally, by the spring of 1944, OKW was convinced that the entire U.S. 1st Army Group, led by the redoubtable Lt. Gen. George S. Patton, Jr., was assembling in Kent to launch the main cross-channel attack at the Pas de Calais. Dummy radio traffic indicated that Patton had twelve divisions. In fact, he did not have a single combat unit.

At the strategic level, German military intelligence work was, in fact, poor to nonexistent throughout the war and a major contributing factor to the eventual demise of the Third Reich. "A weakness of the German Army was the lack of instinct and knowledge in practical intelligence work," General von Geyr commented later. "In the unwritten tradition of the Army, intelligence work had a slight odor of not being respectable—at any rate, not as important as the work of operational personnel who controlled the fighting."[7]

Adm. Wilhelm Canaris, the chief of the *Abwehr*, has been depicted by some authors as a romantic hero and a kind of intelligence genius, who lost his job and later his life in the effort to rid the world of Adolf Hitler. He, in fact, was generally over his head as chief of the *Abwehr* and many of his estimates were very wide of the mark or just plain wrong. In 1941, for example, he estimated that there were 10,000 British troops in Crete, that they were demoralized and would not put up serious resistance against a German airborne assault, and that the native Cretan population would support the Germans against the British. In fact, there were almost 40,000 British troops on Crete. When the German parachute and gliderborne forces landed, the British and their allies put up a fierce resistance and, aided by the native population, inflicted terrible losses on the German parachute corps and almost succeeded in destroying it altogether. Unfortunately for the *Wehrmacht*, this example of bad military intelligence was not an isolated case.

Canaris was not fired by Hitler for attempting to overthrow the Nazi regime. The final straw for the admiral came in February 1944, when he told Field Marshal Albert Kesselring, the OB Southwest in Italy, that there was absolutely no danger of the Allies launching an amphibious assault behind his lines. Acting on this information, Kesselring moved the bulk of his reserves to the front—less than three days before an entire Anglo-Saxon corps landed in his rear at Anzio. Justifiably furious at this latest gross intelligence failure, Hitler sacked Canaris on February 11 and replaced him with Col. Georg Hansen.[8] Shortly thereafter, the entire *Abwehr* was absorbed by the SD (the intelligence agency of the SS) under SS Gen. Walter Schellenberg.

After Hitler cooled down, he selected Canaris to head a minor naval transport staff in the spring of 1944. Only after a German general found Canaris's secret diary, which he had foolishly left lying about (he kept a diary!), was it discovered that he knew about the German resistance, allowed it to flourish in his headquarters, and attempted to shield it. His deputy was, in fact, one of its leaders. The Gestapo promptly arrested him and, in April 1945, stripped him naked and executed him.

The appointment of Schellenberg came too late to help Rommel or have much effect on the overall ineptitude of German military intelligence, which predicted that the invasion would come at Pas de Calais. Field Marshal Rommel, however, did not believe that the Allies would attack the strongest point in the German defensive system just to have a short supply line. He initially predicted that the Allies would come ashore in northern France, probably on the left flank of the 15th Army. He also felt that a secondary invasion would land on the Mediterranean coast of France and push up the Rhone River Valley to take the Atlantic Wall in the rear.[9] (Map 2.1 shows the Western Front.)

Hitler, at various times, predicted that the Allies would come ashore at Gironde, Brittany, the Cotentin, Pas de Calais, and Norway.[10] On March 20, 1944, for some unexplained reason, he changed his mind again and picked Normandy or Brittany as the site of the invasion. Perhaps it was just his intuition acting up again, but he insisted that the Normandy sector be strengthened. "Rommel," B. H. Liddell Hart wrote, "came round to the same view as Hitler. In the last months he made feverish efforts to hasten the construction of underwater obstacles, bomb proof bunkers and minefields" in the Normandy sector from Caen to Cherbourg (Map 2.2).[11] He also strengthened the Normandy sector with

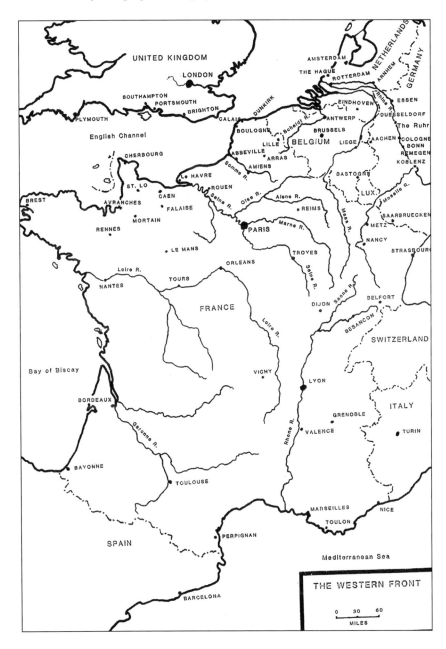

THE WESTERN FRONT

0    30    60
MILES

another first-class German division—the 352nd Infantry—and several independent regiments and battalions. Had Hitler allowed him to, Rommel would have added the 12th SS Panzer Division and the entire III Flak Corps to the Normandy defenses, but that is another story. (Map 2.3 shows the dispositions of OB West on June 5, 1944.)

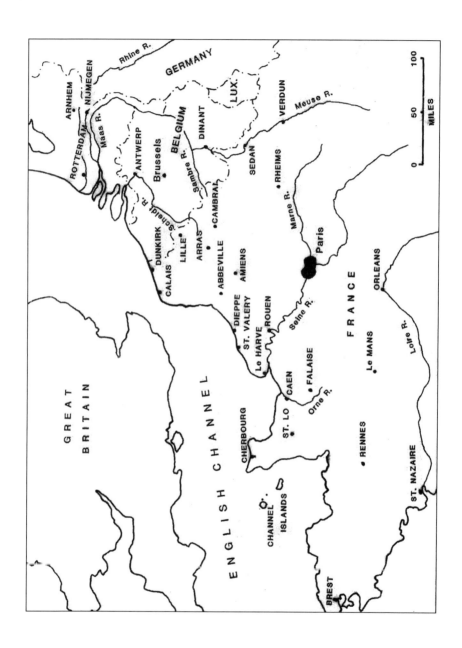

The Allies, under the command of U.S. General Dwight D. Eisenhower, landed in Normandy on June 6, 1944 (Map 2.4). Unfortunately for Germany, Rommel was at home, on his way to a conference with the Fuehrer at Berchtesgaden. He rushed back to his headquarters at La Roche-Guyon (on the Seine) and arrived at 10:30 P.M. on D-Day, but it was June 9 before he and General von Geyr could launch their armored counterattack—at least two days too late. It was repulsed.

From that moment on, all the Germans could realistically hope for was to pin the Allies down in the hedgerows of Normandy, force them into a stalemate, and prevent them from breaking into the interior, liberating France, and pushing on to the borders of the Reich.

Meanwhile, yet another strange metamorphosis occurred at Fuehrer Headquarters. Before the invasion, Hitler had been sure it would come ashore in Normandy. Now that it had gone as he had predicted, he decided that the landings were a feint. The real invasion, Hitler and OKW declared, would come ashore at Pas de Calais, far to the northeast of Normandy, on the Belgian border in extreme northern France. As a result, while the 7th Army and Panzer Group West struggled and bled in Normandy, the much stronger 15th Army lay idle for two months, awaiting an invasion that had already come.

Normandy today is much different than it was in 1944. During World War II, it was covered with hedgerows, which are much different from the simple bushes we tend to think of when hearing the term "hedge." A Norman hedgerow was used to enclose small fields and consisted of an extended mound of dirt about six feet high, covered in brush and undergrowth. They were ideal defensive positions for the Germans. Hedgerows were everywhere in 1944 in Normandy. (Though one can still find hedgerows there, they are much scarcer.)

British Field Marshal Sir Bernard Law Montgomery planned to advance rapidly and push the Germans out of hedgerow country on D-Day; in fact, he hoped to gain up to thirty miles. His armies barely gained five at their deepest point and in many places were only two miles from the beaches on June 7. As a result, Rommel was able to check—but not repulse—the Great Invasion. They would still be in hedgerow country in August.

On June 9, the headquarters of Panzer Group West was located in an orchard twelve miles southwest of Caen. It consisted of four large wireless trucks, with several jumbo office tents and smaller tents standing completely in the open. Von Geyr, an "eastern general," had never faced a tactically sophisticated enemy who possessed complete air supremacy; he did not make any attempt at camouflaging his command post, and his

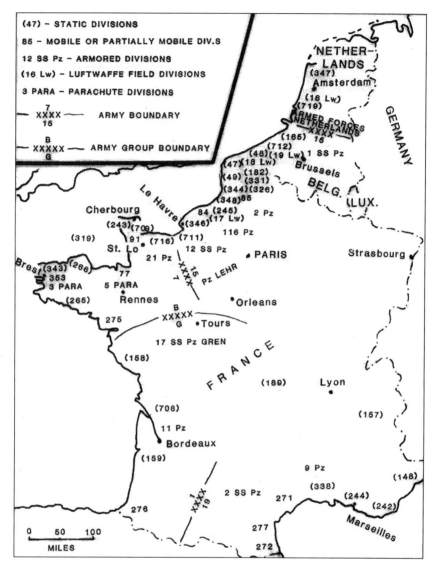

communications security was too lax. It was not difficult for the Allied pilots to identify his headquarters as a major target. As a result, they hit it with a saturation bombing raid and nearly wiped it out. General von Geyr was wounded; his chief of staff, Maj. Gen. Ritter und Elder Sigismund-Helmut von Dawans, was killed; and the group's entire operations section, including the chief of operations, was wiped out.[12] Field Marshal Rommel himself barely escaped the debacle, having left the area only an hour before. Ironically, von Geyr's last words to the Desert Fox as he departed were to warn him to watch out for low-flying enemy aircraft!

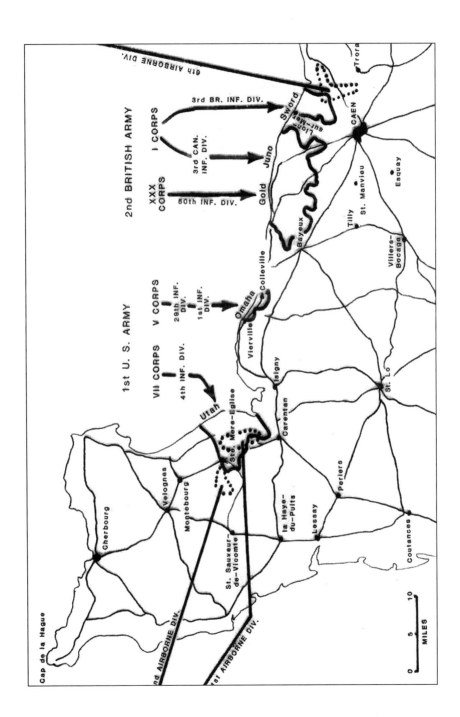

Headquarters, Panzer Group West, had to be withdrawn from the battle and rebuilt. It could not return to action until June 28. When it did, it took charge of the right wing of Army Group B, in the Caen sector of Normandy. The 7th Army continued to hold the left.

That same day, Col. Gen. Friedrich Dollmann, the overworked and overstressed commander of the 7th Army, collapsed with a heart attack and died.[13] Rommel recommended that he be replaced with Gen. of Infantry Kurt von der Chevallerie, the commander of the 1st Army.[14] Instead, Hitler replaced him with Gen. of Waffen-SS Paul Hausser, whom he promoted to SS colonel general.[15] Hausser had retired from the regular army as a lieutenant general and was able, courageous, and energetic, but his record as a corps commander had been uneven, and he was definitely a Nazi. The very capable SS Lt. Gen. Wilhelm "Willi" Bittrich, the commander of the 9th SS Panzer Division "Hohenstauffen," succeeded Hausser as commander of the II SS Panzer Corps.[16] SS Col. Thomas Mueller, the commander of the 20th SS Panzer Grenadier Regiment, became acting commander of the 9th SS Division.

Meanwhile, on the morning of June 25, the British launched their massive Epsom offensive. Their target was the tactically critical Hill 112, southwest of Caen. The main blow was spearheaded by the British VIII Corps, which included the Scottish 15th Infantry, the 11th Armored, and the 43rd Infantry Divisions. They slowly pushed back the 12th SS Panzer Division, and late on June 28, the British 29th Armoured Brigade captured the vital hill.

Rommel and von Geyr had no choice but to counterattack and retake the hill, or Caen was lost and the entire German position in Normandy would be compromised. They threw in every uncommitted unit they could lay their hands on. The British were slow to reinforce the 29th Armoured, and on June 30, Bittrich's II SS Panzer Corps recaptured Hill 112, while the Panzer Lehr Division beat back attacks from Montgomery's 49th and 50th Infantry and 2nd Armoured Divisions a few miles to the west. The German line had been bent but not broken. Field Marshal Montgomery was nothing if not persistent, however. He regrouped and prepared to try again. (Map 2.5 shows the Battle for Hill 112.)

On the evening of June 30, Rommel returned to La Roche-Guyon from another frustrating and fruitless meeting with Adolf Hitler, in which the Fuehrer again refused to allow a timely retreat. It was a heated meeting, and it was to be their last. Rommel was met by a document, drafted by von Geyr and endorsed by Hausser, calling for the evacuation of the Caen sector, a retreat that would put the German forces out of range of the big Allied naval guns and allow them to create an armored reserve. It

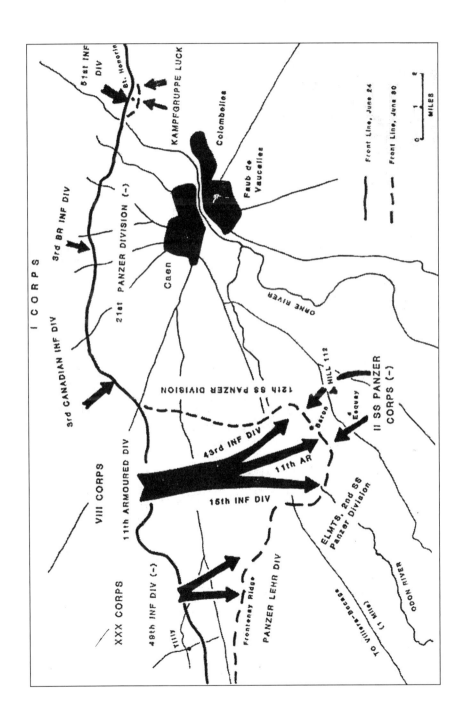

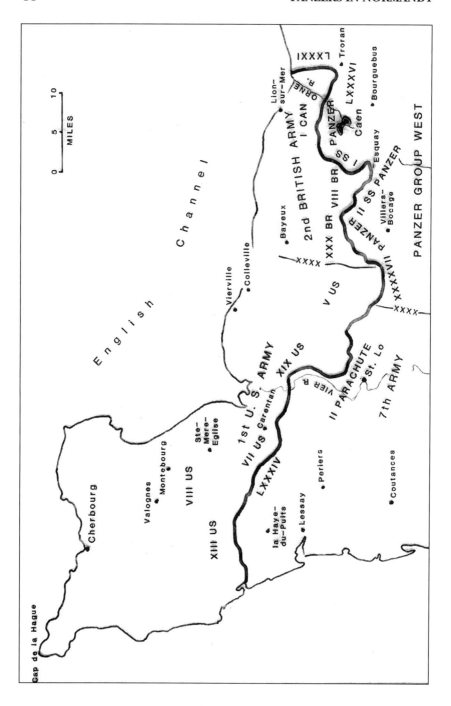

would also, however, put the Allies on favorable terrain for armored operations. Even though Hitler had just rejected these ideas a few hours before, Rommel signed the document anyway and quickly forwarded it to Rundstedt in Paris. Rundstedt quickly endorsed the recommendations a few minutes after midnight on July 1 and forwarded them to Berchtesgaden. Here Jodl recommended that these ideas be rejected and took the documents to the Fuehrer.

The Nazi dictator's reaction to this piece of insubordination was quick in coming. Von Geyr was dismissed from his post and placed in Fuehrer Reserve, thus being removed from active service.[17] Rundstedt was also sacked, but much more politely. One of Hitler's army adjutants, Col. Heinrich Borgmann, arrived at OB West headquarters, presented him with the Oak Leaves to the Knight's Cross, and gave him a handwritten letter from Hitler, courteously ordering him into retirement due to age and health.[18]

Rundstedt reacted with relief. "I thank God that I won't be in command during the coming catastrophe!" he exclaimed to the Desert Fox.[19] Rommel, who was next in line for the post, was passed over in favor of Field Marshal Guenther von Kluge, an "eastern general." Geyr von Schweppenburg was replaced by Gen. of Panzer Troops Hans Eberbach. (Map 2.6 shows the situation in Normandy on July 1, 1944, the day before Eberbach became commander of Panzer Group West.)

**NOTES**

1. Gerd von Rundstedt was born at Aschersleben in the Harz Mountain region on December 12, 1875. His father was a hussar (cavalry) officer. He was educated at cadet schools and graduated from Gross Lichterfelde, the German equivalent of West Point. He entered the army in 1892 at the age of sixteen as a senior officer-cadet and was commissioned second lieutenant in the 83rd Royal Prussian Infantry Regiment the following year. He became a member of the general staff in 1909. He spent most of World War I on the Eastern Front, became a corps chief of staff, and returned home a major. He rose rapidly after the war and assumed command of the 2nd Cavalry Division in 1928. He was briefly commander of the 3rd Infantry Division (1932) before assuming command of Army Group 1 (1933–38). He retired in 1938 but was recalled to active duty in 1939 and led Army Group South in the Polish campaign. He later commanded Army Group B (later South) in France (1940) and southern Russia (1941). Hitler sacked him for the first time in December 1941, but after Sepp Dietrich told the Fuehrer that he had done the commander an injustice, Hitler recalled Rundstedt to duty as OB West in March 1942. For the best biography of Rundstedt, see Charles Messenger, *The Last Prussian: A Biography of Field Marshal Gerd von Rundstedt, 1875–1953* (Washington, DC: Brassey's, 1991). Also see Guenther Blumentritt's earlier *Von Rundstedt: The Soldier and the Man* (London: Odhams Press, 1952).

2. Baron Leo Geyr von Schweppenburg, "Panzer Tactics in Normandy," U.S. Army ETHINT 3, an interrogation conducted at Irschenhausen, Germany, 11 December 1947. On file, U.S. National Archives.

3. Leo Geyr von Schweppenburg, "Panzer Group West (mid-1943–15 July 1944)," Foreign Military Studies MS #B-258, Office of the Chief of Military History, U.S. Army. Hereafter referred to as Geyr MS #B-258. A slightly different version of the same manuscript will be referred to as Geyr MS #B-466. Guenther Blumentritt, who was promoted to general of infantry on April 1, 1944, was born in Munich in 1892. He joined the army in 1911, was commissioned the following year, fought in World War I, served in the *Reichsheer*, and was admitted into the general staff during the Weimar era. He served as a branch chief in OKH (1938–39), I-a of Rundstedt's Army Group South (1939), I-a of Army Group A (also Rundstedt) (1939–40), chief of staff of the 4th Army (late 1940–early 1942), and chief of operations of OKH (January–September 1942). He was dismissed from this post when Hitler abruptly sacked Franz Halder as chief of the general staff and replaced him with Kurt Zeitzler. Blumentritt was immediately reemployed by his friend Rundstedt and served as chief of staff of OB West from September 24, 1942, to September 9, 1944. Later Blumentritt was acting commander of the XII SS Corps (1944–January 1945), 25th Army (January–March 1945), and 1st Parachute Army (March–April 1945). He ended the war as commander of the ad hoc Army Blumentritt. After the war, he wrote a laudatory biography of Rundstedt. He died in the city of his birth in 1967.

4. Geyr MS #B-466.

5. Cornelius Ryan, *The Longest Day* (New York: Simon and Schuster, 1959), 23.

6. Ibid, 26.

7. Geyr MS #B-466.

8. See Heinz Hoehne, *Canaris*, trans. J. Maxwell Brownjohn (Garden City, NY: Doubleday, 1979), for the best account of Canaris's life. Wilhelm Canaris was born in Aplerbek on New Year's Day 1887. He entered the navy as a cadet in 1905 and became an ensign in 1908. He served primarily in torpedo boats and cruisers prior to World War I and was interned in Chile as a spy in 1915. He escaped and made his way back to Germany, where he commanded a torpedo boat and later U-boats, sinking three British vessels. He spent the 1920s and 1930s in a variety of fleet, shore installation, and general staff assignments, commanding the battleship *Schlesien* (*Silesia*) (1932–34). He became chief of the *Abwehr* in 1935 and held the post until February 12, 1944, when he was relieved of his duties and sent into the Fuehrer Reserve. After Hitler's anger over the intelligence failure at Anzio abated, he placed Canaris in charge of a special naval transportation staff. Canaris was arrested by the Gestapo on July 23, 1944, but the evidence connecting him with the July 20 plot was considered insufficient to bring him to trial, and he probably never would have been tried had he not kept a diary at work—including accounts of his part in the anti-Hitler plot—and left it there after his dismissal as chief of the *Abwehr*! This diary was discovered by pro-Nazi Gen. of Infantry Walter Buhle in early 1945. Canaris was executed at the Flossenbuerg concentration camp on April 9, 1945. Unlike most of the conspirators, Canaris seems to have considered his participation in the plot something of an insurance policy, rather than having been motivated by genuine anti-Nazi feelings.

9. Hans Speidel, *Invasion 1944* (Chicago: Regnery, 1950), 33–34.
10. Gordon A. Harrison, *Cross-Channel Attack*, (Washington, DC: Office of the Chief of Military History, Department of the Army, 1951), 138.
11. B. H. Liddell Hart, *History of the Second World War* (New York: Putnam, 1971), 2:548–49.
12. Ritter und Elder Sigismund-Hellmut von Dawans was born in Erfurt in 1899. He was educated in cadet schools and entered the service as a *Faehnrich* in the infantry in 1917. He was discharged from the service after World War I ended but managed to get into the *Reichsheer* as a second lieutenant in 1924. He became a general staff officer and was on the staff of the I Corps (1937–39). Dawans commanded the I/472nd Infantry Regiment (1939–40), was I-a of the 19th Panzer Division (1940–late 1941), and served as chief of staff of the XIII Corps (1941–42), III Panzer Corps (1942–43), and 4th Army (1943), before becoming chief of staff of Panzer Group West on December 1, 1943. He was promoted to major (1938), lieutenant colonel (1940), colonel (1942), and major general (February 1, 1944). After the RAF attack, Dawans and sixteen others were buried together in a mass grave, located in one of the bomb craters.
13. Friedrich Dollmann was a large and physically impressive officer who showed great political skill and adaptability throughout his career. Born in Wuerzburg in 1882, this artillery officer joined the Bavarian Army as a *Fahnenjunker* in 1901. A colonel by 1930, he commanded the 6th Artillery Regiment (1931–32) and was artillery commander VII and deputy commander of the 7th Infantry Division in Munich (1932–33). After serving as inspector of artillery (1933–34), he assumed command of *Wehrkreis IX* (1934–39), the main component of which became IX Corps upon mobilization in August, 1939. Dollmann had commanded the 7th Army since October 1939, but he had seen action only once in World War II—and on a secondary sector, at that. He had commanded an army of occupation in France since 1940 and had never faced the Anglo-Americans in battle. His performance as commander of the 7th Army left much to be desired in 1944. Although he was an early supporter of the National Socialists within the military, he became deeply troubled by their actions and had ceased to support them by 1944.
14. Kurt von der Chevallerie was born in Berlin in 1891. He attended cadet schools and entered the service as an officer-cadet in the 5th Guards Grenadier Regiment in 1910. Commissioned in 1911, he spent the first half of World War I as an infantry company commander and spent three months in hospitals in 1915, recovering from wounds. He spent the second half of the war in staff positions. Admitted to the general staff, Chevallerie commanded the II Battalion/17th Infantry Regiment (1933–34), Goettingen Infantry Regiment, and 38th and the 87th Infantry Regiments (1934–37). Named chief of the 10th Department of the army general staff in 1937, he became chief of the Central Office in 1938. He later commanded the 83rd Infantry Division (December 1939–December 1940), 99th Infantry Division (December 1940–December 1941), and LIX Corps (February 1942–February 1943). Chevallerie was acting commander of the 1st Panzer Army on the Eastern Front from April 21 to June 2, 1944, and acting commander of the 1st Army after that date. He was promoted to lieutenant general on New Year's Day 1941 and general of infantry on February 1, 1942. He was relieved

of his command on September 6 and was never reemployed. Chevallerie was in Kolberg on April 18, 1945, when the Soviets overran the city and was never seen since. His younger brother Hellmut became a lieutenant general and successfully commanded the 13th Panzer Division. Hellmut survived the war.

15. Paul Hausser, perhaps the single greatest influence of the military development of the *Waffen-SS*, was born in Brandenburg in 1880, the son of a Prussian officer. He was educated in the cadet schools and graduated from Gross Lichterfelde (located in Berlin-Lichterfelde), Imperial Germany's equivalent of West Point, in 1899. Guenther von Kluge was one of his classmates. Hausser was assigned to the 155th Infantry Regiment and served eight years of regimental duty. He became a member of the general staff in 1912, held several general staff positions during World War I (and also commanded an infantry company), and served with the *Freikorps* against the Poles after the war. He joined the *Reichsheer* in 1920 and retired as a major general in 1932, with an honorary promotion to lieutenant general. He joined the SS as chief training officer for the *SS-Verfuegungstruppe* (SS-VT), the embryo of the *Waffen-SS*. He soon became responsible for the military training of all SS troops except Theodor Eicke's "Death's Head" concentration camp guards. In late 1939, he was named commander of the SS-VT Division, which he led in France in 1940. This unit later became the 2nd SS Panzer Division "Das Reich," which Hausser led until October 1941, when he was badly wounded on the Eastern Front and lost his right eye. After he returned to active duty in 1942, he was named commander of the SS Panzer Corps (later II SS Panzer Corps), which he led on the Eastern Front in 1943–44, with uneven results. He was nevertheless promoted to SS colonel general and named commander of the 7th Army in Normandy, which he led until he was severely wounded during the breakout from the Falaise pocket. He escaped, but two-thirds of his command did not. A poor to mediocre army commander, he was nevertheless promoted to the command of Army Group G when he returned to duty in January 1945. By now he was thoroughly disillusioned with Hitler and the Nazi leadership. He was sacked in late March 1945 because he objected to one of Hitler's senseless hold-at-all-costs orders. Despite his long association with the *Waffen-SS*, Hausser was not subjected to a long imprisonment after the war. He remained a staunch defender of the Waffen-SS until his death in 1972, at the age of ninety-two.

16. Wilhelm Bittrich was born in February 26, 1894, in Wernigerode am Harz, the son of a German trade representative. He joined the 19th Reserve Jaeger Battalion when World War I broke out and ended the conflict as a second lieutenant and fighter pilot. He was a member of the Freikorps von Huelsen in the early 1920s and fought against the Poles in the Eastern Marchlands. Later, he was a civilian employee of the *Luftwaffe*, working as an instructor pilot, and was involved in training aviators at the secret German air base in Russia. He joined the Nazi Party in 1932 and entered the SS in July 1933. A member of the SS-VT, the forerunner of the *Waffen-SS*, Bittrich was almost immediately given command of a battalion, the I/SS "Germania" Regiment, because of his solid and varied military background, and was an SS colonel commanding the SS Regiment Deutschland in late 1940. He took charge of the 2nd SS Panzer Division after Paul Hausser was wounded in 1941 but had to give it up after he fell ill in early 1942. In May 1942, Bittrich assumed com-

mand of the 8th SS Cavalry Division "Florian Geyer," which he led against partisans in the Balkans. On February 15, 1943, he assumed command of the 9th SS Panzer Division "Hohenstaufen," which was just being formed. Bittrich assumed command of the II SS Panzer Corps when Hausser was promoted to the command of the 7th Army. Promoted to *SS-Obergruppenfuehrer und General der Waffen-SS* on August 1, 1944, he made a number of unguarded, derogatory remarks about Himmler and the Nazi leadership. The *Reichsfuehrer-SS*, Himmler, ordered him recalled to Berlin, but this move was blocked by Field Marshal Model, who protected him. Bittrich led the II SS until the war's end. He held the Knight's Cross with Oak Leaves and Swords, which was awarded on May 6, 1945, a week after Hitler's suicide and several days after Himmler had been stripped of his posts. He surrendered to the Americans at the end of the war, but they turned him over to the French, who held him until 1954, when he was finally released. He was then tried for war crimes committed in Bordeaux but was acquitted. See Jost W. Schneider, *Verleihung Genehmigt!*, ed. nd trans. Winder McConnell (San Jose, CA: R. James Bender Publishing, 1977), 35–37. General Bittrich died April 19, 1979, in Wolfratshausen, Upper Bavaria. Ernst-Guenther Kraetschmer, *Die Ritterkreuztraeger der Waffen-SS*, 3rd. ed (Preussisch Oldendorf, Germany: K. W. Schuetz-Verlag, 1982), pp. 220–23.

17. Von Geyr's forced retirement lasted only a few weeks. On July 21, 1944, the day after the unsuccessful attempt on Hitler's life, his friend Heinz Guderian became the new chief of the general staff of the army. The following month, Guderian managed to get von Geyr installed as his successor as inspector general of panzer troops. Captured by the Americans at the end of the war, von Geyr was a prolific writer about military affairs. Until the end of his life, von Geyr maintained that he was right and Rommel wrong concerning the use of German strategic reserves in Normandy. It is difficult to follow his logic, however. He died at Irschenhausen on January 27, 1974.

18. Rundstedt was recalled to active duty on September 5, 1944, and resumed command of OB West. He led it until March 9, 1945, when Hitler removed him for a fourth and final time. Captured by the Americans at Bad Toelz at the end of the war, Rundstedt was held by the Allies until 1949, when he was released because of ill health. He died at Castle Oppershausen near Celle on February 24, 1953.

19. William B. Breuer, *Hitler's Fortress Cherbourg* (New York: Stein and Day, 1984), 256.

# CHAPTER 3

# The Battles of the 5th Panzer Army, July 3–August 9, 1944

After his capture on August 31, 1944, General Eberbach was sent to various prisoner-of-war camps. In late 1947, he was transferred from British to American custody and thus fell into the hands of American officers, some of whom were military historians. Seeing that they had a unique opportunity, they allowed and encouraged their German prisoners to write about their experiences. Much of the rest of this book is taken from the memoirs of General Eberbach, which suffer from only one flaw: The general had access to only a few maps, none of which had any wartime information, and he did not have access to wartime documents or diaries, with the exception of one report written by a lieutenant. Eberbach therefore had to rely almost entirely upon his memory. But fortunately, that was very good indeed.

I have occasionally added a comma or modified a sentence for the sake of clarity. Writing without notes or his units' war diaries, for example, General Eberbach occasionally confused the 708th Infantry Division with the 711th Infantry Division. Where he made this error, I corrected it. Other than that, I have not changes the facts at all. When I wished to add facts, I did so in italics, brackets, or in the endnotes.

## MS #B-840: REPORT ON THE FIGHTING OF PANZERGRUPPE WEST (5TH PANZER ARMY) FROM 3 JULY–9 AUGUST 1944

### by Heinz Eberbach, *General der Panzertruppen*

*Introduction.*

After having fallen ill on the Eastern Front, where my last assignment had been that of commander of Army Detachment

Nikopol, I was assigned as Inspector of Panzer Troops of the *Heimatheer* (Army of the Zone of the Interior) [the Home Army] after my recovery in February, 1944.

On June 5, 1944, I flew to Russia to Army Group Model (i.e., Army Group North Ukraine) to take over the command of one of the three panzer corps which were to undertake an attack with a limited objective in the northern sector of this army group. Upon my arrival at Staff Model, I was informed that the invasion had begun in the West.

The invasion was soon reflected on the activities on the Eastern Front. The beginning of our offensive on that front was delayed for the time being. One intended to first wait for the developments in the situation in the west. On about June 12, 1944, entraining orders were received to transfer one of the three panzer corps destined for the offensive in the east, II SS Panzer Corps, to the west. Thus the intended attack had become an impossibility. It was cancelled. On June 16, 1944, I left Lemberg [now Lvov, Poland] in order to once more take up my former activity as inspector of panzer troops until further notice.

On June 30, 1944, I received orders to fly to the west—together with Field Marshal Guenther von Kluge—on July 1, 1944, in order to take over the command of Panzer Group West on the invasion front.

### Assumption of Command of Panzer Group West.

Field Marshal von Kluge, who was to replace von Rundstedt as the commander of the entire Western Front [i.e., OB West], informed me on the way that his orders from OKW were to put up a stubborn defense and, if possible, not to give up one inch of soil until the further enemy landing intentions had been clarified and so many German forces had been concentrated at a decisive point that a counterthrust could be carried out.

After reporting to the chief of staff, OB West, General of Infantry Guenther Blumentritt, and the chief of staff of Army Group B, Lieutenant General Hans Speidel (Field Marshal Rommel was at the front),[1] I arrived, on July 2, 1944, at the headquarters of Panzer Group West; was initiated by my predecessor, General of Panzer Troops Geyr von Schweppenburg; and took over the command of the panzer group on July 3, 1944.

The staff of Panzer Group West had, in its time, not been set up as an army staff in order to save men and material; it was a *Fuehrungsstab* [operational staff], with the result that, for example, it did not have eight signal communications companies normally available to an army headquarters but only had three, and also had no rear supply services. With the beginning of the invasion, Panzer Group West was put in charge of the Caen area; the invasion front was thereby subdivided into the right sector under Panzer Group West and the left one under 7th Army.

General von Geyr was under the direct command of Army Group B (Rommel), while he was dependent on 7th Army for his supplies.

A few days after the beginning of the invasion, the staff of Panzer Group West had been so badly shattered by pattern bombing that it had to be withdrawn and reorganized. It was not until June 24, 1944, that it could again take over the command in the frontal sector of Caen.

## The Situation at the Assumption of Command of Panzer Group West

### *The Enemy.*

The boundary between Panzer Group West and 7th Army generally coincided with the boundary between the British and American troops.

Panzer Group West was opposed by one British and one Canadian army. According to our intelligence reports, the enemy had at least one and a half times as many divisions as we had. Besides, the enemy divisions were considerably stronger in men and materiel than ours and were all fully motorized. Additional American and British divisions were being held in readiness on the other side of the Channel.

The greater experience in warfare of our troops and the superiority of our more recent types of tanks, compared with those of the Western powers, were points in our favor. On the other hand, the number of tanks available to the enemy amounted to approximately three times as many as our own—according to our calculations.

On about July 20, 1944, my senior artillery officer reported to me that the number of enemy batteries identified in our sector amounted to 344. At that time we had 133 batteries at our disposal.

In the air, however, the Anglo-American superiority was complete, and the cooperation between ground and air forces was highly developed.

The same situation prevailed on the sea: the enemy could—according to our observations—more or less undisturbedly carry out his shipping and landing operations according to schedule without being disturbed. His naval artillery effectively complemented the artillery on the land.

What were the intentions of the enemy?

Rommel and the staff of Panzer Group West considered a second landing in western France (Calais–Le Havre) as improbable because such a landing (apart from the landing in southern France, which was being considered as certain) would have required an unheard-of amount of materiel. The advantages of the defense—such as mines, obstacles, and fortified defense systems—would have had to be once more surmounted by the attack with an ensuing expenditure of men and materiel, and the risks connected with every landing—such as the weather and moments of weakness during the initial stage—would have had to be borne once more. A second landing would have afforded the defense the advantage of concentrating its forces, first against one of the bridgeheads and then against the other, with the result that at least partial successes could probably have been obtained. Such a second landing was therefore not to be expected. According to information received and opinions expressed, which I have no knowledge of, OKW was, at least up to the month of August 1944, of a different opinion. In a conversation with a reporter of the London *Daily Telegraph* (see edition of June 22, 1945), and during his examination in Nuremberg, Colonel General Alfred Jodl [the chief of operations at OKW] characterized the estimate of OKW of that time as a distinctive mistake.[2]

What were the enemy intentions in Normandy? In the beginning, the enemy was being compressed into a disagreeably narrow bottleneck. He had to get out of this bottleneck; that is to say, he had to attack. According to his strength, he could put up a point of main effort in the American sector, as well as in the British sector of the front. When considering the course of the front and the more favorable terrain for an attack, a point of main effort in the British sector seemed more likely. If the enemy succeeded in piercing Panzer Group West's front, the German Normandy front would have been unhinged, with the resulting threat of the divisions of 7th Army being pocketed in the Normandy peninsula or being pushed back to the south. Oppose the American front, however, and the terrain could at first be abandoned without grave consequences. This point of view was supported by the assumption that the British troops, being more experienced in warfare, would be chosen to force a decision. The state of training, the quality of leadership, and the spirit of sacrifice of the American troops were, at that time, still unknown to us.

It was to be assumed that in the sector of Panzer Group West, the British leadership would attempt to thrust as rapidly as possible into the open terrain between Caen and Falaise, which was advantageous to attacking forces, and by supporting its left wing on the Seine, would have launched one spearhead in the direction of Paris, the other into the rear of 7th Army. Apart from the terrain, our estimate was also confirmed by the fact that the Canadian army, which had no combat experience, had been committed on the right wing of the British army group and had thereby been given only a secondary mission for the time being.

### Our Own Troops.

What was the situation of our own troops?

OB West and Army Group B (Rommel) had drawn the necessary conclusions from the above-mentioned evaluation of the enemy intentions—as far as the contradictory estimate of OKW would permit. All available forces—with the exception of 15th Army in the Calais–Le Havre sector—had been moved up or were being brought up.

Rommel had built up a German center of gravity in the Panzer Group West sector in order to counter the main enemy thrust, which was to be expected in this area. For this purpose, the following seven panzer divisions had been concentrated: 2nd Panzer, 21st Panzer, Panzer Lehr, 1st SS Panzer "Leibstandarte Adolf Hitler," 9th SS Panzer "Hohenstafen," 10th SS Panzer "Frundsberg," and 12th SS Panzer "Hitler Jugend" (or Hitler Youth). In addition, army artillery, including railway guns, III

Flak Corps (under *Luftwaffe* Lieutenant General Wolfgang Pickert), and two rocket launcher brigades were subordinated to Panzer Group West.

*The III Flak Corps had no divisional headquarters in mid-1944. It consisted of the 1st, 2nd, 3rd, and 4th Flak Assault Regiments and 103rd Air Signal Battalions. The 1st Flak Assault Regiment comprised five standard flak battalions, which had been stationed in the Lille area. The 2nd Flak Assault Regiment was established in the summer of 1942 from the staff, 5th Flak Training Regiment, in Hamburg. It included four standard flak battalions and one heavy flak battalion. The 3rd Flak Assault Regiment had been the 37th Flak Regiment, which fought on the Eastern Front and was destroyed at Stalingrad. It was rebuilt around the staff of the Flak Lehr Regiment and was composed of two flak battalions and a light flak battalion. The 4th Flak Assault was the former 79th Flak Regiment, which had been stationed in Kaiserslautern, Lille, and Nantes. It had three standard flak battalions and a light flak battalion.[3]*

There were, however, only five infantry divisions available, with the result that in order to build up a somewhat continuous defensive front, at least strong elements of all panzer divisions had to be employed as infantry troops at the front, instead of being held in readiness for concentrated counterthrusts. Thus, their strength in men and materiel diminished with frightening rapidity.

The only reserves available to Panzer Group West were elements of these panzer divisions.

Nevertheless, by moving up elements of the flak corps for ground fighting at the focal point south of Caen, the defense had been deployed to such depth that the danger of a British breakthrough did not seem imminent for the time being.

As for the artillery forces, the number of guns at my disposal was considerable (133 batteries, without counting the flak batteries, by mid-July). But since ammunition was so scarce that firing had to be kept at a ratio of 1:10 to the British expenditure, the many guns and rocket launchers were of little use to me. The army artillery of the panzer group consisted of guns from nearly all European countries. For instance, twenty-four Italian heavy guns fired so badly and had so little ammunition that I suggested their demolition after expenditure of the few available shells.

The troops had deterioriated since 1941 as far as morale, the quality of officers, and the training condition were concerned.

Most of the divisions had neither had sufficient time, nor ammunition, nor POL [petroleum, oil, and lubricants] for their training. The coordination of weapons was therefore unsatisfactory except with a few divisions. The infantry divisions and the 21st Panzer Division had been activated or reorganized and trained in France. The long time they had been lying around in the communications zone had been of detrimental influence. The best officers and men had, in addition, been transferred to the east. Considering these circumstances, their performance was, in general, surprisingly good. Their training was sufficient for defensive operations. Although the soldiers had grown tired of war, their morale was altogether still undaunted, despite the depressing superiority of the enemy.

The equipment of the German divisions with weapons, etc., though quite heterogeneous and nowhere complete, was still sufficient. Of course, the horse-drawn infantry divisions proved to be no longer equal to the modern warfare in the west.

The German losses were high due to the material superiority of the enemy. I estimated them as at least as high as the losses of the enemy, who was in a better position to replace them than we were in. Within two to three weeks, the divisions employed at the focal points had been burned to cinders. Troop replacements arrived only slowly and in insufficient numbers. During July 1944, they covered only about one-sixth of our losses. Thus the infantry companies mostly had a combat strength of only fifteen to twenty-five men. By reassigning supply personnel, transferring artillery men, and holding on to minor casualties in the field hospitals, the lower commands took their own emergency measures. Despite high losses, the panzer divisions proved to be more resistant during this process of attrition than the infantry divisions.

If the front were to hold out, this war of attrition peremptorily demanded constant and timely moving up of additional divisions.

The supply situation was particularly harassing. At first the supplies for Panzer Group West had to be procured via 7th Army. The destruction of the railroad net and the demolition of the bridges, in particular the Seine bridges, threatened the supply system.

Panzer Group West had about 700 tanks and self-propelled assault guns at its disposal—that is, in theory. In reality, more than half of them had been lost due to direct hits and technical deficiencies, or they were being repaired. Tank replacements and spare parts arrived at an approximate ratio of 1:6 to the requirements. In addition, the tank replacements had to cover a distance of 200 kilometers [124 miles] from the detraining point to the front. Since the training of the drivers was only mediocre because of the shortage of POL, and since also many tanks suffered from constructional defects, half of the new tanks were eliminated already during their approach.

The motor vehicle situation was tense. There was no supply of new motor vehicles. No division was fully equipped with motor vehicles. Apart from the normal expenditure, motor vehicle losses from air attacks occurred daily. In addition, the destruction of the railroads resulted in an extension of the supply routes, POL had to be picked up in Paris, and spare parts for the tanks often had to be brought up from Magdeburg.

### The Situation in the Sectors of the Adjacent Armies.

Fifteenth Army in the Calais–LeHavre sector was not under attack and was holding the positions of the Atlantic Wall, the construction of which was relatively advanced in this sector. For this reason, and because of the separation by the Seine, communications with 15th Army were restricted to conferences on the moving up of divisions which were to be transferred from the army to Panzer Group West.

Seventh Army had—apart from a number of infantry divisions, one flak division and one rocket launcher brigade, and two panzer divisions—2nd SS Panzer "Das Reich" and 17th SS Panzer Grenadier "Goetz von Berlichingen." As a consequence of the loss of Cherbourg and the American advance on St. Lô, the 7th Army front had started to crumble in the beginning of July 1944. Shortly after my arrival, Panzer Group West was forced to transfer the Panzer Lehr Division to support 7th Army; 7th Army therefore had three panzer divisions at its disposal, against six assigned to Panzer Group West.

Our relations with 7th Army were close from the very beginning. Close cooperation between commanding officers and chiefs of staff respectively was assured by regular telephone communications and also by occasional personal meetings.

A special boundary detachment ("Naht-Kommand 2"), consisting of a reinforced battalion, was being held in readiness at the army boundary to avoid surprises the enemy might contemplate at this point.[4]

*As difficult as the situation was for Panzer Group West on the German right flank, it was much more difficult on the left, where the 7th Army was crumbling.*

*On June 9, Lt. Gen. Wilhelm von Schlieben launched a major attack on the U.S. 82nd Airborne Division's bridgehead west of Ste.-Mere-Eglise. His objective was to threaten the American beachhead at Utah Beach, but he was checked by U.S. Brig. Gen. James M. Gavin's battle group in heavy fighting. Schlieben then retreated to the western edge of the American perimeter, in order to defend Cherbourg, sixteen miles northwest of the Utah beachhead. Here he established a line manned by surviving elements of the 243rd Infantry Division, 91st Air Landing Division, and his own 709th Infantry Division. As a result of casualties, none of these units was at more than regimental strength. Schlieben, however, collected an impressive array of artillery, including a battalion of the 243rd Artillery Regiment, the 456th and 457th Motorized Artillery Battalions, a battery of six French 155 millimeter guns from the 1261st Army Coastal Artillery Regiment, the remnants of the 1709th Artillery Battalion (from his own division), five flak batteries from Flak Group Koenig, and part of the 100th Mortar Regiment. Schlieben placed all of the artillery under Maj. Friedrich Wilhelm Kueppers, a fine officer despite his low rank.*

*As soon as the Americans had established some depth to their beachhead, they began a campaign to capture Cherbourg, which would give them their first significant port on the European mainland. Their plan was to push to the west, cut the Cotentin peninsula in half, and then turn north against Cherbourg. U.S. Lt. Gen. J. Lawton Collins was placed in charge of this effort. His VII Corps included the 4th, 90th, 79th, and 9th Infantry Divisions and 82nd Airborne. After several days of probing and fighting, the Americans broke through on June 15.*

*The breakthrough occurred south of Maj. Gen. Rudolf Stegmann's 77th Infantry Division. This veteran commander realized that if he did not react quickly, his division would be cut off in Cherbourg and doomed, along with the rest of Group von Schlieben. Accordingly, he launched a breakout to the south— much to the surprise of the Americans. As a result of this brilliant maneuver, about half of the 77th Infantry escaped, though not General Stegmann. His body was ripped apart by 20-millimeter shells from an American fighter-bomber.*

*Although the 77th helped the LXXXIV Corps establish a thin line in the hedgerow country south of the U.S. VII Corps, it could not prevent Collins from cutting the Cotentin in half and isolating Cherbourg on June 18. The next day, Collins turned north, driving on the city itself. (He was not nicknamed "Lightning Joe" for nothing.) The drive was slowed by Kueppers's brilliant handling of the artillery and a huge storm that wrecked the American artificial port at Omaha*

*Beach, but nothing could save the garrison of Cherbourg. On June 22, it was attacked by about 1,000 aircraft. By the morning of June 24, Schlieben was signaling that he had no more reserves and the fall of the fortress was inevitable. Some German units were fighting tenaciously; in others, morale collapsed altogether. The fortress fell quickly. Schlieben surrendered at 1:30 P.M. on June 26. Major Kueppers was killed shortly thereafter. The last pocket of resistance surrendered on July 1.*

*During the battle of Cherbourg, Collins's corps lost 22,000 men, including 2,811 killed. The Germans lost approximately 47,070 killed, wounded, or captured, including 826 officers and 6 generals.[5]*

*The German situation would have been even worse had not Rear Adm. Walter Hennecke been naval commander, Normandy.[6] It was his task to destroy the port of Cherbourg before the Americans captured it. Hennecke, a man who had a tremendous talent for destruction and disorganization, conducted what the U.S. official history called "the most complete, intensive, and best-planned demolition in history."[7] It would be weeks before the Americans could get the slightest use out of the place. In short, the capture of Cherbourg did not solve the Allied supply problems in Normandy, as the Anglo-American leaders had hoped it would. Hitler was so delighted by Hennecke's accomplishment that he awarded him the Knight's Cross, even though the admiral was in captivity.*

### Cooperation with the Ranking Commands.

The conceptions of OB West [von Kluge] and Army Group B [Rommel] coincided with that of Panzer Group West with reference to the general situation as well as with details. Since the top commanders were fully aware of the difficulties experienced at the front, as a result of frequent inspection trips, the collaboration was homogeneous and harmonious. All requests and wishes expressed by Panzer Group West received as much support from these two commands as a situation, their own limitations and their orders from OKW would admit.

The orders from OKW were 1) a rigid defense; 2) no considerable weakening of 15th Army in favor of the Normandy front; 3) commitment of the panzer divisions for the defense of the front; and 4) adherence to the plan of annihilating the enemy at the right time by concentrating all forces. How this plan could finally be realized despite the enemy air supremacy, his superior land forces, and the insufficient German supply services remained an unanswered question.

*As of June 18, the Allies had brought 600,000 men ashore. By July 1, they had brought 929,000 men to Normandy. Rommel's Army Group B had about a third that number at or near the front. From D-Day to the third week of July, the U.S. 1st Army and British 2nd Army had lost 117,000 men. The 7th Army and Panzer Group West had lost 2,722 officers and 110,357 men over the same period. Only 10,078 of the German casualties had been replaced. The Allied casualties had been fully replaced.[8]*

Practically speaking, every withdrawal had to be authorized by OKW [Hitler]. Since these authorizations were often delayed for a long time, they frequently arrived too late. Thus occasionally actions had to be taken against orders, or one arrived at harmful compromise solutions.

By July 17, for example, the U.S. 1st Army had pushed the weak and battered II Parachute Corps to the outskirts of St. Lô. SS General Hausser signaled headquarters, Army Group B, and asked permission to abandon the town. Hausser's chief of staff, Maj. Gen. Max Pemsel, telephoned Col. Hans Tempelhof, the I-a [chief of operations] of Army Group B, to stress the urgency of the request and the need for a prompt decision. Pemsel wanted the request forwarded to OB West and then to OKW, which meant Hitler, in accordance with existing procedures. Tempelhof, however, knew that this approach was impractical, because he knew that Hitler would never approve it. "You take whatever measures you think are necessary," he told Pemsel. "If you have to withdraw, go ahead, just report to us afterwards that the enemy penetrated your main line of resistance in several places and that you barely succeeded in reestablishing a new line to the rear."[9]

The subterfuge worked. St. Lô fell on July 19, but the II Parachute Corps was saved.

I had no authority of command over the elements of the *Luft-waffe* and Navy stationed in the panzer group area; Army Group B and OB West had no authority over them either. This resulted in frequent frictions and idling of forces. While, for instance, an increase in transportation space would often have been of decisive importance to the armies, hundreds of motor vehicles belonging to the *Luftwaffe* and Navy remained idle.

*Neither Adm. Theodor Kramcke, the pro-Nazi commander of Naval Group West, nor Lt. Gen. Wolfgang Pickert, the commander of the III Flak Corps, were*

*subordinate to OB West or any of the army generals. They usually did not cooper-
ate with their army counterparts. Luftwaffe Field Marshal Hugo Sperrle, the commander in chief of the 3rd Air Fleet, would cooperate more frequently than the
other two. On the other hand, the* Luftwaffe *field divisions had been transferred
to the army on November 1, 1943. Most of their commanders were now army generals—even those who were not tactically and administratively subordinate to the
army.*

There were numerous V-1 and V-2 projector ramps with their
personnel within the panzer group area. The leadership and
troops were thereby given the impression that new weapons
would soon be employed very extensively. There was no precise
information on the time when they would be launched, or on
their effectiveness.

### The German Luftwaffe.

Numerous German fighter planes of a superior new type were
supposed to arrive within a short time. Actually, however, the
enemy air force exclusively dominated the skies. The consequences were very grave:

A) German attacks of some importance were, due to enemy
air supremacy, only possible in bad weather or during the night.
A German offensive seemed scarcely feasible, were it for this reason alone. Even a successful defense, because of the intensive
employment of the enemy air force (pattern bombing) without
German interference, was possible only by accepting high losses,
which could hardly be borne for any length of time.

B) While the enemy recognized every movement of ours from
the air, we had practically no air reconnaissance of our own.
Thus the enemy alone could make use of the element of surprise.

C) While the enemy directed his artillery fire by observation
planes without being disturbed, we never had this advantage.

D) Our daily losses in men and materiel from close support
airplanes and fighter-bombers were high in good weather. Their
effect on the morale of our soldiers also was considerable. On
the other hand, the enemy suffered practically no losses from
our planes.

*A joke made the rounds on the German side of the Western Front at this time: "If the airplane above you is silver, it is American. If it is camouflaged, it is British. If it is invisible (not there at all), it is Luftwaffe."*

E) The enemy was able to carry out displacements and supply operations by day and night without any interference whatsoever. All our movements in clear weather, however, could be accomplished during the night, which was six to eight hours long. During these few hours, we experienced overloading of the road and railroad network with resulting traffic jams. The consequences were 1) all our movements could be executed only slowly, and with many difficulties and losses; it was therefore necessary to plan in advance and prepare those movements very thoroughly; 2) the enemy was able to execute his movements at least twice as fast as we carried out ours; 3) movements of our units during daytime and good weather bogged down because of air attacks and caused heavy losses; 4) the supply situation was bound to become increasingly difficult; 5) the moving up of reinforcements was a tedious operation. Delays entailing critical situations had to be taken into account.

*By now, the "German glance" had arrived in Europe. It was a fugitive glance over the shoulder, looking for diving enemy airplanes.*

## Consequences of the Situation

### Strategic Conclusions.

A) After the successful Anglo-American landings, the military situation of Germany as a whole was such that one could continue the fighting only in order to still obtain not too stringent peace conditions. The aim of our fighting in the west therefore had to be to gain time to enable the political leadership to initiate armistice negotiations.

B) A large-scale German counterattack to push the enemy back into the sea was no longer possible because of 1) lack of sufficient army forces; 2) lack of air support; and 3) insufficient supplies.

C) The defense against the Anglo-American forces and containing them within the Normandy peninsula could still be continued for some time, if all forces available in the west [i.e., 15th Army] would immediately be moved up for the establishment of a defense in depth and the improvement of rear positions.

D) The forces available at present could hold the front for a few weeks, at best. In order to make these available forces suffice for some time, the defense had to be carried out in such a manner that the troops would not be completely exposed to the superior enemy materiel—pattern bombing and concentrated artillery fire—and that the good German panzer divisions would repeatedly be in a position to execute strong counterthrusts at advantageous points. The transition to a *mobile defense system,* however—which was essential for this type of operations— entailed the decision of giving up southern and central France and of preparing a timely withdrawal to the Seine–Yonne–Vosges position. This decision could only be successfully carried out if it were taken soon and on a voluntary basis.

The decision for the execution of such plans went beyond the scope of the mission of Panzer Group West. I know that Field Marshal Rommel shared my point of view and that he squarely supported it with his ranking commands.

### Tactical and Organizational Conclusions:

A) Avoid unneccessary bloodshed. For this purpose: 1) early withdrawal to the Orne position; 2) defense echeloned in depth; and 3) construction of rear positions.

B) Building up of a center of gravity south of Caen.

C) Constant urging for the transfer of additional infantry divisions in order to withdraw the panzer divisions from the front.

D) Extension of the staff of the panzer group to an army staff.

E) Execution of measures for the improvement of the supply services, particularly the organization of supply installations assigned to Panzer Group West.

### The Commanders and Troops Subordinate to Panzer Group West

My chief of staff was Lieutenant General Alfred Gause, formerly chief of staff of Rommel in Africa.[10] We got along well. Most of the time I went to the front, but sometimes he also drove there. In the evening, we made the necessary decisions and issued the relevant orders as far as that had not been done on the spot. My I-a was Major von Rottberg.

We changed command posts every two weeks. This measure proved effective. The command posts we had left usually were bombed out shortly after our departure, and that despite their remoteness.

The senior artillery officer of the panzer group, Major General Gerhard Grassmann, was directly subordinate to the Army Artillery.[11] I have already pointed out its motley composition and the shortage of ammunition which prevailed.[12] The two rocket projector (*Werfer*) [rocket launcher] brigades subordinate to panzer group, the bulk of which was concentrated at the center of gravity south of Caen, were also subordinate to the senior artillery officer. Their employment suffered from shortage of ammunition, which was never to be eliminated, and the inferior range of projectors. The mission of the senior artillery officer was to coordinate all batteries of panzer group down to division level. After the end of July 1944, he had a fire-control battery at his disposal for the purpose of concentrating the fire.

In the beginning of July, 1944, panzer group received two artillery PaK [antitank gun] battalions with 88-millimeter guns for commitment in the terrain which was advantageous for armored attacks. Since their artillery equipment was missing, they could only be used as static antitank guns in the depth of the main defensive area.

Some of the elements of the III Flak Corps under *Luftwaffe* Lt. Gen. Wolfgang Pickert took over the air-raid protection in the panzer group area.[13] The other batteries formed an antitank net at 6 to 12 kilometers [3.7 to 7.4 miles] distance behind the main line of resistance, thereby giving the defense a depth which, for a long time, permitted it to intercept the major attacks launched by the British.

The right-wing corps of the panzer group, LXXXVI Corps, was subordinate to General of Infantry Hans von Obstfelder.[14] His chief of staff was fifty-five-year-old Colonel Helmut von Wissmann of the Officers' Reserve Corps. Subordinate to the corps were:

A) The 711th Infantry Division (with only five battalions) was employed along the coast from Deauville to Merville. A so-called "static" division, it had only makeshift equipment. The divisional commander was Lieutenant General Joseph Reichert.[15]

B) The 346th Infantry Division was under the command of Lieutenant General Erich Diestel.[16] It was employed between Merville and the forest area east of Escoville. The division had suffered considerable losses during the preceding fighting.

C) The 16th Luftwaffe Field Division was in the adjacent sector, astride the Orne as far as Authie, west of Caen. The divisional commander was Lieutenant General Karl Sievers.[17]

D) The 21st Panzer Division was under the command of Major General Edgar Feuchtinger.[18] After having suffered considerable losses, it had just been relieved by 16th Luftwaffe Field Division and had been moved to the area north of Mezidon for its reorganization. This panzer division had been organized on a makeshift basis. Its equipment was partly different from that of the other panzer divisions. Also, it did not have the good, battle-tested cadre of officers and men the other panzer divisions had. This deficiency could not be completely equalized by its good commanders.

Adjacent to the west of LXXXVI Corps was I SS Panzer Corps under SS General Josef "Sepp" Dietrich.[19] His chief of staff was SS Colonel Fritz Kraemer.[20] Subordinate to the corps were:

A) The 12th SS Panzer Division "Hitler Jugend," which, judged by the quality of the troops, their combat morale, equipment, and training, was the best division in the west. Its divisional commander was SS Colonel Kurt Meyer. The division fought in the Authie–Carpiquet–Verson sector. It was reinforced by elements from the 1st SS Panzer Division "Leibstandarte." High losses had resulted in the greatly diminished combat strength of the 12th SS Panzer Division.

B) The 1st SS Panzer Division "Leibstandarte," only elements of which had arrived. The division commander was SS Major General Theodor Wisch.

The II SS Panzer Corps, under the command of SS Lieutenant General Willi Bittrich, held the Odon sector. His chief of staff was SS Lieutenant Colonel Peipkorn.[21] The corps was newly organized. Nevertheless, it was good. Subordinate to the corps were:

A) The 9th SS Panzer Division "Hohenstaufen," under the command of SS Oberfuehrer Sylvester Stadler.[22]

B) The 10th SS Panzer Division "Frundsberg," under SS Colonel Heinz Harmel.[23]

All the SS divisions suffered from a shortage of officers who had received thorough training for a number of years. For this reason, these divisions lacked good coordination of weapons. A similar situation also existed in the case of some of the army infantry divisions. On the other hand, the army panzer divisions still had good officers, but their equipment was worse than that of the SS panzer divisions.

The left-wing corps, XXXXVII Panzer, was under the command of General of Panzer Troops Baron Hans von Funck.[24] His chief of staff was Colonel Walther Reinhard. Subordinate to the corps were:

A) The 273rd Infantry Division, under Lieutenant General Albert Praun, which held the sector from Moyers to west of St. Vaast.[25]

B) The 2nd Panzer Division, under the command of Lieutenant General Baron Heinrich von Luettwitz,[26] commanding the area west of Caumont.

C) The 326th Infantry Division, commanded by Lieutenant General Victor von Drabich-Waechter,[27] in the area south and west of Caumont.

## The Loss of Caen

At the time of my arrival, the center of gravity of the fighting in the panzer group sector was in the Caen area, where the British were attempting to eliminate our bridgehead across the Orne, and north of Esquay, where the Canadians wanted to capture Hill 112, which dominated the terrain south of Caen, and which was being defended by II SS Panzer Corps.

The 16th Luftwaffe Field Division had just relieved the 21st Panzer Division, which had seen combat since the first day of the invasion and which had been greatly weakened. The *Luftwaffe* field divisions had so far not shown a combat efficiency equivalent to that of the Army units. The 16th Luftwaffe Field Division had nevertheless been committed in the center of gravity, only because no other division was available. Also, 16th Luftwaffe Field Division was numerically strong and properly equipped with materiel, had a good divisional commander, and had received more extensive training than other divisions of this type. In addition, twenty tanks of the 21st Panzer Division remained in the

16th Luftwaffe Field Division's sector, as support and for the purpose of counterthrusts.

The British fought very systematically. They did not take any risks, but always played for safety. They were never in a hurry. They preferred to avoid shedding too much blood during individual attacks, even though they missed out on several great opportunities. The British attacks mostly took place in the following manner: First they laid down pattern bombing of 2 to 3 kilometers [1.2 to 1.8 miles] width and depth, as well as heavy barrages, which annihilated the defending troops or softened them up. Then the British tanks advanced until they came under strong fire from German tanks or antitank guns, and then only came the British infantry, which was being sparsely used to occupy and hold the terrain which had been gained. The coordination of weapons on the British side was good.

To oppose these tactics, the defending party had to keep the main line of resistance only sparsely occupied, had to intercept the attack in the depth of the defensive position, and had to turn the tide by a rapid counterthrust. This procedure made high requirements on the troops with reference to training condition, morale, and ability of the troop commanders.

On July 7, 1944, strong elements of the British Army launched a large-scale attack on Caen in the above-mentioned manner. According to reports from my senior artillery officer, General Grassmann, the British fired approximately 120,000 shells on this day. Pattern bombing caused heavy losses among the battalions of the 16th Luftwaffe Field Division committed north of Caen. Nevertheless, the enemy at first succeeded in making only a few slight penetrations. Counterthrusts pushed back the British at certain points, but there remained gaps in the front. The 12th SS Panzer Division, which had also been attacked near Authie and Carpiquet, had, despite its weakness resulting from the heavy losses incurred during the preceding battles, repelled all attacks and had put out of action a great number of British tanks. During the night of July 7–8, the front north of Caen was withdrawn about 2 kilometers [1.24 miles], and the construction of a new defensive position was again being attempted. An additional battalion of 16th Luftwaffe Field Division was being moved to the western bank of the Orne as support. By this time Caen had—due to the burst of bombs and the artillery fire of the

British—become a pile of debris, which could only be passed through with difficulties, and where the inhabitants were recovering their dead and wounded with admirable courage. All bridges were being prepared for demolition.

When, on July 8, the British continued their attack with the same intensity, the 16th Luftwaffe Field Division front, north of Caen, collapsed. If the British armored units had made a daring thrust across Caen into the rear of 12th SS Panzer Division, this would have meant the annihilation of this division, which, on this day also, had again repelled practically all enemy attacks with heavy losses to the British. But by the evening of July 8, elements of the 16th Luftwaffe Field and one regiment of the 21st Panzer Division succeeded in stopping the British, who were hesitantly advancing, at the northeastern and northern city limits of Caen. Some elements of the units of the 12th SS Panzer Division, however, which were in the sector near Authie, were caught from the rear and were finally shattered. Altogether, about eighty British tanks were put out of action during these two days, the majority of them in the vicinity of Carpiquet.

The bridgehead had now become so narrow that it could no longer be considered the basis for a sortie at a later date. It was now only a salient in the panzer group front, which required strong forces and cost many lives, quite apart from constituting a threat of complete annihilation to the forces stationed beyond the Orne. On July 9, the British attacks diminished in strength. I therefore gave orders for a gradual withdrawal behind the Orne by the morning of July 10. This withdrawal was successfully accomplished. The bridges were blasted. Only the demolition of the railroad bridge near Colombelles did not succeed, but it was accomplished during one of the following nights, despite the vigilance of the enemy.

Since the corner of terrain between the Orne and the Odon Brook was an unfavorable position, I first withdrew our front to the heights of Eterville, and later to Maltot.

In order to enlarge his bridgehead across the Orne east of Caen, the enemy heavily attacked during the next days in the direction of St. Honorine and Colombelles, with weaker thrusts toward Vancelles. St. Honorine and Colombelles were temporarily lost, but were retaken by counterthrusts. Finally, the front had to be withdrawn a little near St. Honorine, while Colombelles remained in the hands of the 16th Luftwaffe Field Division, which fought well at this point.

The enemy intention of thrusting out of his Orne bridgehead could now already be recognized. Since he took his time, we had sufficient time to organize the defense south of the river. By employing the gradually arriving PaK and flak units, I ordered the building up of a main defensive area in depth. Rear positions were being determined, and their improvement was being undertaken by rear-echelon troops.

Half of 21st Panzer Division was withdrawn from LXXXVI Corps (Obstfelder) and used for the improvement and occupation of a reserve position which was situated approximately 3 to 4 kilometers [1.86 to 2.49 miles] behind the most advanced line.

The I SS Panzer Corps was assigned the advance elements of the 272nd Infantry Division (Lieutenant General Friedrich-August Schack) and committed them to the front as soon as they arrived.[28] Thus the corps could gradually withdraw strong elements of 1st SS Panzer Division in order to build up reserves behind the front. The remnants of the 12th SS Panzer remained on the line. It was thanks to the combat performance of the 12th SS Panzer Division that the Germans had not been defeated at Caen at the beginning of the invasion and during the recent fighting.

## Fighting for Hill 112

The main line of resistance of II SS Panzer Corps had at first been situated along the Odon Creek, with its combat outposts along the Caen–Villers road. Now that the combat outposts were being pushed back, it became obvious that the slope toward the Odon was too easily overlooked to maintain troops at this point against an enemy whose artillery was so superior, unless heavy losses were to be taken into account. Thus the front was at first withdrawn to the Verson–Fontaine–Baron line, and after Baron had been lost at the beginning of July, to the Verson–Hill 112–Bougy line. The Canadians very stubbornly attacked this frontal sector practically every day.

Their attack methods were different from the British. Although their advance was also preceded by bombing attacks and a heavy barrage, the forces committed to following up rarely exceeded one regiment and up to fifty tanks. Attacks on a larger scale were rare. This method might partly have been conditioned by the terrain, which was more difficult to survey than usual. In general, however, the Canadian attacks seemed to be lacking some of the sureness and planning with which the British were being conceived. According to the impression we were given, the coordination of weapons also was not up to the standard reached by the British. On the other hand, the Canadians were perhaps less calm, more enterprising, more daring, and tougher than the soldiers from the mother country. I had the impression that the individual Canadian was a brave child of nature, and that therefore his average combat efficiency was superior to that of the British city dweller. The lower command of the Canadians also was good. On the other hand, the British leadership of larger units seemed superior to me.

Hill 112 changed hands several times. Again and again, the SS recaptured it by counterattacks. Since finally both sides were claiming its possession, I myself went up there. The situation was as usual in similar cases: Both sides occupied parts of the wide, flat height, but in such a way that the enemy, after all, was refused a view into the plain south of Caen. I found the report of my special-mission staff officer on this trip to the front among my letters. Since it contains a number of interesting points, I am attaching it here:

Billet Area, July 13, 1944
SUBJECT: Inspection Trip to the Front of General of Panzer
        Troops Eberbach on July 13, 1944.

6 A.M.: Departure from the command post of Panzer Group West. Drive to the Caen combat area, sector of II SS Panzer Corps. Across the demolished Orne bridge at St. Andre to Feugerolles to the command post of SS Grenadier Regiment Schulz, a unit belonging to 10th SS Panzer Division.

7:30 A.M.: SS Colonel Schulz reports that the present combat strength of his regiment still amounted to 400 men, which were forming three battalions. The army commander [Eberbach] advises assembly into two battalions, 114 men arrive as replacements on wagons which had been dispatched by the replacement-training battalion on July 12, 1944.

The army commander points out that it is essential that the present MLR [main line of resistance] be held at all costs because of the employment of special combat measures [revenge weapons]. The unit commanders were to search for means of sparing lives. When questioned on his combat experience, SS Colonel Schulz points toward the necessity of occupying the MLR as densely as possible, like a string of pearls; otherwise there was a danger of individual grenadiers being taken prisoner during the night. For this reason, he was against echelonment in depth because of the shortage of manpower.

In rejecting these arguments, the army commander emphasizes the necessity of organizing the main defensive area as far back as possible, if possible in three waves, in such a manner that, during daytime, only one-third of the men would be stationed in the MLR or in front of it, respectively, while two-thirds stayed in the depth of the main defensive area. During the night, one additional third can be moved up to the front in order to avoid that individual sentries be cut off by surprise raids.

SS Colonel Schulz points out that the establishment of the MLR along the course of the Caen-Evrecy roads within the area of Hill 112 was proving effective, because there the northern road ditches afforded cover and gave an opportunity for digging into foxholes. Moving the MLR farther up front did not serve any useful purpose, because it could be overlooked from the terrain features in the vicinity of Carpiquet and would become a target to direct fire. The supplies of close-combat weapons and ammunition were satisfactory. There was a shortage of mines, in particular of stray mines.

8 A.M.: The itinerary leads to Hill 112, where the observation post of the SS artillery was located. Splendid observation point for the entire sector of Hill 112, which was being contested.

8:30 A.M.: Continuation via Esquay (some corpses of SS men, which had not been buried, at the exit from the village) to the southern rear slope of Hill 112. No harassing fire. The closer one approaches the contour line, the denser are the strikes, about 90 percent of which are of light caliber. In the perimeter of the knoll, the terrain appears as if it were perforated by the many hundreds of impacts and scraped by a coarse hoe. The scattered ammunition, shelter-halves, etc., attract attention. On the hill, three tanks are in well-camouflaged positions. The tim-

ber forest on the western part of the hill is completely smashed
up. In the forest and on hill terrain are disabled enemy and
German tanks, shattered antitank guns and carriages. There is a
clear view of the enemy positions north of the Caen-Evrecy road
from the most forward infantry line. The enemy continues to
remain quiet. SS grenadiers were relieved during the night.
Most of the soldiers are lying around idle in their foxholes.
Nobody is digging anywhere. A visual reconnaissance officer
reports favorable experiences made with covering slit trenches
and shelters only slightly with beams and planks. They resisted
two direct hits without major damage. The grenadiers in the
front line praise the Panzer IV–type tanks very highly. The fact
that the expected continuation of the enemy attack on Hill 112
did not take place is being attributed to our own strong artillery
fire, supported by rocket projectors, which, during the hours of
the night, was directed against traffic and preparations respectively, observed in Baron, Garvus, [and] Tourmauville. Because
of our satisfactory supply of ammunition, our artillery fire was
very intensive.

It was only upon our departure from Hill 112 that the enemy
fired a few rounds of light caliber shells into the reverse slope of
the hill.

9:45 A.M.: At the command post of 10th SS Panzer Division
"Frundsberg," the I-a first reports on the successful employment
of artillery during the night. The troops have two more issues of
ammunition. The I-a explains the inactivity at the front up to
this hour by expressing the belief that the enemy—after we had
retaken Hill 112 with the support of tanks and had repelled
another enemy attempt to capture the hill—considered the
continuation of attacks against a panzer corps as senseless.

Among other details, SS Colonel Harmel reports on the combat tactics used by the enemy that they fire dummy grenades up
to the last second before starting their attack and also already
during the advance of their infantry, without interrupting the
general barrage for a single second. When the smoke of the last
dummy grenade vanishes, the enemy is already within our own
position. They also use plenty of smoke. The army commander
recommends trench periscopes and observation by telescope as
countermeasures. Digging in was absolutely essential. For this
purpose, engineers had to be taken to the front line in difficult

terrain, such as Hill 112. "We must hold out under all circumstances; we must therefore dig in to save manpower and thereby cut down on casualties!"

The commitment of engineers as boundary detachments is therefore impossible. More work has to be accomplished everywhere.

Furthermore, the army commander suggests that the division command post be established on Hill 120. The collection of equipment and ammunition, as well as of cattle, and the milking of the cattle, which were unattended in the vicinity, was of vital importance to the troops. Still more men from the trains and rear services had to be moved to the front, above all those men who could no longer be used at their present point of employment because of the loss of their wagons and equipment.

In order to provide faster transportation for the infantry units which were to replace the panzer divisions, the army commander requested the divisions which were to be replaced to furnish transportation space of their own. SS Colonel Harmel promised to pick up one battalion a night with his own transportation. SS Colonel Harmel reports the following on new armored tactics: The enemy covers the area with smoke shells. In between the heavy tanks, he sends in some small armored cars, so-called "Scouts," firing rockets against our tanks from the smoke screen in a fan-type pattern. After short, quite effective fire, the small cars immediately disappeared again.

A very revealing enemy map was captured; it showed imprinted results of air and ground reconnaissance and reports from agents. This type of map is issued daily on a 1:25,000 scale. The interpretation of this map shows that the enemy is surprisingly well informed on our positions, preparations, and billeting areas. The map will be taken to his command post by the army commander to serve as a datum. The army commander repeats the comments he has already made at his conference with SS Colonel Schulz, and points out the special need for digging in and echeloning in depth the main defensive area by leaving at the most one-third of the combat strength in the MLR area during daylight.

11:10 A.M.: Upon arrival at the command post of II SS Panzer Corps, and as a result of reports received from SS Lieutenant

General Bittrich and SS Colonel Pipkorn as well as the conferences at the command posts of Regiment Schulz and 10th SS
Panzer Division and the inspection of Hill 112, the most essential matters can be summarized in three points which are to be
acted upon: 1) the units are to be echeloned in depth; 2) every
man has to disappear underground in order to save lives during
heavy artillery fire and enemy zone fire; for this reason, the
improvement of positions has to be rapidly and extensively
achieved; and 3) the infantry units have to be moved up rapidly,
to relieve the panzer divisions. For this purpose, all available
transportation space of the divisions which are to be relieved
will be allocated to the infantry divisions.

These three most essential measures must be carried out all
the more rapidly, since the present situation and the evaluation
of enemy intentions make a new, early major enemy attack at
the focal points of the present fighting, also in the Hill 112
area, seem an absolute certainly.

Noon: Return trip to the panzer group command post. On
the way back, a disabled Panther tank, which stands about 6
kilometers [3.7 miles] east of Thury-Harcourt on the Thury-
Harcourt-Falaise road, attracts our attention. (It could be made
use of by the maintenance workshop.) Farther along the same
road, 7 kilometers [4.35 miles] west of Falaise, we find an extensive lumber dump with thick beams for covering trenches and
foxholes.

12:30 P.M.: Arrival at the panzer group command post.

(Signed): Lutz Koch
Lieutenant

In order to satisfy some of the complaints of the front with reference to the British artillery superiority, I ordered my senior
artillery officer to execute a surprise fire in the II SS Panzer
Corps sector. After many efforts and extensive preparations, we
scraped together the ammunition for the attack. The artillery
proudly reported that 2,500 rounds had been prepared for the
artillery concentration. Once it had started, there really was
some detonation. But I soon observed that the greater part came
from the enemy side. Actually, the British had—with the greatest
of ease—returned 22,000 rounds for our 2,500. We were con-
ducting a poor man's war. By building up centers of gravity of

ammunition and by surprise fire on enemy preparations, we attempted to equalize our inferiority in ammunitions. On an average, we have never had more ammunition than one issue. The shortage of ammunition was critical during the days of large-scale fighting.

The Anglo-Canadian radio discipline generally was good. I insisted upon the installation of an efficient intercept service from the beginning, also for the supervision of German radio discipline. As a result, we soon succeeded in decoding some of the British radio messages. They were our most important source of intelligence information. Among other results, the bombing of staff headquarters, which the enemy intended in our area, could mostly be made ineffective by intercepting the messages and by their rapid transmission to those who were being threatened.

## The Major British Attack

We were aware of the fact that the attacks on the II SS Panzer Corps front also were to serve the purpose of distracting our attention and of diverting our reserves from the preparations which were being made in the vicinity of Caen. Neither of these two Allied hopes was justified. We had a fairly clear picture of the intentions of Montgomery. Air reconnaissance carried out by night—it was impossible to do so by day—and ground observation confirmed our estimate. Among many other reports, we received some on armored concentrations north of Caen, commitment of new batteries in the same area, and bridge constructions across the Orne. The interception of enemy radio messages also confirmed our estimate of the enemy intentions.

There were no signs of an impending airborne landing or landing from the sea in the rear of our front. Both types of landings would have been extremely dangerous to the panzer group. Reserve groups against airborne landings were formed from corps rear elements.

I was somewhat worried by the imminent large-scale attack. The remnants of the 12th SS Panzer Division had been transferred from the panzer group to OKW reserves and had been moved to the Lisieuz area. All I could scrape together in the way of reserves were elements of the 1st SS Panzer Division, which, after their heavy fighting and losses, could not be considered very highly. The combat strength of the infantry regiments, which belonged to divisions employed at the front, was on the average only about 500 men.

There were no indications as to the probable date of an enemy attack.

On July 18, 1944, we were awakened in the early morning by a British artillery barrage. A hailstorm of more than 100,000 shells descended upon our positions. Two thousand two hundred British and American planes flew wave after wave over our front from 5:45 A.M. to 10 A.M., without being interfered with, and dropped 7,000 tons of bombs. The area of annihilation, which was thereby created, was for the first time six kilometers wide and six kilometers deep. No German plane was to be seen. The greatest battle of materiel since the beginning of the invasion had begun.

It was annoying that no news whatsoever got through for hours, both on enemy or German troops. But after all, everything possible for intercepting the attack had been done, and two armored wedges with altogether 150 tanks were being held in readiness for a counterthrust against the flank of the enemy armored forces.

At 10 A.M., the alarming news finally arrived that the enemy had penetrated our front to a depth of 10 kilometers [6.21 miles], that hundreds of tanks had reached Bourguebus and were continuing their irresistible advance.

What had happened?

The hail of enemy artillery shells and bombs had simply swept away not only the remaining half of the 16th Luftwaffe Field Division, but also the elements of the 21st Panzer Division, which had been assigned to the second position in its rear. The local reserves had been annihilated or shattered, their guns smashed before they ever fired a shot. When the enemy tanks penetrated into our front, they found no resistance. In addition, the telephone communication lines had been cut. The radio stations of the intermediate command staffs, insofar as they had not been damaged, had been put out of commission by dust and concussion. The observation posts, even insofar as they were not situated in the sector under attack, saw for hours nothing but a screen of smoke, dirt and flames. Thus the batteries which were left intact did not know where to fire. And if they fired all the same, then enemy fighter bombers immediately dived onto them and silenced them with machine-gun fire and bombs.

The situation was critical. The new-type battle of materiel of the enemy seemed to be completely successful. Considering the enemy superiority in tanks (800 against 160), a breakthrough seemed to be unavoidable.

I launched the armored group of the 21st Panzer Division, which had been further reinforced by an army Tiger battalion, from the Bellengreville area and the armored group of the 1st SS Panzer Division from the Fontenay area for a counterthrust against the flanks of the enemy armored wedge. Both groups were to meet at Hubert Folie, within the enemy wedge. The point of the enemy wedge was to be stopped by the 88-millimeter flak guns of General Pickert.

Both of our armored groups were to start their movement at noon, but the group of the 21st Panzer Division had suffered such severe losses from pattern bombing that it reported unable to start before 2 P.M. Some tanks had received direct hits; others had turned over or had fallen into bomb craters. The tank turrets had been immobilized by the dirt, which had been whirled up; the optical and radio installations of the tanks had been incapacitated. On the basis of this report, I postponed the counterthrust to 2 P.M., which was very much against my wish. Where would the enemy tanks be by then?

Shortly before 2 P.M., the 21st Panzer Division reported that Panzer Group Oppeln (under Colonel Hermann von Oppeln-Bronikowski, the commander of the 22nd Panzer Regiment) could not start before 3 P.M.[29] I had considered the joint attack of the two armored wedges as decisive for the success of the counterthrust, but now it was too late to stop the 1st SS Panzer Division. Its attack had been launched. Group Oppeln, however, actually did not start off until 4 P.M., and then only with a small group of tanks which had been repaired. Even then this group did not really get ahead. It seemed as if it were paralyzed.

But how far had the enemy tanks meanwhile advanced in their rush? Something which was incomprehensible for any armored expert had happened: The enemy tanks had stopped during the decisive hours between 10 A.M. and 3 P.M.

Thus started an armored battle, which continued all through the afternoon and lasted until the evening. We succeeded in repelling the enemy tanks at their flanks and to definitely stop their advance points. By the evening, 150 enemy tanks had been put out of action. The German losses were not even one-third of this number.

But at Troarn, also, the situation had become critical. There the enemy had penetrated into the city. And there we had no troops, no more reserves capable of stopping them, if they continued to powerfully advance. In addition, there was a 5-kilometer [3-mile] gap in the front to the south of Troarn as far as Cagny, and behind this gap there were no other troops but a few detachments of flak near Argences. There the enemy only had to march, then they would have achieved a breakthrough. These were difficult hours for us. The *Daily Telegraph* wrote at that time: "Dramatic results may develop in the very near future."

One German battalion, which was completely encircled, still continued to fight near Colombelles. In Vancelles, elements of 1st SS Panzer Division had repelled all Canadian attacks, partly by counterattacks, despite the hail of artillery shells and bombs. Farther to the south, on the Orne, our units were standing with their backs to the river near Bourgebous. If the rear elements of the British armored divisions turned against these German forces, these battalions, together with all their guns, could not have escaped complete annihilation.

Finally, it became dark. The British had continued to stay immobile, as if a miracle had happened. Under the protection of darkness, the forces which had been cut off were successfully disengaged from the enemy. We built up a new defensive position along the approximate line Herouvillette–Troarn–Cagny–Bourgebus–St. Andre. The last reserves of Corps Obstfelder recaptured Troarn. The worn-out 12th SS Panzer Division, which had once more been subordinated to me upon urgent requests, closed the wide gap between Troarn and Cagny before daybreak.

Thanks to the hesitations of the British and the inactivity of the enemy during the night, the enemy breakthrough on the first day of attack had thus been prevented. On the morning of July 19, 1944, the British and Canadians were thus once more facing a continuous front. But this front was thinly spread. It no longer had the protection of the Orne. The armored reserve groups of

the 21st Panzer Division and the 1st SS Panzer Division, fleeced
and tired from the preceding day, constituted our only reserves.
Should the enemy repeat his devastating attack methods of the
preceding day, a breakthrough seemed inevitable.

But again a miracle happened: The enemy did not summon
up his strength for another large-scale attack. Although a few villages were lost as a result of his scattered thrusts, which he continued during the whole day, and although the fighting went back
and forth, the front held out. And on this second day of attack,
the losses of British tanks were again high. Especially in this open
terrain, the wider range and force of penetration of our Panther
and Tiger tanks made itself felt against the British Shermans. The
enemy had now lost more than 200 tanks within two days. One
company of German assault tanks (*Sturmpanzer*) drove toward the
strongly occupied town of Cagny and annihilated [British forces
defending] the town by bursts of its 150-millimeter shells.

The British radio announced [they had lost] 2,500 men captured, which is proof of the excellent way in which our troops
fought.

During the night of July 19–20, strong elements of the 2nd
Panzer Division, which had been withdrawn from my left wing
corps, arrived in the St. Stilvrain area. The weather on July 20
was rainy; the enemy planes could therefore not intervene. And
we knew that the British would not attack without their support.
Also, during the night, our artillery had effectively concentrated
its fire on preparations [and assembly areas] recognized on the
enemy side, as well as on relief operations of armored divisions
by infantry units.

On July 21, 1st SS Panzer Division captured an entire British
battalion—300 men—by a coup de main.

The major Anglo-Canadian attack had been repelled.

The losses of men, PaK, and artillery, which had to be sacri-
ficed for this defensive success, were high. We could not repeat
such sacrifices very often. To the simple soldier, the resistance
against such superiority must have seemed hopeless. One had to
give him an objective, which gave his holding out some sense; one
had to fix a date or state some well-founded hopes. I therefore
requested repeatedly that a leading personality from OKW look
over the situation at this point and formulate the ideas and plans
of OKW to us. Field Marshal von Kluge supported my requests.

## Reorganization

The British successfully hid from us their further intentions. The troops at the front reported several times enemy preparations in the sector south of Caen. On several occasions, British artillery barrages seemed to indicate a major attack in this sector. The London radio announced the imminence of a new British offensive. Everything seemed to point toward a continuation of the attack toward Falaise. We had to take countermeasures against it.

The construction and improvement of rear positions was accelerated, mines were being brought up, switch positions were being constructed for the artillery, etc.

The main effort, however, tended toward the creation of reserves.

The LXXXVI Corps, the sector of which now extended only as far as Troarn, was given reserves of its own by the withdrawal of elements of the static 711th Infantry Division from the coastal sector.[30] In the present situation, I considered an enemy landing in our rear as improbable.

Only remnants were left of the infantry troops of the 21st Panzer and 16th Luftwaffe Field Divisions after the conclusion of the British attack. The artillery of both divisions had also suffered considerably. I effected a merger of the two divisions by the absorption of the *Luftwaffe* field division by the 21st Panzer Division. This merger took place in the LXXXVI Corps area, but the division was, during that time, directly subordinate to Panzer Group West.

The I SS Panzer Corps, which was responsible for the sector from Troarn to the Orne, continued to keep strong elements of the 1st SS Panzer Division as reserves. The corps was given the mission of energetically persevering in the reorganization of the 12th SS Panzer Division, despite its continued commitment at the front. Among other items, division was short 11,000 carbines, 800 submachine guns, and half of its artillery. Practically all its company commanders had been killed or wounded. Here 1st SS Panzer Division had to intervene, since it had excess equipment. The rear services of both divisions were of such numerical strength, which consisted almost exclusively of young men, that from the service troops of these two divisions alone, several hundred men could be assigned to front duty. By subordinating Army

Tiger Battalion 503 and one assault tank battalion—equipped with Panzer IV chassis and with strong armor and 150-millimeter howitzers—to this division, its armored forces also once more had striking power. The 272nd Infantry Division had proven its value.

There were no changes at II SS Panzer Corps.

The XXXXVII Panzer Corps received orders to straighten out its front in order to make two infantry divisions suffice for its occupation. The 2nd Panzer Division, which had thereby become available, was moved into the Afran–St. Silvain–Urville area as panzer group reserves, together with 116th Panzer Division (commanded by Major General Count Gerhard von Schwerin), which was arriving after July 25.[31]

While several fully equipped army staffs were idle in France during this period, the staff of Panzer Group West, which had been committed in the focal point of fighting, still had only emergency equipment. This fact presented disadvantages, which we attempted to equalize, but which were to show their detrimental effect on the leadership and the course of the fighting in the long run. Finally, my requests for improvement of the staff were granted.

The shortage of signal communications equipment of the staff made itself particularly felt, since this equipment was essential for the command of so many units. Instead of a signal regiment with eight companies, we had a battalion with three companies. By the assignment of a regimental staff and one company by army group, and the incorporation of the signal battalion of the 16th Luftwaffe Field Division (two companies), one signal regiment could be formed by the end of July. It consisted of six companies.

Trucking space for 350 tons was diverted from the truck convoys of 7th Army at the beginning of July and was assigned to the panzer group for its own supply services. I had an excellent O Qu (quartermaster officer) in Reserve Lieutenant Colonel Colsmann, who quickly organized an efficient quartermaster battalion, and who extended the supply services of Panzer Group West in such a manner that there was a marked improvement. The supplies of artillery ammunition, in particular, could be increased so much that the ratio of expenditure improved at times from 1:10 to 1:3. The use of Seine shipping for our supply services by the capable O Qu of Army Group B, Colonel Eberhard Finckh, also contributed to the increase in supplies.[32] But the supply situation continued to be critical. Because of the long distances separating the railheads from the front, enforced by the enemy bombing attacks, the horse-drawn vehicles of the infantry divisions, with their low capacity of tonnage and their reduced radius of action, could no longer suffice [for] the supply requirements of the troops. The horses ate, needed disproportionately many men for their care, and were, in this type of warfare, of practically no value. Since the troops at the front shared this impression, they left only the worst personnel with the trains. These men cared little about good traffic discipline and contributed in a large measure to the often disastrous obstruction of the roads. The horse-drawn vehicle was useless in the west. The supply services of the infantry divisions would have been insufficient without the use of the trucking space furnished by the adjacent panzer divisions.

The staff of the 16th Luftwaffe Field Division was assigned by me as command staff for the army rear area. A military police battalion was formed from the remnants of the division, in order to maintain discipline behind the front and to regulate the traffic.

The continuous air attacks on important bridges and other objectives necessitated the maintenance of damage clearance and repair service crews at certain points. They had to be taken from the front, which anyhow was so thinly spread. Requests for the allotment of army engineers and construction battalions were rejected by OKW. Even now, OKW used these units still exclusively for the improvement of the Atlantic Wall.

At the end of July 1944, Panzer Group West was redesignated 5th Panzer Army.[33]

## Developments in the Situation Up to July 26, 1944

Even though there was no major attack up to July 26, not one day passed without minor enemy thrusts. The evening attacks, favored by the Canadians, were particularly disagreeable.

They usually succeeded, by plentiful commitment of materiel, to "fire" (*herausschiessen*) us out of a position and thereby to advance 2 to 3 kilometers [1.24 to 1.86 miles]. During daytime, we often succeeded in regaining the lost position by a quick counterthrust. But the situation was still too confused for counterthrusts during the night, especially since the troops also were no longer sufficiently trained. Thus the Canadians had time to dig in during darkness and to organize the defense. On the next morning, they could only be driven back with losses which we could not afford. This is how the Canadians expanded their bridgehead.

Apart from the 380-millimeter shells of the "Rodneys" [i.e., naval gunfire by HMS *Rodney* and *Nelson*], the so-called "*Schein-Granaten*" [dummy shells] fired by the Canadians were very inconvenient. These glass shells exploded with the same detonation as ordinary grenades, but they had no effect. The enemy used these shells immediately before the assault, thus keeping the defensive forces under cover while the attacking troops could advance unharmed and surprise the defending forces before they were ready for combat.

The enemy pressure in the I SS Panzer Corps sector was being maintained. Along the Orne, the fighting for St. Andre was very stubborn, and this town, as well as St. Martin, finally remained in Canadian hands.

Maltot was captured by the enemy in the II SS Panzer Corps sector. The fighting for Hill 112 continued; the height remained in German hands.

Violent thrusts against the right wing of XXXXVII Panzer Corps in the vicinity of Noyers were repelled by the commitment of the first company of a *Jagdpanther* [tank destroyer] battalion, equipped with 88-millimeter guns, and with the support of the 9th SS Panzer Division, after minor losses of terrain.

There were scarcely any partisans in the 5th Panzer Army (Panzer Group West) area. Cases of sabotage were rare. The population was friendly. By maintaining strict discipline among our troops, we attempted to keep up the friendly spirit of the population. Wherever the inhabitants were being endangered by the combat actions, they were evacuated into the rear areas of the army according to plan and in an orderly manner, together with their belongings.

## The Situation at the End of July 1944

Statements by prisoners, our own observations, the results of radio intelligence, individual air reconnaissance, and reports from our agents indicated that the landings of American and British divisions were continuing in the bridgehead. Since the British and the Canadian armies, which had so far appeared opposite the panzer group, consisted of about the usual number of divisions, the presence of an additional British army had to be taken into consideration. It was possible that the same fact applied to the American sector. Not only the narrowness of the bridgehead, but also political and strategic considerations necessarily would force the enemy to use his new units as early as possible for an offensive.

Where would they be employed?

The enemy strength and superiority were sufficient for a full-scale attack along the entire front. He now had to attempt to achieve a breakthrough. The favorable terrain between Caen and Falaise ought to attract him now as ever. In the comparatively open terrain in that sector, he could fully deploy his superior materiel. If he achieved a breakthrough, Paris beckoned as a magnificent reward. Since the bridges across the Seine had been demolished below Paris, the river offered effective flank cover to the advancing British forces. If, in addition, the German forces could be pushed back away from the Seine toward the south, their supply problems would become acute and their annihilation possible. The objection to this plan, however, was that the first British attempt to break through in the direction of Falaise had failed. From the experiences of World War I, however, it was quite likely that this objection would not deter the British leadership from attempting a reinforced attack at the same point. It was at this point, therefore, that one had to build up strength.

The possibility of a secondary British thrust west of Caen for the purposes of diversion and for the possession of the hilly terrain of Mont Pincon near Ondefontaine and east of St. Martin was not excluded. This attack would encounter terrain difficulties, but would have to deal with only two widely extended infantry divisions.

Also, a British attack in this sector for the support of the Americans was conceivable.

The Americans had so far acted very independently and had obtained surprisingly great successes. They were obviously in no way only an appendix to the British. They might support the to-be-expected British attempt at a breakthrough toward Falaise by a thrust on Vire, or they might also thrust independently, as they had done so far, either from St. Lô in the direction of Avranches, in order to encircle strong elements of 7th Army, or attack along the coast toward the south. According to the latest news from the adjacent army, the Americans were engaged in carrying out the latter plan. Their objective would then be Paris and the annihilation of the German troops in Normandy, in conjunction with the British on the lower Seine.

How was the German leadership to react to this situation and the possibilities arising from it?

Our inferiority in men and materiel had further grown since the beginning of July, because of the continuous landing of additional Allied divisions in Normandy and the German losses. Everything that has already been said on the subject of strategic conclusions was still valid, only increasingly so.

In contrast to the days of four weeks ago, 7th Army could now abandon just as little terrain as 5th Panzer Army, if they were to restrict the enemy to the Normandy bottleneck.

Was it now still possible to keep the enemy compressed in that area? The German front was considerably longer and had therefore grown proportionately. Even if OKW had now decided to employ all available forces on the Caen–Avranches front, they would have arrived too late to prevent the enemy breakthrough out of the Normandy peninsula. But the withdrawal of the German Normandy armies to the Seine position was now still possible, if it were ordered immediately, and if the divisions of 15th Army and other German forces were taking up a covering position along the Seine.

In any case, it had now become necessary to assign to 7th Army also a sufficient number of panzer divisions. Thus 9th Panzer Division was transferred from the Marseilles area to 7th Army during these days, and I was advised of the imminent transfer of the 116th Panzer Division, and shortly afterwards of that of the 2nd Panzer Division, to 7th Army. Thus 7th Army would then have six panzer divisions (Panzer Lehr, 2nd SS Panzer, 17th SS Panzer Grenadier, 2nd Panzer, 9th Panzer, and 116th Panzer Divisions) at its disposal, while 5th Panzer Army had five (1st SS Panzer, 9th SS Panzer, 10th SS Panzer, 12th SS Panzer, and 21st Panzer Divisions). These forces were insufficient for a counterattack against an enemy so vastly superior. In addition, the shortage of infantry divisions in the 7th Army sector also had necessitated the commitment of all panzer divisions at the front, with the exception of the 2nd and 116th Panzer Divisions, which were now on the approach march.

I do not know at what time OKW had come to the realization that no second landing was to be expected in western France. In any case, it was around this time that the transfer of additional infantry divisions was being promised. But their moving up was desperately slow.

OKW rejected all suggestions referring to a withdrawal. It maintained the rigid defense of Normandy. It was to be attempted to take measures accordingly. The deep main defensive area which was needed for this purpose was nowhere available—except south of Caen—because the available forces were insufficient for this purpose. In order to intercept the breakthrough, which therefore was feasible anywhere, the panzer divisions had to be available for a counterthrust. Apart from 2nd and 116th Panzer Divisions, which now were to be transferred, and the 21st Panzer Division, which was undergoing emergency reorganization, this was not the case. The withdrawal of additional panzer divisions had to be attempted as soon as additional infantry divisions could be moved up. Panzer divisions which were being held as reserves could then quickly intervene at any threatened point, considering the short distances within the army area.

When the American offensive in the direction of Coutances started on July 25, the fact that it would eventually lead to the breakthrough, and that it could no longer be stopped by local forces, was probably not immediately realized.

*On the Allied right flank (the German left), the American generals were not at all satisfied with their latest offensive, which had ended on July 19. They had captured St. Lô, true enough, but with a dozen divisions, they had advanced a maximum of seven miles in seventeen days and suffered 40,000 casualties—90 percent of them infantry—in the process, and they were still deep in hedgerow country. Gen. Omar Bradley's U.S. 1st Army had fifteen divisions (counting the three just down from Cherbourg). They faced SS Gen. Paul Hausser's 7th Army, which had nine divisions, but four of these were* Kampfgruppen—*divisions reduced by casualties to regimental strength. The Americans also outnumbered the Germans 750 to 110 in tanks. The pressing problem that the Americans faced was the* bocage *(hedgerow) country, where every advantage of terrain accrued to the defense. They simply had to break out of hedgerow country or they would never be able to fully bring their superior firepower and mobility to bear.*

*To break the stalemate, Omar Bradley decided to employ air power on a massive scale. He committed all the heavy bombers of the U.S. 8th Air Force, all the medium bombers of the U.S. 9th Air Force, the fighters and the fighter-bombers of the U.S. 8th Air Force, the 2nd Tactical Air Force of the RAF, and the U.S. IX Tactical Air Command—2,500 airplanes in all. Their mission was to obliterate all German positions and units in a 7,000-yard-wide and 2,500-yard-deep rectangular target area due south of the Periers–St. Lô Highway. Once the German front was smashed, Bradley planned to commit the entire U.S. VII Corps—six divisions, three of them armored and three motorized infantry. The offensive was code-named Operation Cobra.*

*Lt. Gen. Fritz Bayerlein's Panzer Lehr Division lay entirely within the rectangle. It controlled 2,500 combat effectives, plus 450 combat troops from the 275th Infantry Division, the 15th Parachute Regiment from the 5th Parachute Division, and a few elements of the 2nd SS Panzer Division—about 3,200 men in all. When the battle of Normandy began, the Panzer Lehr Division had 15,000 men and more than 200 tank, but now only about 45 of these were still running.*

*On July 25, Panzer Lehr was pulverized by a bomber stream 100 miles long. The American airmen dropped 60,000 bombs in the rectangle, nearly annihilating the German tank division and the adjacent 13th and 15th Parachute Regiments. They dropped an amazing total of 12 bombs for each German soldier in the rectangle. German tanks were tossed into the air like plastic toys. Outposts, command posts, and entire companies simply vanished because they were completely wiped out. The 901st Panzer Grenadier Regiment and 15th Parachute Regiment ceased to exist as effective combat forces. General Bayerlein survived only because he was visiting a regiment that had headquartered in a Norman chateau whose walls were ten feet thick. By the time the aerial bombardment was over, the Panzer Lehr's sector looked like the surface of the moon. Bayerlein estimated that his division had suffered 70 percent casualties, although some of these men were only stunned or shocked and would be available again within forty-eight hours.*

*On July 26, General Collins committed the American mobile reserve—three armored and three motorized infantry divisions—which was soon running free in the rear of the German 7th Army. The Americans had achieved their decisive breakthrough.*

*The magnitude of the catastrophe was compounded by the fact that Field Marshal Kluge was slow to recognize what had happened. For some inexplicable reason, he spent July 27 inspecting Panzer Group West, where he still expected the main American blow to fall. He did dispatch reinforcements to the 7th Army, but not nearly enough.*

On July 27, 5th Panzer Army received orders to transfer 116th and 2nd Panzer Divisions, as well as the staff of XXXXVII Panzer Corps [to the right flank of 7th Army]. They started on their march during the night of July 27–28 (daytime marches were impossible because of enemy air attacks) along two different roads which were barred to any other traffic. [It would, however, take them days to reach their destinations.]

The 2nd and 116th Panzer Divisions were at this time the only ones in France which were still approximately fully equipped in men and materiel.

The staff of the LXXIV Corps arrived just at the right time to take the place of the staff of the XXXXVII Panzer Corps (von Funck). Its commanding officer was General of Infantry Erich Straube,[34] and its chief of staff was Colonel Zoellner. The corps took over the left wing sector of my army.

*Meanwhile, on the right flank of the 7th Army, the 2nd SS Panzer and 17th SS Panzer Grenadier Divisions and the 6th Parachute Regiment of the LXXXIV Corps were crushed on July 28. SS Col. Christian Tychsen, the stocky, scar-faced thirty-four-year-old commander of the 2nd SS Panzer Division, was killed near Coutances in a firefight with an American patrol. At the same time, Hausser's command post was cut off by the rapid American advance. Hausser was fired at by an American armored car and escaped death or serious injury only by throwing himself into a muddy ditch.*

*On July 29, the LXXXIV Corps disintegrated, as its men streamed south to avoid encirclement. When the Americans fully occupied the Coutances area two days later, they counted 66 tanks, 204 other vehicles, and 11 guns destroyed, and 56 tanks and 55 vehicles damaged or simply abandoned.*

*Meanwhile, a huge German traffic jam developed at Roncey, about four miles south of Coutances. Horse-drawn and motorized vehicles were stacked up for two miles, three abreast in some places. American fighter-bombers immediately pounced upon it and, in what became known as the Roncey massacre, attacked it for six hours. They destroyed 100 tanks, 250 motorized vehicles, and a huge number of horse-drawn wagons. By sunset on July 28, the 91st Air Landing, 243rd Infantry, 77th Infantry, 17th SS Panzer Grenadier, 5th Parachute, 353rd Infantry, 275th Infantry, and Panzer Lehr Divisions had been reduced to* Kampfgruppe *strength or were in remnants.*

*That same day, Kluge finally made a quick inspection of the 7th Army area and clearly (and to some extent correctly) blamed Hausser for the disaster. Hausser could have established a mobile reserve prior to Cobra but had failed to do so, despite Kluge's suggestions. Kluge either did not have the authority to sack the SS general or, more likely, did not dare to do so for political reasons, but he did denounce the army's entire performance as "farcical, a complete mess," and stated that "the whole army [is] putting up a poor show."[35] He sacked Max Pemsel, the army's chief of staff,[36] and replaced him with Maj. Gen. Rudolf-Christoph von Gersdorff, who had once been Kluge's own chief intelligence officer. He also tried to make Gen. of Infantry Dietrich von Choltitz a scapegoat for the disaster, relieving him of his command and replacing him with Lt. Gen. Otto Elfeldt.[37]*

*Hausser, meanwhile, was missing. Elements of the U.S. 4th Armored Division had advanced twenty-five miles in thirty-six hours and had taken Avranches at nightfall on July 30. They also had passed within 200 yards of the farmhouse that housed Hausser's command post, without realizing it was there. Hausser, Gersdorff, and much of the rest of the army's staff had to infiltrate between American armored columns to reach German lines.*

There were further indications for the attack which was to be expected on the 5th Panzer Army front, but it did not yet come off. Now, as ever, the area south of Caen seemed a probable point of main effort. We were glad for every day the enemy gave us. The 21st Panzer Division, our only reserve after the transfer of the 2nd and 116th Panzer Divisions, thereby gained time for the emergency reorganization it needed so badly. We were aware of the fact that its combat efficiency, of necessity, still was unsatisfactory. A training period would have been needed in order to once more make the division fully capable.

*Eberbach was, of course, mistaken in thinking that the 5th Panzer Army would be the point of the Allied main effort, although it would face some very serious attacks in the Caen sector from the British 2nd Army and 1st Canadian Army.*

The [5th Panzer] Army had been promised the transfer of the 271st Infantry Division (commanded by Major General Paul Dannhauser) and the 85th Infantry Division (Lieutenant General Kurt Chill).[38] Each battalion was to be committed upon its arrival, thereby allowing for the withdrawal, at first of elements, and later on of the entire 9th and 10th SS Panzer Divisions, as well as of the 1st SS Panzer Division. Would the enemy give us sufficient time even for this operation?

The situation remained troublesome. On July 30, the American armored spearheads reached Avranches. The breakthrough in the 7th Army seemed inevitable. What was then to happen?

*The 7th Army had, in fact, already been broken through. Patton's U.S. 3rd Army was now activated. (The map on the following page shows his advances in Brittany and south of Normandy during the period August 1 to 16.)*

When, in the course of July 30, I was questioned by Field Marshal von Kluge whether I was in the position to transfer additional panzer divisions to 7th Army, the British offensive on Vire had meanwhile started. There were also indications for an imminent attack on Falaise. I therefore had to report that a British breakthrough was to be anticipated in my area, should additional forces be withdrawn from my army before the arrival of the two promised infantry divisions.

The Normandy front could not be held with the forces which were then available, neither defensively nor still less offensively. Field Marshal Kluge shared this opinion.

Meanwhile, I did everything to accelerate the approach of the 85th and 271st Infantry Divisions by picking up their units with the trucks which were at my disposal. I had tried in vain to obtain trucking space for this purpose from the idle *Luftwaffe* and navy. By the battalion, without field kitchens or artillery, which arrived only several days later because of their slow horse traction, these units were moved up to the front. But the relief could nevertheless take place at the earliest only during the first days of August, when strong elements of 1st and 9th SS Panzer Divisions could be withdrawn.

## Vire

On July 29, British forces attacked my left-wing division—326th Infantry Division. At first the division was able to hold its own. Until well into the afternoon, it seemed that LXXIV Corps (Straube) would succeed in stopping the attack by committing the *Jagdpanther* battalion, and that despite the pattern bombing by 1,000 bombers which was again being used at this point. Only during the afternoon did it become obvious that this was a large-scale offensive, apparently carried out by a new British army. The brave commander of the 326th Infantry Division, Lieutenant General Victor von Drabich-Waechter, had been killed during the counterthrust; the thin front had been pierced; major enemy armored forces were advancing toward the hilly terrain south of Caumont (Le Beny Bocage and to the east thereof).

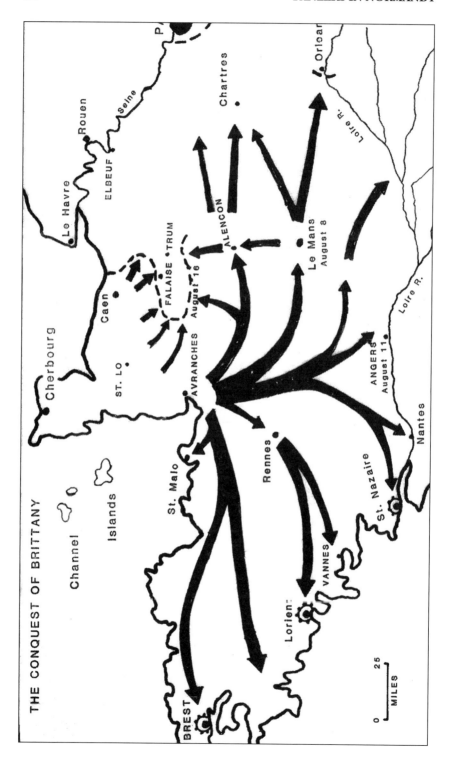

THE CONQUEST OF BRITTANY

The only division which at that time was at my disposal was the 21st Panzer Division. On July 29, once the situation began to clear, the division was issued orders to send an armored group under Colonel von Oppeln, reinforced by one Tiger battalion, to Straube's corps. The group was to carry out a thrust against the wing of the enemy, who had broken through, was to stop them and, if possible, throw them back, and hold the hilly terrain east of St. Martin. On the basis of further news, which reached me by the evening, I dispatched also the remaining forces of the 21st Panzer Division to the same sector with the identical mission. But the British had reached the St. Martin area during the night, where the remnants of one German infantry battalion were still holding out. On the morning of July 30, the enemy had also occupied the hilly terrain east of St. Martin. Oppeln had lost time. He probably wanted to wait for the arrival of the remainder of the 21st Panzer Division. The division launched the counterthrust only on the afternoon of July 30. It was repelled. Then they attempted to intercept the enemy. But on July 31, their thin security lines were pierced, and the division was pushed back toward the east. On August 1, the points of the British Guards Armoured Division reached the small town of Vire, which was being held by a weak garrison of paratroops of II Parachute Corps (General of Parachute Troops Eugen Meindl) of the 7th Army.[39] By noon, Vire was in British hands. While the paratroopers were still holding out west of Vire against American forces, which had advanced together with the British to the identical point, there was a 10-kilometer [6.21-mile] gap in the front, east of the town, through which the British armored divisions could pour into the flank and rear of the two German armies without being interfered with.

Meanwhile, the situation in the 7th Army's sector had taken a disastrous turn by August 1. American divisions were advancing into Brittany and toward the south without being checked. In view of this situation, I suggested to army group to order the withdrawal behind the Seine in order to avoid a disaster, but OKW did not agree to a withdrawal.

We had meanwhile succeeded in withdrawing the bulk of II SS Panzer Corps from its position along the Odon Creek and replacing it by 271st Infantry Division. Since the combat value of this division amounted to only a fraction of that of the panzer corps, the relief was a hazardous undertaking, but it had to be ventured; II SS Panzer Corps was to be transferred to 7th Army. The breakthrough near Vire forced Army Group B to leave II SS Panzer Corps subordinate to my army in order to close the gap between 7th and 5th Panzer Armies. On August 1, I therefore ordered SS Lieutenant General Bittrich to throw back the enemy by a launching a counterattack into the flank of the advancing British wedge, and to close the gap in the front.

The II SS Panzer Corps could not carry out all attack preparations before the afternoon of August 2, cover the distance of the approach march, and establish contact with the enemy. The enemy therefore had at least twenty-four hours of complete liberty of action. But it was our luck that the British, in general, stood still during this period. On August 2 and 3, Bittrich thrust into the enemy forces astride the Conde-Vire road—10th SS Panzer Division on the right, 9th SS Panzer Division on the left— and with approximately 80 tanks of his own, annihilated 150 British tanks while suffering only insignificant losses, recaptured Vire, and pushed back the British so far that the gap in the front between 21st Panzer Division and the paratroopers was closed.

But the British attack had meanwhile extended over a wider area. In the entire area between Orne and Vire, British divisions with numerous tanks attacked 271st Infantry Division (Dannhauser), which had only just been committed for the relief of II SS Panzer Corps, as well as 273rd Infantry Division (Praun). This sector of the front had only just been taken over by LXXIV Corps (Straube), while Bittrich now took over the command on the left wing. The two infantry divisions had very wide frontal sectors, little artillery, and only ten self-propelled assault guns (*Sturmgeschuetze*) per division. They were unable to resist the enemy assault. They gradually retreated, step by step, to the approximate line of Thury–Harcourt–Vire. The rear positions which had been constructed rendered good services. The situation became critical on several occasions, but the troops succeeded again and again in resisting effectively.

In this fighting, the enemy was supposed to have taken altogether 10,000 prisoners. If this number was correct, this would clearly indicate the lowering of the combat morale of our infantry divisions.

Since there had not yet been any large-scale attacks on the Caen front, which was against all expectations, and since II SS Panzer Corps—instead of reinforcing 7th Army—had been pinned down near Vire in my sector, Army Group B ordered, on August 3, that 1st SS Panzer Division be transferred to 7th Army. The divisional elements (such as the tank destroyer battalion, the engineer battalion and the flak battalion), however, were put on the march twenty-four hours after the panzer and panzer grenadier units, because they had to wait until they were relieved by elements of the 85th Infantry Division, which were just arriving on the Normandy battlefield. The 5th Panzer Army also transferred the equivalent of one flak division and one rocket projector brigade to 7th Army.

The situation in the 7th Army sector had meanwhile continued to grow worse. Its left wing was being pushed back farther. Mortain was taken by the Americans; all of Brittany, with the exception of Brest, was in enemy hands;[40] and American divisions advanced toward Orleans. Our insufficient forces had not even been able to hold their own on the defensive. To all of us, the only possibility seemed to be a withdrawal. But OKW decided to issue orders to 7th Army to make a counterthrust on Avranches without supplying the Normandy front with new forces worth mentioning and without real reinforcements for our *Luftwaffe*. According to the plans of OKW, however, this thrust was to be the start of a German offensive.

On August 3, General of Artillery Walter Warlimont from OKW paid us a visit.[41] We described our situation to him with complete candor and clearness. We suggested a retreat to the Seine as the only possible solution. He answered that Hitler would never accept that. He was unable to give us an objective or hope for a positive solution. Those at the top expected everything from the counterthrust of 7th Army on Avranches, which we considered as hopeless.

On the same day, Sepp Dietrich flew to the headquarters of OKW. We had asked him to describe the plain facts of the situation in Normandy and to state our point of view that it was senseless to hold on to the present front any longer or even think of carrying out a counteroffensive. He promised to do so. The result of his conversations remained unknown to me. Sepp Dietrich was at that time promoted to colonel general of the *Waffen-SS*.

## The Canadian Attack on Falaise

The 85th Infantry Division, which was numerically strong but was still lacking combat experience, had replaced not only the 1st SS Panzer Division but also the weary 272nd Infantry Division (Lieutenant General Friedrich August Schack) in the I SS Panzer Corps area. The 272nd Infantry Division was to get a little rest in the quieter sector of the 12th SS Panzer Division and was at the same time to relieve this panzer division, which by now was the only one still available in the area south of Caen; an army reserve was thereby again to be created.

This withdrawal of the 12th SS Panzer Division had only just begun on August 6, when the enemy attacked the front of the inexperienced 85th Infantry Division—after pattern bombing, allegedly carried out by 1,000 bombers, during the preceding night as well as an artillery barrage. The attack took place between Hubert Folie and St. Andre. This division was unable to resist such an onslaught. Its front was pierced, and the division was thrown back into the forests west of Bretteville sur Leize. It was once again the 12th SS Panzer Division which prevented a gap in the front by executing a counterthrust with those of its elements which already had been relieved. Many antitank guns were lost during the withdrawal. The old positions had been mined. There were scarcely any mines left for the new positions to which the I SS Panzer Corps front had to be withdrawn. For the first time, we encountered a great number of "stragglers" without weapons.

The situation was serious. Once more it had been the hesitating advance by the British rather than our own forces which had prevented a breakthrough. Had the enemy attacked energetically and stubbornly, he would have encountered such weak forces that a gap in the front would have been inevitable.

When I returned from the front on this day, I was informed that the counterthrust toward Avranches in the 7th Army sector had bogged down after some initial successes. The third panzer division, 1st SS Panzer Division, to be transferred out of my army would have prevented a defeat in my sector, while it had been unable to bring about a success in the 7th Army counterattack.

*On Hitler's orders, Kluge and Hausser assembled five panzer and panzer grenadier divisions on the western edge of the German front. Under the command of Gen. of Panzer Troops Baron Hans von Funck and his XXXXVII Panzer Corps, they had the objective of attacking west and capturing Mortain and then Avranches on the sea, twenty miles away. The strike force, which included the 116th Panzer, 2nd Panzer, 2nd SS Panzer, and 1st SS Panzer Divisions, along with the remnants of the 17th SS Panzer Grenadier Division, attacked in the predawn darkness of August 7. If they could reach the coast, they would split the U.S. 1st and 3rd Armies and cut Patton off from the main invasion force.*

*They had no way of knowing that Bradley had anticipated just such an attack, and his intuition had been confirmed by the Ultra code breakers in London. The Allied general had already assigned the task of keeping the twenty-mile-wide Avranches corridor open to Collins's U.S. VII Corps, which included the 30th, 1st, 9th, and 4th Infantry Divisions, as well as strong elements of the 2nd and 3rd Armored Divisions. Just in case a crisis developed, however, Bradley had already recalled Maj. Gen. Paul Baade's 35th Infantry Division from Fougeres in Brittany and ordered Patton to halt the three divisions of the XX Corps (the U.S. 35th and 80th Infantry and French 2nd Armored) in vicinity of St.-Hilaire, much to the disgust of "Old Blood and Guts." Not in on the Ultra secret that the German military code had been broken, Patton was amazed when the Germans attacked exactly when and where Bradley said they would.*

*In addition to deploying his reserves in the best possible manner, Bradley planned to attack the XXXXVII Panzer Corps with several hundred Jabos, as the Germans called the Allied fighter-bombers, just as soon as it committed itself.*

*During the Normandy campaign, the American air forces had gotten a reputation for developing a tendency to attack every vehicle they saw—not just the vehicles of the Wehrmacht and Waffen-SS. A joke made the rounds that when the RAF attacks, the Germans take cover. When the Luftwaffe attacks, the British and Americans take cover. And when the American aviators attack, everyone takes cover. It was no laughing matter to Funck and his men on August 7, however, as they were pelted by hundreds of American Thunderbolts, Mustangs, and Lightnings, each with two 500-pound bombs under its wings, supported by ten squadrons of British rocket-firing Typhoons. For the Germans, it was three hours of uninterrupted hell. In all, the Jabos destroyed eighty-one Tigers, Panthers, and Panzer Mark IVs and damaged another fifty-four, while twenty-six German tanks were simply abandoned, their crews escaping their metal coffins before the fighter-bombers could incinerate them. Hundreds of German trucks, armored cars, Volkswagen staff cars, artillery pieces, antitank guns, assault guns, and supply wagons were also lost.*

*The divisions of the XXXXVII Panzer Corps had been slaughtered.*

*Meanwhile, to the south, the XV Corps of Patton's army had moved too fast for Gen. of Panzer Troops Adolf Kuntzen, the commander of the LXXXI Corps. Kluge had assigned the 708th Infantry and 9th Panzer Divisions to him, but the Americans struck his vanguards before they could arrive and deploy. Instead of giving ground and assembling his units in some defensible position east of LeMans, he committed each regiment piecemeal, as far forward as possible, as soon as it arrived. As a result, Patton's men swamped each unit individually, and the LXXXI Corps was not able to even slow down the U.S. XV Corps. About half of the 708th Infantry Division was destroyed, the 9th Panzer's reconnaissance battalion was almost totally wiped out, and much of the rest of the division was severely damaged.*

On [the evening of] August 8, the Americans took Le Mans, which until then had been the supply base for 7th Army.

*General Hausser was among the last to leave, skulking out of the city of 75,000 in a single armored car, with only his orderly and driver. Meanwhile, Bradley ordered Patton to turn the XV Corps north, toward Alencon and Argentan (see map on facing page). The encirclement of the 5th Panzer and 7th Armies was already taking shape.*

Fifth Panzer Army received orders to withdraw also [its] 10th SS Panzer Division from the front near Vire, without consideration for the consequences, and to transfer the division to 7th Army. This could only be achieved without tearing the front, which had only just barely been patched in this sector, because 10th SS Panzer Division—after being committed to combat for such a long time—scarcely had the strength of one regiment with some artillery and a dozen tanks. After that, 5th Panzer Army had only three panzer divisions at its disposal—against eight in the 7th Army sector. Of these three divisions, 9th SS Panzer could be considered as only half a division, while 12th SS Panzer and 21st Panzer Divisions were only a miserable handful of troops. It is all the more remarkable that their morale did not give way, but that they continued to fight to the bitter end.

*By August 7, Patton had a dozen divisions south of Avranches and his spearheads were only a dozen miles from Alencon. In the meantime, General Montgomery's 21st Army Group began its drive to the south, toward Falaise. Excited by the success of Operation Cobra, Monty and Gen. Henry D. G. Crerar, the commander of the 1st Canadian Army, planned Operation Totalize, which was to be preceded by a massive employment of strategic bombers. The ground attack was to be directed by Lt. Gen. Guy G. Simonds, the competent but ambitious and ruthless commander of the II Canadian Corps. Its target was the 89th Infantry Division.*

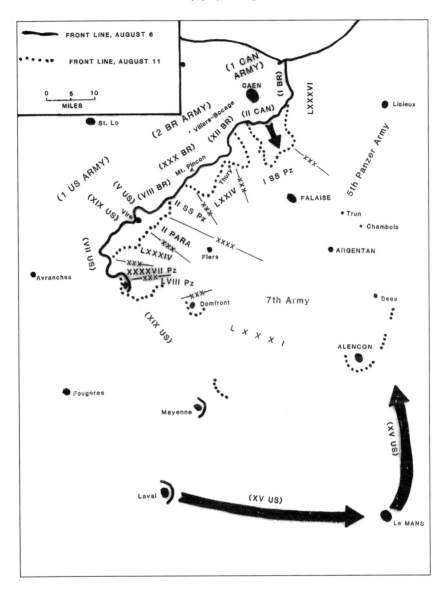

*Lt. Gen. Conrad-Oskar Heinrichs's 89th Infantry ("Horseshoe") Division had been formed in Norway in early 1944 and had led a relatively easy existence until August 2, when it was suddenly rushed onto ships, transported to Holland, and hurriedly trucked to Normandy, where it replaced the 1st SS Panzer Division at the front near Caen on the night of August 4–5. It had been in the line less than seventy-two hours when it was attacked by 1,020 Halifax and Lancaster heavy bombers shortly before midnight on August 7. It was pounded for more than an*

*hour, then shelled by 360 guns. Finally, the 2nd Canadian Infantry and 51st British Highland Divisions advanced along a narrow six-mile sector between the villages of St.-Martin and Soliers, supported by hundreds of Cromwell tanks and other armored vehicles. This was more than the green German division could stand; its men panicked and fled, some of them throwing away their rifles as they ran.*

*General Eberbach had stationed the veteran 272nd Infantry Division behind the 89th, but it was too depleted to halt the British and Canadians and soon gave way as well. Fortunately for the Germans, SS Oberfuehrer Kurt Meyer was nearby with his 12th SS ("Hitler Youth") Panzer Division. The 12th was also very much understrength; of the 214 tanks it had on D-Day, only 48 were still operational. The thirty-four-year-old Meyer walked out into the middle of the road and, with a cigar in mouth, personally rallied many of the fleeing infantrymen, temporarily checking the Allied advance. On the morning of August 8, however, Meyer still did not have nearly enough firepower to halt the entire II Canadian Corps. But the expected major attack did not come. Meyer was puzzled. Except for his two badly understrength battle groups and 48 tanks, the road to Falaise was open. Why did the Canadians not resume their attack? he wondered. He had no way of knowing that the inexperienced Allied tank commanders were exhibiting excessive caution because they were not sure of themselves. In any case, Meyer decided not to wait. A veteran of two years on the Russian Front, he realized that the entire sector was on the verge of collapse and his best chance of keeping it intact was to launch a spoiling attack of his own. The Hitler Youth went forward at 12:30 P.M.*

*On the Allied side of the line, General Simonds was preparing to commit the Canadian 4th Armoured and Polish 1st Armored Divisions through the Canadian 2nd Infantry and British 51st Highland Divisions when Meyer struck. On the left, one battle group, consisting of eight 62-ton Tigers and fourteen 45-ton Panthers, drove toward Cintheaux; on the right, 20 Tigers advanced along the road toward St.-Aignan-de-Cramesnil. As they attacked, 492 Flying Fortresses from the 8th U.S. Air Force appeared and blasted the area around the area from whence the 12th SS had just left. Had they not attacked, the Hitler Youth battle groups would have been slaughtered, and the road to Falaise would have been wide open. Although elements of the division were hit by stray American bombs, it had been very lucky.*

*The Polish and Canadian armored divisions, which were also struck by errant bombs, did not feel so lucky. In addition to losing several dozen soldiers, they lost one of their best-loved commanders, Maj. Gen. R. F. L. Keller, the leader of the 3rd Canadian Infantry Division. Nicknamed "Captain Blood" by his men because of his red hair, the forty-four-year-old Keller had not lived up to the expectations of his commanders, Simonds, Crocker, and Montgomery, but was very popular with the rank and file. Keller's headquarters was one of the places mistakenly attacked by the American bombers. Keller wound up in a coma for a week and had to be invalided out of the service.*

*After being bombed by the Americans, the Canadians and Poles were hit by the SS panzers. Meyer's lefthand column burst into Cintheaux and took the town from the Canadians. The righthand battle group plowed into Gen. Waldimar Maczek's 1st Polish Armored Division, which destroyed six of its twenty panzers. The SS gunners, however, knocked out twenty-six Polish Shermans. Meyer's counterattack was halted in fierce fighting, but Montgomery's advance was, for the moment, also completely derailed.*

*The cost on the German side had also been heavy. Among those listed as missing in action was SS Lt. Michael Wittmann, considered by many to be the leading tank ace of World War II. When last seen, he was being attacked from three sides by five or six Shermans. Wittmann had destroyed 141 enemy tanks and 132 antitank guns. He remained missing until 1987, when a French road construction crew accidentally discovered his body and those of his crewmen. Despite this damaging loss, however, "Panzer" Meyer had achieved his objective. That evening, the British, Poles, and Canadians dug in, eleven miles short of their goal. Falaise remained in German hands.*

On August 9, the enemy renewed his attacks in the direction of Falaise. Again he achieved a penetration. Again 12th SS Panzer Division had to seal off the point of penetration. And again the front had to be taken back during the following night, whereby it became still longer and more thinly spread.

While I was at 85th Infantry Division headquarters and I SS Panzer Corps headquarters, General of Infantry Walter Buhle from OKW[42] visited my chief of staff, General Gause. He gave Buhle a true picture of our situation and explained to him that the day the enemy chose to break through our front and the consecutive disaster exclusively depended on the enemy. Buhle asked Gause whether a repetition of the thrust toward Avranches with a concentration of all forces—in particular, of all panzer divisions—seemed promising to him. Gause replied in the negative and pointed out that the enemy would meanwhile not stay inactive and that his continued thrusts into our rear would make any offensive on our part an impossibiity. He, Gause, was of the opinion that there was only *one* conclusion which could be drawn from the situation at the Normandy front.

When I returned from the front in the afternoon, I received orders by telephone from Field Marshal Kluge to immediately constitute an emergency staff as Panzer Group Eberbach and to prepare and execute with a number of panzer divisions as a repetition of the counterthrust on Avranches, which had failed. For this purpose, I was to report this very day to the commander of the 7th Army, SS Colonel General Hausser, to whom I was to be subordinated for this mission. The command of the 5th Panzer Army was to be taken over by Sepp Dietrich, who had meanwhile been promoted to the rank of *Oberstgruppenfuehrer* [colonel general of SS]. I objected, stating that I considered this entire offensive to be impossible and hopeless. I therefore requested that someone else be put in charge. My arguments were rejected with the indication that speed was essential and that this was an order issued by the Fuehrer.

**Conclusions**

1) The striking power of the American army was being underestimated by the Germans, so 7th Army had therefore perhaps been a little neglected at first.

A contributing factor in underestimating the American troops was that the German authorities did not realize how many more favorable conditions for the organization of armed forces existed in an industrially highly developed state than in the age of a more primitive economy. Even in modern agriculture, man from his early youth is nowadays getting used to disciplined work, working with machines and cooperating with others. These fundamentals formerly had to be acquired by painstaking training. The state disposes of sufficient manpower, used to giving orders and handling other men, in the pool of foremen, headworkmen, department chiefs, etc. They also have the necessary organizational training. Thus a good army can nowadays be more easily rapidly improvised than formerly, supposing that the necessary war materiel is available.

From this knowledge, the Russians have formed battalions of the men from recaptured villages, immediately after retaking them, and have committed these units. Although such battalions suffered from considerable shortages, they nevertheless proved to be useful.

In addition, underestimating the American strength was probably based on not realizing the full value of mass commitment of good materiel, and the American war potential in general.

The most remarkable achievement in my opinion was the rapid training of such a great number of higher commanders and general staff officers for the American Army.

2) While the small standing army had sufficed to furnish the necessary number of good generals and general staff officers for the American troops, this did not seem to entirely apply to the Canadian Army—according to my impression. In this case, the peacetime army probably was too weak to suffice for the training of a sufficient number of higher commanders and their assistants without support of a strong military power.

Whether there were other contributing factors for the difference between American and Canadian troops—such as the lower stage in the industrialization of Canada, less density in population and therefore less integration in the coordination of all men and weapons—cannot be judged by me.

3) The main difference between the American and British leadership is in the greater boldness shown by the Americans. The British invasion army was being led extremely cautiously and schematically. This fact probably is to be attributed to the principle that bloodshed be avoided, which already in World War I led to the battles of materiel at the Somme and in Flanders—and which resulted in extremely high British casualties instead of achieving to spare lives. By using these tactics, the British leadership succeeded in its intention of keeping casualties down during individual engagements. But on the whole, the British method of combat probably had prolonged the war, and had thereby led to higher casualties than if the more daring type of warfare of the Germans and Americans had been adopted, because the cautious, schematic advance neglected making use of the several available opportunities of breaking through our front.

4) The German Army had shown a high degree of daring and mobility during the first three years of the war. [Its mission] had been dictated by politics and, with the available means, could not be solved any better than was done.

The entire picture changed when the politicans not only gave the army its missions, which went far beyond its strength, but also intervened in the command functions and ordered a rigid defense, because that type of defense had, under entirely different circumstances in the winter of 1941–42 against the Russians, to a certain degree appeared to be justified.

In the west, considering the tremendous materiel enemy superiority, a rigid defense meant senselessly sacrificing our own infantry. Against the instructions from OKW, the armies have therefore also used the elastic defense system as far as this could be done without continuous conflicts with the Fuehrer's headquarters.

The hamstringing of the armies by OKW, instead of leaving them—according to our long-standing soldierly tradition—a free hand within the scope of definite missions, had to be atoned for, because it led to many half measures and because many decisions were being taken too late.

5) A German counteroffensive in Normandy could only offer chances of success at the beginning of the invasion and by rapidly concentrating all available forces, including also the bulk of the *Luftwaffe*. OKW realized too late that a German counteroffensive was no longer possible after the end of June, and its assumption was erroneous that a second Allied landing was to be anticipated in western France. Thus the opportunity for concentrating all our forces for the *defense of Normandy*, for the time being, was missed.

Time would have been gained, and German casualties would have been reduced, had all forces been assembled in time for this purpose. The following measures should have been taken:

(a) Commitment of all available infantry divisions;

(b) Their mobility should have been obtained by using the motor vehicles of the idle elements of the navy and the *Luftwaffe*;

(c) Construction of a defensive system in depth, first in Normandy, then along the Seine and the Somme;

(d) Utilization of the panzer divisions should have been restricted to counterthrusts;

(e) Improvements in the supply situation.

6) A people or an army possess a certain amount of psychological strength which is gradually being consumed during the course of a long war.

The Anglo-American troops therefore were fresh and energetic.

The German troops were more seasoned, but had consumed a great amount of their moral capital during the five years the war had lasted by then, and above all during the last year and one half, which had seen so many reverses in Russia. Their moral strength was, in addition, undermined by the dreadful devastations the enemy bomber wings had wrought in the Zone of the Interior. The death of so many women, children, and old folks brought their hearts to despair.

One had to add to this the disastrous materiel inferiority, which made it impossible to give the troops even satisfactory training.[43]

The numerical superiority of the enemy involved complete overexertion of our own troops. The British command withdrew battle-weary divisions from the front and gave them a rest. The German command generally had to leave its divisions in the front line until they were shattered.

The German soldier was so exhausted by continual fighting, guard duty and psychological shocks that people often broke down from exhaustion. After twenty-four hours of sleep and decent food, such people were again willing to go up to the front. Nobody wanted to leave his buddies in the lurch. Comradeship proved to be a strong tie.

At the end of the battles in Normandy, the psychological capital of our divisions was as consumed as their equipment. The perseverance and performance of our troops are worthy of recognition and high praise. But the Supreme Command had greatly overtaxed the strength of the people and the army.

7) According to my information, tens of thousands of workers continued the construction work along the Atlantic Wall right through the entire months of June and July 1944.

At the same time, all requests made by the two German armies in Normandy to obtain labor for the construction of defensive positions were being rejected.

The American breakthrough in the 7th Army area succeeded also because no rear positions were available in the vicinity of Coutances and Avranches, which might have increased our own defensive strength.

8) The belief of OKW that the German forces in Normandy, which were insufficient even for defensive purposes, could—without additional troops being brought up—as if by a miracle, summon the strength for a successful counteroffensive on Avranches is the real cause of the Falaise pocket and the annihilation of the 7th Army.

9) One of the reasons for the German defeat in France was the shortage of supplies at the front. The two main causes for these shortages were:

(a) The continual destruction of all supply installations and all supply routes by the enemy air forces; and even more so,

(b) The situation of the German war economy.

No troops, however brave, can hold out in the long run if the enemy has ten times as much artillery ammunition, fifty times as many planes, and four times as many tanks at his disposal.

The performance of the German war economy was incredibly high. But it could not counterbalance the production of the entire world, and that all the less when its area was continually being reduced and, besides, covered with bombs.

The troops at the front have attempted to replace their shortages by improvising. This only increased their load. In addition, all such expedients did not modify the basic facts.

The German military strength as a whole was on a decline, the rapidity of which was steadily increasing, but the war potentialities of the world were only now being fully employed against us and were still steadily increasing.

Hence, the political conclusion ought to have been drawn by the leadership of the state.

## NOTES

1. Hans Speidel was born in Metzingen, Wuerttemberg, on October 28, 1897. He joined the army as an infantry officer-cadet in late 1914; he fought in World War I and served in the *Reichsheer*; was I-a of the 33rd Infantry Division (1937–39), IX Corps (1939–40), and Army Group B (1940); chief of staff to the military governor of France (1940–42), of the V Corps (1942–43), to the German general with the Italian 8th Army (1943), of the 8th Army (1943–44), and of Army Group B (April 15–September 9, 1944). A lieutenant colonel when World War II began, he was promoted to colonel (1941), major general (January 1, 1943), and lieutenant general (January 1, 1944). During Rommel's absence on D-Day, Speidel performed poorly. He was nevertheless retained as chief of staff by Rommel, Kluge, and Model. Despite Field Marshal Model's efforts to protect him, Speidel was arrested on suspicion of being involved in the anti-Hitler conspiracy, but the Court of Honor did not expel him from the army; he therefore could not be executed, but he did spend the rest of the war in prison. In 1955, he became a lieutenant general in the West German Army, the equivalent of a three-star general in the U.S. Army under the new rank structure, and held high positions in NATO. Speidel retired on March 31, 1964, and died at Bad Honnef on November 28, 1984.

2. Alfred Jodl was born in Wuerzburg in 1890 and joined the Bavarian Army as a *Faehnrich* (senior officer cadet) in 1910. Commissioned in 1912, he fought in World War I, served in the *Reichsheer*, and became chief of operations of OKW in 1938. On October 1, 1938, Jodl began a tour of troop duty when he

became commanding officer of the 44th Artillery Command. He was recalled to OKW as chief of operations and held this position throughout the war. Hitler's chief military adviser, Jodl was promoted to major general (April 1, 1939), general of artillery (July 19, 1940), and colonel general (January 30, 1944). He skipped the rank of lieutenant general altogether. Albert Jodl was hanged at Nuremburg as a war criminal in October 1946. He was later cleared by a West German court. His younger brother Ferdinand (born 1896) rose to general of mountain troops and commanded the XIX Mountain Corps and Army Detachment Narvik.

3. Tessin, *Verbaende und Truppen*, (1979–1986), 5:69; 6:51; 10:161; 12:50.

4. This concept was not new in the German Army. During World War I, the Imperial Army sometimes stationed entire divisions at these sensitive boundaries.

5. Harrison, *Cross-Channel Attack*, 441, 447.

6. Walter Hennecke was born in Bethelm/Hanover on May 23, 1898. He entered the navy as a war volunteer in 1915 and received his commission as an ensign in 1917. He spent most of his career on line ships and, from May to October 1941, commanded the obsolete battleship *Schleswig-Holstein*. He spent most of World War II, however, commanding the Ship Artillery School. He assumed command in Normandy in May 1943, was promoted to rear admiral on March 1, 1944, and was captured on June 26, 1944. He was released from captivity on April 17, 1947, and died on New Year's Day 1984. Hans H. Hildebrand and Ernst Henriot, *Deutschlands Admirale, 1849–1945*, 4 vols. (Osnabrueck, Germany: Biblio, 1988–96), 2:59–60.

7. Harrison, *Cross-Channel Attack*, 441.

8. Friedrich Ruge, *Rommel in Normandy* (San Rafael, CA: Presidio Press, 1979), 343. Vice Admiral Ruge was naval advisor to Army Group B.

9. Martin Blumenson, *Breakout and Pursuit* (Washington, DC: Office of the Chief of Military History, Department of the Army, 1961), 168–69.

10. Alfred Gause was born in Koenigsberg on February 14, 1896. He entered the army as an officer-cadet in the 18th Engineer Battalion in March 1914 and was commissioned in 1915. He spent the entire First World War with the 18th Engineers, fighting on the Western Front, where he was wounded several times. He was promoted to first lieutenant in October 1918. He was stationed in East Prussia, mainly with the 1st Engineer Battalion, from the end of the war until 1927, when he passed his *Wehrkreis* exam near the top of his group and began his general staff training. He graduated in 1931. He was sent to Stuttgart, where he served in the 5th Infantry Division and later became I-a of the V Military District. Gause was promoted to major (1934), lieutenant colonel (1936), colonel (1939), major general (June 1, 1941), and lieutenant general (March 1, 1943). He was sent in 1937 to Berlin, where he headed the important Armed Forces Office in the War Ministry and then was on the staff of OKW. In late 1939, he was named chief of staff of the X Corps and took part in the invasions of Belgium and France. He returned to the staff of OKH in 1940, and after briefly serving as chief of staff of the XXXVIII Corps in France, he was sent to Libya as chief of the German liaison staff to the Italian High Command. This staff was quickly taken over by Rommel, whom Gause served for the next three years. In

September 1941, he became chief of staff of Panzer Group (later Panzer Army) Afrika. He was severely wounded during the battle of the Gazala Line on June 1, 1942, but returned to duty in North Africa late that same year. He was named chief of staff of Army Group Afrika on March 1, 1943, but was sent back to Europe just before the army group surrendered in May. That same month, Gause became chief of staff of Rommel's Army Group B, in which position he served in northern Italy and the west. He and Rommel had a falling out in April 1944, caused by a fight between their wives, and Gause was placed in the Fuehrer Reserve. Rommel tried to have Gause put in command of a panzer division, but the assignment fell through. On June 15, 1944, however, Gause was named chief of staff of Panzer Group West (later 5th Panzer Army), serving under von Geyr, Eberbach, and Dietrich. The SS general took Gause with him when he was named commander of the 6th Panzer Army, but when Gause was relieved on November 20, 1944, Dietrich did nothing to help him. General Gause was in the Fuehrer Reserve until April 1, 1945, when he was named commander of the II Corps in the Courland pocket on the Eastern Front. Gause surrendered his corps on May 10, 1945, and remained in Soviet prisons until 1955. Finally released, he retired to Karlsruhe, West Germany, where he died on September 30, 1967.

11. Gerhard Grassmann was born in Neisse, Upper Silesia, in 1893. He joined the army as a *Fahnenjunker* in 1912, but for some reason, he was discharged two months later—perhaps because of an injury he received during training. In any case, he enlisted as a war volunteer in 1914. Commissioned in the 16th Field Artillery Regiment in 1915, he served in the *Reichswehr* and spent his entire career in the artillery. He was a lieutenant colonel and an instructor at the Artillery School at Jueterbog when World War II began. Later, he was promoted to colonel (September 1, 1940) and major general (March 1, 1943). He was on the artillery staff of Army Group C (1939–40), commanded the 26th Artillery Regiment (1940–42), and 122nd Artillery Command (Arko 122) (1942), and briefly commanded the 333rd Infantry Division on the Eastern Front (December 10, 1942–March 22, 1943). Apparently he was either wounded or fell ill in 1943. Either way, he did not return to active duty until July and was not given another field command until September, when he took over Harko 311, which was supporting the 1st Panzer Army on the Eastern Front. Grassmann assumed command of Harko 309 on January 16, 1944. He became commander of Harko 321 (supporting the 19th Army on the southern sector of the Eastern Front) on November 15, 1944. He held this post until the end of the war. A POW until June 1947, he settled in Aschaffenburg, Lower Franconia, in southwestern Germany, after the war and died there in 1975.

12. Shortly thereafter, the artillery headquarters of Panzer Group West was redesignated 309th Higher Artillery Command (Harko 309) and became independent of the 7th Army. Harko 309 was the former Staff, 309th Artillery Division, which had fought on the Eastern Front in support of the 16th Army.

13. Wolfgang Pickert was born in Posen, southern Prussia (now Poznan, Poland), on February 3, 1897. He commanded the 9th Flak Division on the

Eastern Front, until it was destroyed at Stalingrad. Just before the end, he flew out of the pocket, allegedly because he was wounded. He was promoted to general of flak artillery on March 1, 1945, and ended the war as the general of the flak arm at OKL, the High Command of the *Luftwaffe*. Pickert died in Weinheim, Baden-Wuerttemberg, on July 19, 1984. Throughout his career on the Western Front, he often refused to employ his antiaircraft units as the army generals requested. See Karl-Friedrich Hildebrand, *Die Generale der Luftwaffe*, 3 vols. (Osnabrueck, Germany: Biblio, 1990–92). The III Flak Corps was formed from headquarters, 11th Motorized Flak Division.

14. Hans von Obstfelder was born in Steinbach-Hallenberg, Thueringen, in 1886. He entered the service as a *Fahnenjunker* in 1905 and was promoted to colonel on March 1, 1933, a month after Hitler took power. Promotions to major general (1936), lieutenant general (1938), and general of infantry (June 1, 1940) followed. The pro-Nazi Obstfelder commanded the 28th Infantry Division (1936–40), XXIX Corps (1940–43), LXXXVI Corps (1943–late 1944), 1st Army (December 1, 1944–February 28, 1945), and 19th Army (March 1–28, 1945). He was sacked by Hitler near the end of the war. Obstfelder served in Kassel, Hessen, where he died in late 1976 at the age of ninety.

15. Joseph Reichert was born in Burgfeld, in the Laufen district of Bavaria, in 1891. He joined the Bavarian Army as an officer-cadet in 1910 and was commissioned in the Bavarian 21st Infantry Regiment in 1912. He fought in World War I, served in the Reichswehr, and became commander of the 6th Infantry Regiment in 1938, the year after he was promoted to colonel. He fought in Poland, Belgium, France and the northern sector of the Eastern Front. He led this regiment until September 17, 1941, three days before he assumed command of the 177th Replacement Division in Vienna. Named commander of the 711th Infantry on March 15, 1943, he led it in Normandy and in the battle of the Scheldt. The division was then sent to the Eastern Front and fought in Hungary and Czechoslovakia. Reichert led it until April 14, 1945, when he was seriously injured in an automobile accident in Czechoslovakia. He thus escaped Soviet captivity. He was promoted to major general on September 1, 1941, and lieutenant general on September 1, 1943. Captured by the Americans in May 1945, he was a U.S. POW until July 1947. He settled in Gauting, Bavaria, where he died in 1970.

16. Erich Diestel was a highly capable officer. Born in 1892 in Deutsch Eylau, East Prussia (now Itawa, Poland), he was educated in cadet schools and entered the army as an infantry *Faehnrich* in 1912. He served in World War I and in the *Reichsheer*, and in 1937, he assumed command of the I Battalion/68th Infantry Regiment. Later, he commanded the 188th Infantry Regiment (early 1940–1942), 101st Jaeger Division (1942), 75th Infantry Division (1942), 346th Infantry Division (1942–October 1944), and 331st Special Administrative Divisional Staff (1944–45). He briefly commanded Army Detachment Dietsel (March 23–April 9, 1945) and was deputy commander of Army Detachment Kleffel from April 10 until the end of the war. He was promoted to major general on August 1, 1942, and to lieutenant general one year later. A POW until 1947, he lived near Goslar in the Harz in the 1950s and died in Bad Wiessee in 1973.

17. Karl Sievers was born in Lehrbach, Hesse, in 1892. He joined the army an officer-cadet in 1912 and was commissioned into the 161st Infantry Regiment in 1913. He fought in World War I, served in the *Reichsheer*, and assumed command of the III Battalion/119th Infantry Regiment in late 1938. Promoted to colonel in 1940, major general in 1943, and lieutenant general on October 1, 1944, he led the 168th Infantry Regiment (1939–43), and commanded the War School at Metz (1943), 321st Infantry Division (1943), 16th Luftwaffe Field Division (late 1943–44), and 719th Infantry Division (July 30, 1944–end). He lived in Goettingen after the war and died in 1961.

18. Edgar Feuchtinger was born in Metz (which is now in France) in 1894. He helped with the Nazi Party's Nuremberg rallies before the start of the war and was a favorite of Adolf Hitler and his cronies. He served in the artillery most of his career, which began in 1914, and commanded a horse-drawn artillery regiment, the 227th, in France (1940) and on the northern sector of the Eastern Front (1941–42). He worked with the Fuehrer's secret-weapons program before assuming command of the 21st Panzer Division. A poor field commander and a corrupt one, he was nevertheless promoted to major general on August 1, 1943, and lieutenant general exactly one year later. He had to be fetched out of a Paris nightclub on the night of June 5–6, 1944, to be informed that Allied paratroopers and gliderborne forces were landing in his area of operations. He was relieved of his command and arrested for being away without leave at Christmas 1944, when it was discovered that he went home without permission while his men were battling the Americans on the Western Front. Feuchtinger was saved from execution only because of his Nazi Party connections; he was, however, demoted to private. He lived in Krefeld after the war and worked for the U.S. Army. He died in Berlin in 1960.

19. Josef "Sepp" Dietrich was born in Hawangen, Swabia, on May 28, 1892, the son of a master meat packer. He dropped out of school at age fourteen and became an agricultural driver. Later he was an apprentice in the hotel trade. He joined the Royal Bavarian Army in 1911 and was discharged soon after, but he was recalled to active duty when World War I broke out. He served in the artillery, being wounded by shrapnel in the lower leg and a lance thrust above his left eye. He fought on the Western Front throughout the war, was wounded a third time, and ended up in one of Germany's few tank units. After the war, he fought with the *Freikorps* and joined the Bavarian *Landespolizei* (provincial police) and the Nazi Party. He took part in the Beer Hall Putsch of 1923 on the side of the Nazis, which no doubt accounts for his sudden dismissal from the police. He worked at various jobs in Munich from 1924 to 1929 and in the meantime joined the SS. He became Hitler's bodyguard and one of his favorites at this time. He became a member of the *Reichstag* in 1930 and an *SS-Gruppenfuehrer* (major general) in 1931. In March 1933, Dietrich organized the *Leibstandarte Adolf Hitler* (Adolf Hitler Bodyguard) unit. It eventually grew from 117 men into the 1st SS Panzer Division, with a strength of 21,000 men. Dietrich commanded it for ten years, fighting in Poland (1939), the west (1940), and Russia (1941–43). In July 1943, Dietrich became the commander of the I SS Panzer Corps.

Later he led the 5th Panzer, 6th Panzer, and 6th SS Panzer Armies, rising to the rank of SS colonel general. After the war, Dietrich was sentenced to twenty-five years' imprisonment for the Malmedy massacre, even though he had been nowhere near the place. After passions died down somewhat, he was paroled in 1955, but in 1958 he was sentenced to eighteen months in prison by a West German court for his part in Hitler's 1934 Blood Purge of the Storm Troopers (1934). Released after only five months because of health problems, he retired to Ludwigsburg, where he died in bed on April 21, 1966, at the age of seventy-three.

20. Fritz Kraemer was born in Stettin, Pomerania, on December 12, 1900, and joined the army just after the end of World War II. He was discharged about 1920 and joined the Prussian police, serving until 1934, when he reentered the army as a first lieutenant. He attended the War Academy almost immediately, graduated in 1936, and became a company commander in the 55th Infantry Regiment (1936–39). He served on the staff of the 13th Motorized Infantry Division in Poland and France (1939–40) and became its I-a on October 11, 1940, the same day it became the 13th Panzer Division. He served in this post until August 1, 1943, when he was attached to the SS as an *Oberfuehrer*. In the meantime, he earned the Knight's Cross and promotions to lieutenant colonel (1942) and colonel (January 1, 1943). He served as I-a of the I SS Panzer Corps under Sepp Dietrich (1943–44). Kraemer permanently transferred to the SS in 1944 and was promoted to *Brigadefuehrer und Generalmajor der Waffen-SS* on August 1, 1944. He served as acting commander of the 12th SS Panzer Division "Hitlerjugend" from October 24 to November 13, 1944, when he followed Dietrich to the 6th Panzer Army (later 6th SS Panzer Army) as chief of staff. He held this post until the end of the war. He was sentenced to ten years in the Malmedy massacre trials but did not serve the entire sentence. He died at Hoexter, West Germany, on June 23, 1959. See Mark C. Yerger, *Waffen-SS Commanders*, 2 vols. (Atglen, PA: Schiffer Publications, 1997–99), 1:326–27, and Franz Thomas, *Die Eichenlaubtraeger*, 2 vols. (Osnabrueck, Germany: Biblio, 1997–98), 1:399.

21. Ruediger Peipkorn was a former army officer involuntarily transferred to the SS. He was promoted to full colonel in the SS after the battle of Normandy and given command of the 35th SS Police Grenadier Division on March 1, 1945. He was killed in action during the battle of Halbe (southeast of Berlin) on or about April 28, 1945.

22. The rank *SS-Oberfuehrer* has no exact English translation. It lies between colonel and major general in the German *Wehrmacht* and is sometimes translated "senior colonel." Sylvester Stadler was born in Steiermark, Austria, on December 30, 1910. In his late teens, he attended a technical school and became an electrician. At the age of twenty-three, he joined the Austrian SS, which sent him to Nazi Germany for further training. He attended the SS Junkerschule (Officers' Training School) at Bad Toelz and earned his commission. In 1939, he fought in Poland with Panzer Division "Kempf," a mixed ad hoc force of army and SS men. In 1940, he was a company commander in the "Der Fuehrer" SS Motorized Infantry Regiment during the campaign in the West and in the early weeks of Operation Barbarossa, the invasion of the Soviet Union. He was named commander of the II Battalion,

"Deutschland" SS Motorized Infantry Regiment, in September 1941. Stadler was wounded shortly thereafter, and because he was unfit for field duty, he was used as an instructor at the Bad Toelz and Brunswick SS War Schools. In March 1942, he returned to Russia as a company commander. Shortly thereafter, he assumed command of the II Battalion of the "Der Fuehrer" Regiment. In this position, he distinguished himself in the second battle of Kharkov (May 1942) and earned the Knight's Cross. In June 1943, he was given command of the "Der Fuehrer" and led it in the battle of Kursk and the Mius River battles. In May 1944, he became commander of the 9th SS Panzer Division "Hohenstauffen." He was wounded in action on July 10 but returned to duty five days later. He was again wounded on July 31—more seriously this time—and did not resume his command until October 10. Promoted to SS major general in late 1944 or early 1945, he led the 9th SS for the rest of the war and managed to surrender it to the Americans. He died in August 1995.

23. Heinz Harmel was born in Metz in 1906, the son of a medical doctor. He joined the Nazi Party in 1926 and became an SS man in 1935. By early 1937, he was an SS second lieutenant and platoon leader, and in early 1941, he was on the staff of the II Battalion, "Der Fuehrer" SS Motorized Regiment. He rose rapidly during the campaigns in the East and, in October, 1942, was commander of the SS "Deutschland" Motorized Regiment. On May 1, 1944, Harzer was given command of the 10th SS Panzer Division "Frundsberg" and was promoted to *SS-Oberfuehrer* eighteen days later. On September 7, he was promoted to SS major general. He was awarded the Knight's Cross with Oak Leaves and Swords in late 1944. Kraetschmer, *Die Ritterkreuztraeger*, 760–62.

24. Baron Hans von Funck was born on his family's estate on December 23, 1891. He volunteered for active duty when World War I broke out and was commissioned *Leutnant* in 1915. He spent most of the war with the cavalry on the Eastern Front. One of the pioneers in mechanized warfare, he commanded a motorized machine gun company as early as 1919. He worked closely with Oswald Lutz, the first general of panzer troops, and Guderian in the 1920s and 1930s. Funck was military attaché to Portugal when the war broke out. Later, he led the 5th Panzer Regiment in France (1940), briefly commanded the 3rd Panzer Brigade and 5th Light Division (1940–41), and commanded the 7th Panzer Division on the Eastern Front (1941–43). He was acting commander of the XXIII Corps in late 1943 and became commander of the XXXXVII Panzer Corps on March 5, 1944. Although he did an excellent job as a corps commander in Normandy, Hitler sacked Funck on September 1, 1944. The panzer baron held a minor post in *Wehrkreis XII* (commander of Reserve Panzer Command XII in Wiesbaden) from October 1944 to January 1945, when he was forced into retirement and dismissed from the army by Wilhelm Burghoff, the chief of the Army Personnel Office. Funck was captured by the Russians at the end of the war and spent ten years in Soviet prisons. He died in West Germany on February 14, 1979.

25. Albert Praun was born in Staffelstein in 1894 and joined the Bavarian Army as a *Fahnenjunker* in the 1st Telegraph Battalion in 1913. He spent most of the next thirty-two years in signals units, gaining promotions to major gen-

eral (1942), lieutenant general (1943) and general of signal troops (October 1, 1944). During World War II, he commanded the 696th Signal Regiment (1939–40) and was chief signal officer for the 7th Army (1940), Panzer Group Hoth (1940), Panzer Group Guderian (1940), the military governor of France (1940), and the 2nd Panzer Group/Army (1940–42). In 1942, he commanded the 482nd Infantry Regiment, 486th Infantry Regiment, 4th Panzer Grenadier Brigade, and 18th Panzer Division. He commanded the 129th Infantry Division (August 1942–September 1943) and was chief signal officer for Army Group Center (October 1, 1943–April 1, 1944). He assumed command of the 277th Infantry Division on April 12. After the failed attempt on Hitler's life created several vacancies in the signals branch, Praun became chief signal officer at OKH and OKW on August 11, 1944. He held these posts until the end of the war. He settled in Munich after the war and died there in 1975.

26.  Baron Heinrich von Luettwitz was born on the family estate at Krumpach, East Prussia, in 1896. Unable to secure his father's permission to enter the service when World War I began, Heinrich ran away from home, joined the army as a private, and went to the Western Front at age seventeen. His mother, Klara von Luettwitz nee von Unruh, also came from a military family and used her influence to have Heinrich brevetted second lieutenant two days before his eighteenth birthday. Luettwitz distinguished himself in the trench fighting in France in 1917, during which he was severely wounded. He ended the war commanding a troop of the 1st Uhlan Regiment. He was accepted into the *Reichsheer* as a cavalry officer but was converted to the concept of motorized warfare in 1929 and commanded the 3rd Motorized Battalion in 1936–37. In 1936, he was also leader of the German Olympic Equestrian Team. Because the team did not win the Gold Medal, Luettwitz's career suffered, and he served in backwater posts for several years. He was not sent to the front in Poland until the campaign was decided and, even then, he was unlucky enough to be severely wounded. He was on garrison duty in Poland during the French campaign of 1940. Finally, Maj. Gen. Walter Nehring, future commander of the Afrika Korps and the 1st Panzer Army, rescued Luettwitz from professional exile and gave him command of the 101st Motorized Infantry Regiment in his own 18th Panzer Division. He was abruptly relieved on orders from Berlin in January 1941. Nehring strongly protested, as did Guderian and Hoepner. Luettwitz was then given command of the 59th Rifle Regiment of the 20th Panzer Division, which he led in Russia (1941–42). After Stalin's winter offensive was checked, Luettwitz commanded the 20th Rifle Brigade (1942), 13th Panzer Division (1942–43), and 2nd Panzer Division (1944). He led the XXXXVII Panzer Corps after Funck was unjustly placed in the Fuehrer Reserve in September 1944. He was a very good divisional commander but was less successful commanding a corps, especially in the battle of the Bulge, where he received the answer "Nuts" from the American commander of Bastogne, whose surrender he had demanded. Luettwitz surrendered the XXXXVII Panzer Corps at the end of the battle of the Ruhr pocket and retired to Neuberg in Bavaria, where he again cultivated his horsemanship and acquired a stable from funds saved from his old estates, which were now lost. He died at

Neuburg on October 9, 1969. He was promoted to lieutenant general on June 1, 1943, and general of panzer troops on November 1, 1944.

27. Victor von Drabich-Waechter was born in Strassburg, Alsace (now Strasbourg, France), in 1889. He became a *Fahnenjunker* in the infantry in 1910. Remaining in the *Reichsheer* after the fall of Imperial Germany, he was a colonel and a department head at the Army Personnel Office (HPA) when World War II began. Later he headed an office group at the HPA (1940–42). He was promoted to major general (1940) and lieutenant general (August 1, 1942). He assumed command of the 326th Infantry Division on June 1, 1943, and was killed in action at La Mesnil, Normandy, on August 2, 1944.

28. Friedrich-August Schack was born in 1892 and joined the army as a war volunteer in the 1st Hussars Regiment in 1914. He received a commission as a second lieutenant in the infantry in late 1915. Schack was selected for retention in the *Reichsheer* and, during the World War II era, commanded the 15th Machine Gun Battalion (1938–40) and 392nd Infantry Regiment (early 1940–42), was commandant of the War School at Potsdam (1942–43), and commanded the 216th Infantry Division (1943), 272nd Infantry Division (1943–44), LXXXI Corps (September 4–21, 1944), LXXXV Corps (1944), and XXXII Corps (1945). Promoted to general of infantry on April 20, 1945, he retired to Goslar in the Harz Mountains after the war and died there in 1968.

29. Hermann von Oppeln-Bronikowski was born in Berlin on January 2, 1899. He was educated at various cadet schools and entered the army as a senior cadet in 1917. He was commissioned in the 10th Ulan Regiment later that year. He remained in the cavalry branch until 1940, having been a member of the German Olympic equestrian team in 1936. He commanded II/10th Cavalry Regiment, a reconnaissance unit, in Poland. Later, he served on the staff of the general of mobile troops and led an ad hoc panzer brigade on the Eastern Front in 1941. Here he survived the destruction of his tank by enemy fire on at least three occasions. An incredibly brave officer, he commanded the 35th, 204th, and 11th Panzer Regiments (1941–autumn 1943), but he was not given his own division, almost certainly because he had a drinking problem. He was known to come in drunk at 8 A.M. Oppeln assumed command of the 100th Panzer Regiment in late 1943. He was given command of the 20th Panzer Division on the Eastern Front in October 1944 and was promoted to major general in 1945. A holder of the Knight's Cross with Oak Leaves, Swords, and Diamonds, he survived the war and settled in Hanover. He died in Gaissach, near Bad Toelz, Bavaria, on September 18, 1966.

30. The 711th Infantry Division had only two regiments and an artillery battalion, instead of the usual regiment.

31. Count Gerhard von Schwerin, a holder of the Knight's Cross with Oak Leaves and Swords, was born in Hanover in 1899. He joined the army as a *Faehnrich* (senior officer cadet) in the elite 2nd Guard Regiment of Foot when World War I broke out and was discharged as a lieutenant in 1920. He reentered the service in 1922 and was on the staff of OKH when the Second World War began. Schwerin commanded the I Battalion of the elite Grossdeutschland Motorized Infantry Regiment, the 86th Rifle Regiment, the

Grossdeutschland Regiment itself, and the 200th Special Purposes Regiment (1939–41), before taking charge of the 76th Infantry Regiment (1941–42). After briefly serving as deputy commander of the 254th Infantry Division (1942), he was acting commander of the 8th Jaeger Division (1942) and commander of the 16th Panzer Grenadier Division (1944), which was upgraded to the 116th Panzer Division in the spring of 1944. Schwerin was sacked during the battle of Aachen, but his friends on the general staff saved his career and secured for him the command of the 90th Panzer Grenadier Division in Italy (December 1944). Schwerin commanded the LXXVI Panzer Corps in Italy from April 1 to 25, 1945, and surrendered it to the Western Allies. According to page 319 of Wolf Keilig, *Die Generale des Heeres* (Friedberg, Germany: Podzun-Pallas-Verlag, 1983), he lived in Bonn for a time, but he died in Rottach-Egern, Upper Bavaria, in 1980, at the age of eighty-one.

32. Col. Eberhard Finckh, the former deputy chief of staff of OB West, was deeply involved in the plot to assassinate Adolf Hitler. He was caught, tried, convicted, and executed on August 30, 1944.

33. According to Georg Tessin, *Verbaende und Truppen*, 2:282, Panzer Group West was officially redesignated 5th Panzer Army (*5. Panzer-Armee* [*Pz. AOK 5*]) on August 5, 1944.

34. Erich Straube was born in Elsterwerda, Brandenburg, in 1887. He became an officer-cadet in 1907 and was commissioned in the 62nd Infantry Regiment in early 1909. A major when the Nazis came to power, he was promoted to lieutenant colonel (1933), colonel (1935), major general (1939), lieutenant general (1941), and general of infantry (June 1, 1942). He commanded the 82nd Infantry Regiment (1936–38), War School at Munich (1938–39), 268th Infantry Division (1939–42), XIII Corps (1942), and LXXIV Corps (1943–44). From December 17, 1944, until the end of the war, he led the LXXXVI Corps. He retired to Osterode in the Harz and died in 1971.

35. Albert Seaton, *The Fall of Fortress Europe, 1943–1945* (New York: Holmes & Meier Publishers, 1981), 121.

36. Josef Johann "Max" Pemsel was born in Regensburg on January 15, 1897, and entered the army as an officer-cadet in the 11th Bavarian Infantry Regiment in 1916. He later joined the mountain troops branch and was I-a of the 1st Mountain Division when World War II began. He became chief of staff of the XVII Mountain Corps in late 1940 and held this post prior to joining the 7th Army as its chief of staff in May 1943. After being relieved by Kluge, he was named commander of the 6th Mountain Division in Norway in late August and was promoted to lieutenant general in November, proving that Berlin did not hold him responsible for the Cobra or Roncey disasters. He was named battle commandant of Berlin in the last weeks of the war. Fortunately for him, his airplane was grounded by bad weather in Norway, and by the time he arrived in the capital, the post had been filled by another officer—much to Pemsel's relief. Jodl named him chief of staff of the Ligurian Army in northern Italy as a sort of consolidation prize, and Pemsel left the doomed capital as quickly as he could. He narrowly avoided being killed by Italian partisans before he surrendered to the Americans at

the end of the war. In 1955, he reemerged as a general in the West German Army, and by 1958, he was commander of the II Corps in Ulm. He retired as a lieutenant general (the equivalent of an American three star general in the new rank structure) in 1961 and died on June 30, 1985.

37. Otto Elfeldt was born in Mecklenburg in 1895 and joined the army as an artillery cadet in 1914. He served as commander of the II Battalion/56th Artillery Regiment (1935–39), and 619th Artillery Regiment (1939), on the staff of Army Group A (1939–40), as chief of staff to the general of artillery at OKH (1940–42), and as commander of the 302nd and 47th Infantry Divisions (1942–44). He was captured in the Falaise pocket on August 8. After the war, he lived at Bad Schwartau, between Luebeck and the Baltic Sea, and died in 1982.

38. Paul Dannhauser was born in Regensburg in 1892. He joined the Bavarian 15th Infantry Regiment as a *Fahnenjunker* in 1911. He fought in World War I, served in the *Reichswehr*, and was a lieutenant colonel on the staff of the 106th Infantry Regiment in 1936. By 1939, he was a colonel, commanding the 214th Infantry Regiment. He successively commanded the 550th Infantry Regiment (1940), 36th Infantry Regiment (1940), 427th Infantry Regiment (1940–42), and 256th Infantry Division (1943–late 1944). He was promoted to major general in 1942 and lieutenant general on March 1, 1943. His last assignment was as commander of prisoner of war camps in *Wehrkreis XII* (Wiesbaden area). A POW himself from May 8, 1945, to June 1947, he lived in Landshut, Bavaria, after his release from the camps. He died there in 1974. Kurt Chill was born in Thorn, Pomerania (now Torun, Poland), in 1895 and volunteered for the army in 1913. Commissioned in the infantry in 1915, he fought in World War I, was discharged in 1920, and joined the police. He reentered the army as a major in 1936. He was a battalion commander when the war broke out, successively commanding the 45th Infantry Regiment, 122th Infantry Division, 85th Infantry Division, and LV Corps (February 1945). He was acting commander of the XXVI Corps on the Eastern Front at the end of the war. He nevertheless seems to have managed to surrender to the Western Allies. Released from prison in 1947, he settled in Groemitz, Holstein, where he died in 1976. Keilig, *Die Generale*, 60; Kurt Mehner, *Die Geheimen Tagesberichte der deutschen Wehrmachtfuehrung im Zweiten Weltkrieg, 1939–1945*, 12 vols. (Osnabrück, Germany: Biblio, 1984–95), 12:447.

39. Eugen Meindl was born in 1892 in Donaueschingen, Baden. His father was a forestry official for the prince of Fuerstenberg. After school, Meindl joined the 67th Field Artillery Regiment in Hagenau, then in German Alsace. During World War I, he was a platoon and battery commander and a regimental adjutant on the Western Front. He was retained in the *Reichsheer* and, in 1935, was a major, commanding a battalion in the 5th Artillery Regiment. In 1938, he was given command of the 112th Mountain Artillery Regiment, which he led in Poland. In 1940, he made a parachute jump at Narvik, even though he had no parachute training. Later that year, he transferred to the *Luftwaffe*, commanding the Airborne Storm Regiment, which he led at Crete. Here he was seriously wounded. During the winter of 1941–42, Meindl created the first *Luftwaffe* field division, which was initially called

Group Meindl. In October 1942, he was named commander of the XIII Air Corps, the headquarters responsible for creating and organizing twenty-two *Luftwaffe* field divisions. In November 1943, Meindl was given command of the II Parachute Corps, which was then in Italy. He was promoted to general of parachute troops on April 1, 1944. After Falaise, the II Parachute fought the British at Cleve and Nijmegen. In 1945, Meindl fought at Venlo and defended the Wesel bridgehead on the lower Rhine. He surrendered his corps to the British in Schleswig-Holstein. Released from prison in 1947, he died in Munich on January 24, 1951. Reinhard Stumpf, "Eugen Meindl," in David G. Chandler and James Lawton Collins, *The D-Day Encyclopedia* (New York: Simon & Schuster, 1994), 360–61; Rudolf Absolon, comp., *Rangliste der Generale der deutschen Luftwaffe nach dem Stand vom 20. April 1945* (Friedberg, Germany: Podzun-Pallas-Verlag, 1984), 28; Ernst Martin Winterstein and Hans Jacobs, *General Meindl und seine Fallschirmjaeger: Vom Sturmregiment zum II. Fallschirmjaegerkorps, 1940–1945* (Braunschweig, Germany: Suchdienst des Bundes Deutscher Fallschirmjaeger, 1976).

40. Brest was held by the 2nd Parachute Division with several smaller formations under *Luftwaffe* Lieutenant General Ramcke.

41. Walter Warlimont was born in Osnabrueck in 1894 and joined the Imperial Army in 1913 as an eighteen-year-old officer-cadet in the 10th (Lower Saxony) Foot Artillery Regiment at Strasburg, Alsace. He attended the War School at Danzig (1913–14) and was commissioned in 1914. During World War I, he served as a battery officer, adjutant (battalion, regiment, and brigade), and battery commander on the Western and Italian Fronts. He was a first lieutenant in the *Maercker Freikorps*, which was accepted into the *Reichsheer* in its entirety. Warlimont underwent clandestine general staff training (1922–26), and as a captain, he was named second assistant to the chief of the general staff in 1926. Later, he served in the economics section of the Defense Ministry and in the foreign armies intelligence section. He spent a year attached to the U.S. Army to study industrial mobilization (1929–30). After spending a year as a battery commander in the 1st Artillery Regiment in Allenstein, he was promoted to major on the staff of the industrial mobilization section of the defense ministry. He became section chief in 1935. As lieutenant colonel, Warlimont was Reich military plenipotentiary to General Franco (1936–37) and commanded the II Battalion/34th Artillery Regiment at Trier and the 26th Artillery Regiment at Duesseldorf (1937–38). In 1938, he was named chief of the national defense section of the general staff in OKW, and during Jodl's tour of troop duty, he was chief of operations at OKW (1938–39). From September 1939 to September 1944, Warlimont was deputy chief of operations at OKW and was successively promoted to major general (1940), lieutenant general (1942), and general of artillery (April 1, 1944). He was placed in Fuehrer Reserve in September 1944 and was never reemployed. After the war, he was sentenced to twenty-five years' imprisonment as a war criminal. His sentence was later commuted, and he retired to Rottach-Egern. He died in Kreuth, Upper Bavaria, on October 9, 1976, at age eighty-two.

42. Walter Buhle was born in Heilbronn, Wuerttemburg, on October 26, 1894. He joined the Imperial Army as a *Fahnenjunker* on July 10, 1913, received his

commission when World War I broke out, and served with the infantry during the war. He alternated among infantry, cavalry and general staff assignments in the 1920s and 1930s, and as a lieutenant colonel, he became chief of operations of *Wehrkreis V* in 1937. A promotion to colonel followed. Recognized as a hard worker, an expert on armaments, and a dedicated Nazi, Buhle was summoned to Berlin in 1939 and named chief of the Organizations Section of OKH. (Ironically, his principal assistant in this post was Col. Count von Stauffenberg.) Buhle established a personal relationship with Adolf Hitler while at Fuehrer Headquarters and was named chief of the army staff at OKW in early 1942. He was promoted to major general (1940), lieutenant general (1942), and general of infantry (April 1, 1944). He was Hitler's first choice to succeed Zeitzler as chief of the general staff, but it took Buhle weeks to fully recover from his July 20 wounds, so the appointment went to Guderian. In early 1945, Hitler named Buhle to replace Himmler in one of his many posts—chief of armaments for the army. General Buhle survived the war and subsequent trials and retired to Stuttgart, where he died on December 28, 1959.

43. By early 1944, the average American fighter pilot already had more than 400 hours of flight time before he was posted to a combat squadron. The average *Luftwaffe* pilot had only about 110 hours.

Field Marshal Gerd von Rundstedt, commander in chief of OB West in 1942–44 and again in 1944–45. Named honorary colonel of the 18th Infantry Regiment in 1938, he always wore his colonel's uniform with his field marshal's insignia on the shoulder boards, laughing whenever he was mistaken for a colonel. COL. ED MARINO

Gen. Miles C. Dempsey, who commanded the British 2nd Army against Eberbach in Normandy. U.S. NATIONAL ARCHIVES

General of Panzer Troops Hans Eberbach.

A Hummel. Used as an assault gun and self-propelled howitzer, it featured a 150-millimeter gun mounted on a PzKw III or PzKw IV chassis, weighed twenty-four tons, and had a crew of six.

Gen. of Flak Artillery Wolfgang Pickert, commander of the III Flak Corps. His refusal to cooperate with Rommel and the other army generals did nothing to help the German defense of Fortress Europe.

Field Marshal Guenther von Kluge, commander in chief of OB West starting on July 2, 1944, and commander of Army Group B starting on July 17. Implicated in the attempted assassination on Hitler, Kluge was relieved on August 15 and committed suicide four days later.

Michael Wittmann, one of the leading tank aces of all time. He distinguished himself at Villers-Bocage but was later killed in action north of Falaise.

U.S. NATIONAL ARCHIVES

Field Marshal Erwin Rommel, "the Desert Fox" and commander in chief of Army Group B. Critically wounded by an Allied air attack on July 17, 1944, he was eventually implicated in the attempt on Hitler's life and forced to commit suicide on October 14.

Field Marshal Walter Model replaced Kluge at the head of OB West and Army Group B. He shot himself near Duisberg on April 24, 1945.

Heinz Guderian, the "father of the *blitzkrieg*" and chief of the panzer inspectorate. Eberbach served as his deputy until a disagreement over the deployment of armored divisions in France led Eberbach to seek a combat command.

The *Leibstandarte Adolf Hitler*, the elite SS bodyguard of Adolf Hitler, circa 1934. Formed in 1933, the LAH was later expanded into the 1st SS Panzer Division, commanded by Sepp Dietrich until 1943. U.S. MILITARY HISTORY INSTITUTE

Part of the carnage in the Falaise pocket, August 1944. U.S. MILITARY HISTORY INSTITUTE

German infantry dug in near a camouflaged tank. U.S. MILITARY HISTORY INSTITUTE

Gen. of Panzer Troops Baron Hans von Funck, commander of the XXXXVII Panzer Corps in Russia and Normandy, 1943–44. One of Eberbach's subordinates in the Mortain-Falaise battles, he was sacked by Hitler in early September 1944.

Lt. Gen. Hans Speidel, chief of staff of Army Group B, shown here as a general in the postwar West German Army.

Gen. of Panzer Troops Fridolin von Senger und Etterlin, commander of the XIV Panzer Corps in Italy, 1943–45. Eberbach conferred with Senger about new tank models and armored tactics.

A Panther tank.

With its thick armor and excellent 88-millimeter gun, the Tiger tank terrorized Allied formations in 1944 and 1945. U.S. MILITARY HISTORY INSTITUTE

A Panzer Mk IV and an American Sherman during the Battle of the Bulge, January 1945.

A Tiger tank.

An artillery forward observer and his radio operator look for targets on the
Eastern Front. They are members of the 29th Motorized Division, which worked
closely with Eberbach's 5th Panzer Brigade in 1941. U.S. NATIONAL ARCHIVES

The leading generals of the Western Front, September 1944. Left to right:
Walter Model, commander of Army Group B; Rundstedt, commander in chief in
the west; and Gen. of Infantry Guenther Blumentritt, Rundstedt's chief of staff.

Preparing for the D-Day
invasion, spring 1944. From
left to right are Col. Gen. Hans
Salmuth, commander of the
15th Army; Field Marshal
Rommel, commander of Army
Group B; and Rundstedt.

The U.S. Army comes ashore on D-Day, June 6, 1944.

A German grenadier killed on the Western Front, 1944. Because he is holding a live grenade, his body has not been disturbed. U.S. NATIONAL ARCHIVES

A light mortar team from a *Luftwaffe* field unit. These units proved to be ineffective in combat on any front in 1944.

A StuG assault gun. Built cheaply on a PzKw III chassis, these weapons proved to be remarkably effective. To Guderian's dismay, Hitler kept them within the artillery branch. U.S. NATIONAL ARCHIVES

SS Lt. Gen. (later Col. Gen.) Sepp Dietrich (left), commander of Hitler's bodyguard unit, speaking with Gauleiter Wilhelm Brueckner, Hitler's chief adjutant, in 1934. Dietrich later commanded the I SS Panzer Corps in Normandy and the 6th Panzer (later 6th SS Panzer) Army in the Ardennes. WALDO DALSTEAD

Gen. of Panzer Troops Baron Leo Geyr von Schweppenburg, who became commander of Panzer Group West in October 1943. Hitler fired him on July 2, 1944, and replaced him with Eberbach.

Members of the *Leibstandarte Adolf Hitler* in an armored personnel carrier.

A mixed German combat team in Normandy, 1944. U.S. NATIONAL ARCHIVES

Col. Gen. Hermann Hoth issuing orders on the Eastern Front. Eberbach worked closely with this outstanding officer several times. U.S. NATIONAL ARCHIVES

Field Marshal Erich von Manstein, considered by most German officers to be their best general of the war.

A German self-propelled 88-millimeter antiaircraft/antitank gun, destroyed by an Allied fighter-bomber in Normandy, 1944. U.S. NATIONAL ARCHIVES

A Tiger tank. U.S. NATIONAL ARCHIVES

German engineer troops spearhead an attack across a French river, 1940.

SS Col. Gen. Paul Hausser, commander of the II SS Panzer Corps and later the 7th Army in Normandy. The 7th was on Eberbach's left flank in July 1944 and faced the U.S. 1st Army.

Allied air cover in Normandy. Air power was the key to victory for the Allies. The aircraft on the ground are British gliders. U.S. NATIONAL ARCHIVES

A German gun prepares to fire. U.S. NATIONAL ARCHIVES

A German soldier kneels at the grave of a fallen comrade in Normandy.

British general Bernard Montgomery and American general George S. Patton in 1943.

A German antitank gunner receives a decoration for destroying an Allied tank, 1944.

Col. Claus von Stauffenberg (far left) watches Hitler greet a guest at his headquarters in Rastenberg, East Prussia, in July 1944. Within a week, Stauffenberg would attempt to assassinate Hitler and overthrow the Nazi regime—a plot to which Eberbach was privy. The officer on the far right is Field Marshal Wilhelm Keitel, the commander in chief of OKW. U.S. NATIONAL ARCHIVES

A German PzKw III tank. Although it was the workhorse of the panzer force in 1941, the Mk III was obsolete by 1944 but still in use. U.S. NATIONAL ARCHIVES

The American army liberates Paris, August 25, 1944. Eberbach was captured less than a week later.

# CHAPTER 4

# Panzer Group Eberbach

**My Dismissal as Army Commander**

On August 8 or 9, Field Marshal von Kluge gave me over the phone the order to turn the command of the 5th Panzer Army over to SS General Sepp Dietrich. The attack on Avranches, according to an order from Hitler, was to be repeated. With an emergency staff, I had to take over the command of the panzer divisions provided for this attack, and I was to be subordinate to the commander in chief of the 7th Army, SS Colonel General Paul Hausser.

I immediately put forth again that I considered the attack as hopeless and my assignment to this post would therefore be very unpleasant to me. It did not help; the order was maintained. I had to go to the 7th Army on the same day.

*Eberbach was particularly distressed over the appointment of Sepp Dietrich as 5th Panzer Army commander. "Dietrich's totally unqualified for the job!" he cried to his aides.*[1]

The 7th Army was obviously not very pleased with my turning up there. The insertion of my staff between the army staff and the corps' staffs was unnecessary and meant, in the prevailing situation, a very unpleasant lengthening of the command channel.

I think that the distrust against army generals after July 20 was decisive in my dismissal as an army commander. Otherwise, it would have been unaccountable to take away from me the army after a faultless command for seven weeks, to give it to SS General Dietrich, who was unable to fulfill this task, to subordinate me to the C-in-C of the neighboring army commander, SS General Hausser, to carry out an attack which I had repeatedly declared as hopeless, and for which, moreover, I was unnecessary.

## Organization of the Staff of Panzer Group Eberbach

My staff received the designation of "Panzer Group Eberbach." The initial organization was made by OB West. Owing to the swift events and repeated shifts, parts of the staff never did reach me. I had never more than three radio stations, two of which were very often out of order. The staff was therefore able to function only with the aid of the staff of the 7th Army or one of the corps' staffs. It was a burden for these staffs. During the commitment I had repeatedly reported this fact and requested to dissolve my staff as worthless and without any meaning. OB West agreed with this. The Armed Forces High Command admitted this point of view only after the battle of Falaise, when the staff consisted only of one truck, one special missions staff officer, the driver, and myself.

As chief of staff, I asked the field marshal to appoint his son, Lieutenant Colonel Hans Guenther von Kluge. [Eberbach's chief of operations was Maj. Arthur von Eckesparre, Rommel's former chief supply officer.]

## Situation of the 7th Army

The panzer divisions which had taken part in the first offensive on Avranches (1st SS Panzer, 2nd SS Panzer, 2nd Panzer, and 116th Panzer Divisions) had in the meantime fallen back practically to the starting positions and were there engaged by the pursuing enemy. They would not be available for the second attack until after they disengaged. The infantry was numerically absolutely insufficient to relieve them. A shortening of the front had to be made in order to make the relief possible at all. This shortening also benefited the enemy. First of all, all these measures took much time. For five days, we could not even think of the second attack. What, however, did the enemy do in the meantime? Nothing stood in his way to close the trap in which the 7th Army already stood [see map on facing page]. It was unaccountable that OKW could not see this, after Stalingrad, Tunisia, Crimea, and Krementschug. During all that time, OKW formed its decisions on the present situation without taking into account the possible actions of the enemy.

The blow against Avranches could not take place directly from east to west, because surprise would be entirely lacking if the attack came from this direction. Consequently, the army had

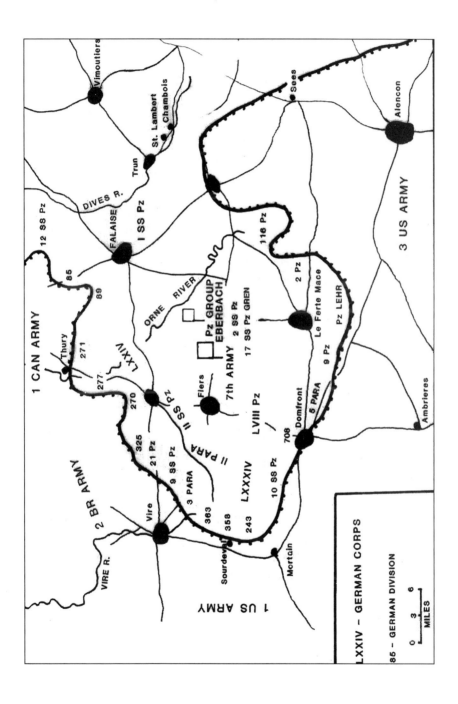

LXXIV – GERMAN CORPS

85 – GERMAN DIVISION

0   3   6
MILES

to start from the Beenton–St. Hilaire area, and from there advance to Avranches and Pontaubault. It therefore had to make an advance of 65 kilometers [40.4 miles], instead of 40 kilometers [24.9 miles], and afterwards to hold a comparatively longer front. The appropriate forces for this were not available.

Without the aid of strong air forces, this longer attack had even less prospect for success than the first one. Our air forces were now weaker than ever before. Of course, they promised to add the 9th Panzer, 9th SS Panzer, and 10th SS Panzer Divisions to those already present, but all these divisions were so worn out and battle-weary that only one-third of the tanks that took part in the first, shorter, unsuccessful attack were now available. At best, they now had only 120 tanks. Besides, it was clear that the weakening of the 5th Panzer Army would inevitably lead to a British breakthrough on Falaise.

The ammunition and fuel situation of the 7th Army was bad. Le Mans was about to fall. Alencon was threatened. Accordingly, the situation of the supply services also did not promise success after a second attack on Avranches.

At first I verbally reported this estimate to the 7th Army. On the next day, I made it out in writing and repeated again that I believed the attack would be unsuccessful. At the same time, I pointed to the necessity of throwing back the enemy at Alencon in order to keep open the supply and retreat routes and so to avoid a catastrophe.

Besides 7th Army, my report also went to Army Group B. On the same day (August 10), the report was read in my presence to Field Marshal von Kluge at his headquarters. The 7th Army (Hausser) agreed with my point of view.

In order to secure even the minimum amount of freedom of action, it was imperative to prop up the deep flank of the 7th Army and to evacuate the "finger" of the 7th Army at Mortain. These necessities were clear. OKW had by its unfeasible illusions of an attack on Avranches prevented the accomplishment of these objectives until now. Now even OKW could not close its ears to the necessity of making an immediate attack on the flank of the enemy advancing toward Alencon and Laigle and throwing him back. On this point, it agreed to Kluge's proposal. However, OKW would not authorize quitting the "finger" but, as if hypnotized, held to the thought of an assault on Avranches. Thereby, Hitler made it impossible for the 7th Army to put immediately at my disposal the panzer divisions necessary. These half measures had necessarily to lead to a catastrophe, if the enemy acted in the right way, i.e., quickly. He did. Overall, the measures taken at that time were "two days too late!"

Perhaps this would have been the right time for Field Marshal Kluge to act against Hitler's order to save the two armies (7th and 5th Panzer), but after July 20, he was watched in such a sharp way that it would have been especially difficult for him.[2] The result would simply have been his replacement by a more manageable tool.

### The Preparation for the Counterattack at Alencon

*Time and Forces.*

For the counterattack at Alencon, I was allotted the LXXXI, XXXXVII Panzer, and II SS Panzer Corps. The LXXXI Corps (General of Infantry Adolf Kuntzen) consisted of the remains of the 9th Panzer Division, the remnants of the 708th Infantry Division, one heavily battered security regiment, and parts of a parachute antitank battalion, the arrival of which, however, could not be awaited.[3]

The units of the LXXXI Corps could not be taken into account for an attack. Excepting the paratroopers, who were not yet at hand, nothing could be expected of these units, even for defense.

The XXXXVII Panzer Corps (General of Panzer Troops Baron Hans von Funck) included the 116th Panzer, 1st SS Panzer, and 2nd Panzer Divisions. The vanguard of 116th Panzer was to arrive at Argentan on August 12. The 1st SS Panzer Division (the "Leibstandarte") and 2nd Panzer were ordered to move into assembly positions in the forest area north of Alencon.

The II SS Panzer Corps (SS Lieutenant General Willi Bittrich), with the 2nd and 9th SS Panzer Divisions, was scheduled to arrive on August 15.

*Intention.*

It was to be foreseen that the arrival of the II SS Panzer Corps could not be awaited. My intention was, therefore, to assemble the XXXXVII Panzer Corps in the forest north of Alencon.

The movement was to be covered by the 9th Panzer Division, and as soon as possible, probably in the evening of August 14, the panzer corps had to attack the enemy flank, either north or south of Alencon, depending on the development of the situation.

### The Loss of Alencon.

At about noon on August 11, my chief of staff and I arrived at the headquarters of the LXXXI Corps northeast of Alencon. My staff, so far as it had been formed, was also expected to arrive there. General Kuntzen informed us that since this morning, the weak 9th Panzer Division was being attacked by at least one armored division. From his weak security detachments, Kuntzen also expected bad news.

Late in the afternoon, the 9th Panzer Division reported that superior enemy forces had broken through. The remainder of the division was assembling itself at the edge of woods north of Alencon and tried to hold the position there. The strength of the division was only about one infantry battalion, one artillery battalion, and a half a dozen panzers.

According to this report, the enemy could be expected to arrive at the corps headquarters at any moment. Kuntzen gave orders for the immediate departure for the region east of Argentan. At the same time, tank artillery fire was heard at a very short distance, and enemy airplanes made any movement impossible. Enemy shell fire hit. Around us, smoke clouds were rising from burning cars. My staff did not arrive.

It was evening before we could break camp. A bakery company was taking defensive positions at Sees. On all streets, rear services flooded northwards. I sent an officer to the 116th Panzer Division with the order to push to Sees at night and hold its position there. To the commander of an antiaircraft artillery regiment, who reported to me in order to get permission to retreat from Argentan, I gave the order to arrange defensive positions there and to hold them.

### The Enemy Attack on Argentan (August 12).

As the point of gravity of my panzer group for the next few days lay with the XXXXVII Panzer Corps, on the next morning we drove to the corps headquarters, which, having no information about the new situation, had established itself near Vieux Pont, 14 kilometers [8.7 miles] southwest of Argentan. General von Funck had, however, already made contact with the remnants of the 9th Panzer Division and taken command over them. Parts of a reconnaissance detachment and parts of his signal battalion were covering the headquarters at a distance. No report had yet arrived from the 116th Panzer Division. Whether Sees was still in our hands was not known. The whole day, machine-gun fire was heard from a short distance. Any moment the enemy might appear at the headquarters. Enemy fighter-bombers, however, made the transfer of the headquarters impossible.

In the afternoon, at last, the report arrived. Two infantry battalions and one artillery battalion of the 116th Panzer Division, without tanks, were advancing toward Sees, but owing to a tough resistance from the enemy, they made but slow progress. In the evening, another report reached headquarters. According to this, the parts of 116th Panzer Division had been destroyed by heavy artillery fire from massed enemy tanks. The enemy was forcing his way toward Argentan.

In the night, both of the headquarters made a shift to the region of Chenedouil, 20 kilometers [12.43 miles] west of Argentan. Notwithstanding the short distance (30 kilometers [18.64 miles]), this shift took six hours. Already it could be felt that the whole supply service for one and a half armies was congested on the few roads between Falaise and Argentan. As the weather was good, for the most part, the columns were only able to move in the eight hours of night. The large number of burned-out motor vehicles created many bottlenecks. In consequence, all streets were congested, and the traffic was moving merely at a walk. Shifting of troops took several times more time than under normal conditions. The supply service was endangered.

The loss of Alencon deprived the 7th Army of its supply basis. It was now entirely dependent on the 5th Panzer Army. I had instructed their quartermaster on August 11 to deliver gasoline and ammunition to the district south of Argentan for the panzer attack.

At night the remnants of the 116th Panzer Division reached the area of Argentan. Together with the antiaircraft regiment, they held a thin line on both sides of the town against heavy attacks and knocked out several enemy tanks.

*The Battle North of Alencon (August 13–14).*

By noontime on August 13, weak elements of the 1st SS Panzer Division had reached the forest area north of Alencon. Difficulties with the release and congestion of the roads were to blame for the artillery arriving first, without infantry protection. The signal battalion arrived next and, much later, the tanks, while the mass of the infantry did not arrive until the next day. Besides, most of the units were cut to pieces on the march by air raids. The 2nd Panzer Division arrived in a better condition, but had at first only half of its forces. In spite of different routes, both divisions got mixed up at night. The commanders, pursued by fighter-bombers, were trying to get their units together. Many companies had not reached their march objectives but, owing to incessant air raids, had sought the nearest shelter.

The news about the destruction of the 9th Panzer Division had not gotten through to the lower units yet, and therefore they considered themselves more or less secure in the woods north of Alencon.

Right into this confusion the enemy was now forcing his way. He went around the remnants of the 9th Panzer Division. A crisis took place. Units of the 2nd Panzer Division had to rescue elements of the 1st SS Panzer Division and vice versa. The forest area north of Alencon was lost. From the region southeast of Argentan, the enemy was pressing westward over the Orne. We succeeded in stopping him at the Cance Brook. By evening, the 9th Panzer Division had but the strength of a company.

*On the southern face of the German front, the 9th Panzer Division was down to a strength of 260 men, 12 tanks, and a few pieces of artillery. The 1st SS Panzer Division could field only 352 men and 29 tanks and assault guns. The 2nd Panzer had 2,230 men, a dozen tanks, and 5 assault guns. These three divisions and a handful of other battered units were facing an American corps of 70,000 men and 650 tanks.[4]*

During the night of August 13–14, further units of the two divisions arrived, and we succeeded in building up a thin front. The 1st SS Panzer Division defended the line La Fert Maci–Carrouges–Chahain, and the 2nd Panzer Division defended the west bank of the Canze brook from Carrouges-Chahain to Ecouche. There it contacted the 116th Panzer Division as before.

The II SS Panzer Corps succeeded in arriving with strong units on August 16.

With the loss of Alencon and Sees, the situation had changed entirely. As the enemy stood close to Falaise in the north, the mouth of the encirclement had a width of only 30 kilometers [18.6 miles]. The ammunition and fuel situation was dreadfully serious. For the supply of the one and a half armies, only three roads were available at nighttime. Because of the lack of fuel, a number of tanks of the 1st SS Panzer Division had to be blown up. The 9th Panzer Division was annihilated. I fully described this situation in my report to the army group and stressed once again the necessity of an immediate and quick retreat on a large scale; otherwise a complete collapse was unavoidable. Just at that time, the panzer group received by wireless an order from Hitler, which in broad lines read as follows: "The attack, ordered by me, southwardly past Alencon toward the east is to be effected under all conditions immediately as a preparation for an attack on Avranches."

Thereupon, on August 14, I sent my last special-missions staff officer to army group with the following report:

"Enemy attack with a presumable strength of two armored and one infantry division. He has surprised the 2nd Panzer Division and the 1st SS Panzer Division (Leibstandarte) while assembling in the forest north of Alencon and thrown them back to the line La Ferte–Carrouges–Cance Brook, causing heavy losses to them. Parts of 116th Panzer Division annihilated at Sees. Rest holds against heavy enemy attacks on both sides of Argentan. Panzer strengths: 1st SS Panzer Division, 30; 2nd Panzer Division, 25; 116th Panzer Division, 15. The 9th Panzer Division still has company strength. Owing to fighter-bombers at daytime and traffic congestion at night, fuel and ammunition situation very serious. Lack of fuel caused 1st SS Panzer Division to blow up a number of tanks. Under flank protection, a quick withdrawal of 7th Army from encirclement is imperative in order to avoid catastrophe. Execution of order of Supreme Command . . . not possible before August 16. Success improbable."

At the same time, the officer had to report the condition of my staff and propose centralized command by 7th Army. He arrived wounded at the HQ of Army Group B on August 14 and delivered the report. On August 14, the 1st SS Panzer Division ("Leibstandarte") was attacked during the whole day. Its parts were not all assembled and in the course of that day and on

August 15, it was slowly driven back. The 2nd Panzer Division held its sector. On both sides of Argentan, however, the enemy succeeded in penetrating in some places the thin line of the bleeding 116th Panzer Division. West of Argentan, the enemy pushed 2 kilometers [1.4 miles] over the Orne and took Ecouche. East of Argentan, he penetrated into the Foret de Gouffern and endangered Chambois.

The morale of the German troops in the west suffered at that time a blow from which it did not recover. The Atlantic Wall was, for too long a period, described by our propaganda as unconquerable; the invasion as a sure defeat for the enemy. For a long time, the soldier had been told of the coming of new arms, masses of new German aircrafts and submarines, and instead of all of this, he had now to wage a war of the poor man against an enemy who had everything in abundance, and who was fresh, while the German soldier had already been engaged in hard fighting for five years and, moreover, during the last two years only suffered defeats. At the shore, he saw hundreds of enemy vessels; every day, he saw hundreds of enemy airplanes flying to Germany entirely undisturbed and coming back again as from a parade, apparently without any loss. From home, he received news of destroyed towns. A glance at the map was sure to suggest doubt even to the common soldier whether he was commanded in a reasonable way. He had no time for thinking, but his feeling told him that this war could no longer be won.

He felt himself betrayed. He no longer fought with a belief in victory and a reliance on his command, but only from a soldier's pride and for fear of defeat. But not all of the soldiers had this sense of duty and this kind of pride. For the first time, not only Poles and Alsatians, but even single Germans deserted to the enemy.

The sinking of the soldier's spirit was even more evident in the "morale of the arms." Some tanks were left standing without being blown up, machine guns were thrown away, guns were left lying, and stragglers without arms were numerous. "Catch lines" in the rear of the front had to be inaugurated. Even the SS was no exception to this rule. The 1st SS Panzer Division ("Leibstandarte") had never before fought so miserably as at this time.

The fighting morale of the German troops had cracked. This I openly reported to Field Marshal Model on August 18 at a meeting in Fontaine L'Abbe. Lieutenant General von Gersdorff mentions in his work of October 17, 1945, that I had just gone face-to-face with Kluge because I considered this fact as an important basis for all decisions of the High Command.

Achievements such as the breakout of the encirclement and the counterattack of the II SS Panzer Corps on Trun should therefore be ranked very high.

On the fourteenth and fifteenth, the situation as to fuel and ammunition remained equally bad, as the fighter-bombers blew up the majority of fuel tank vehicles.

## The Falaise Encirclement

### Argentan.

As soon as the arrival of the II SS Panzer Corps was completed on August 15 and 16, together with fuel for 20 to 30 kilometers [12.4 to 18.6 miles], it was immediately committed to relieve the desperate situation on both sides of Argentan. Despite the fact that the number of tanks of each division lay below twenty, they succeeded in cleaning out the forest area east of Argentan.

At that time, also, two projector (rocket launcher) brigades were allotted to me. However, they had almost no ammunition for their projectors and could therefore be used only as infantry forces.

All divisions subordinated to me could at best be considered as regiments at that time. Also, their artillery had often only the strength of an artillery battalion. Officers and men were extremely tired and hungry.

Since August 15, the command post (CP) of the 7th Army lay in the immediate vicinity of my staff. We were in personal contact daily. Our views on the situation coincided. The army CP did much to keep traffic on the supply roads moving by a segregation of the horse-drawn vehicles and by establishing one-way traffic to and from the front. The results were poor. Orders could not get through in such a situation.

### Field Marshal Kluge's Last Visit.

On August 15, I was visiting the 116th Panzer Division in Pommainville. There I received a wireless order to meet Field Marshal Kluge in Necy. I waited three hours for him. He did not come.

In the evening, I received an order by radio from Army Group B, asking what I knew of the fate of Field Marshal von Kluge. Soon after that, another radio inquiry came from Hitler's HQ with the same text. In reply to my answer, I received a second message from Hitler's headquarters: "Ascertain whereabouts Kluge. Report results hourly."

This matter gave us much anxiety, but at midnight Kluge arrived at my CP. The fighter-bombers had shot up his car and his two radio stations. Afterwards, he got mixed up in the chaotic night traffic. Thus he had personally experienced the desperate situation of the rear service routes.

Only in the prisoner-of-war camp did I hear that these inquiries of the Supreme Command were not prompted by an anxiety for the personal fate of Kluge, but by the suspicion that he might have had a meeting with American officers in order to capitulate or surrender personally. Through investigations he had made in the meantime, Hitler had ascertained that Kluge had previous knowledge of the July 20 assassination attempt.

Kluge discussed the situation with SS General Hausser, General von Funck, and I, each in turn. Each of us told him that an attack, with divisions now bled white, without air forces, and without a safe supply service, was unthinkable. Only a quick withdrawal from the encirclement could perhaps avoid a catastrophe. Kluge was now ready to give all orders for the evacuation of the finger, as we had proposed, but only after having communicated with Fuehrer Headquarters. Without its approval, he did not dare to make such a far-reaching decision. The people there, he said, lived in another world, without any idea of the actual situation here, as he knew from our reports and what he himself had experienced in the last twenty-four hours.

*No one at or near the front knew that at 7:30 P.M. on August 15, Hitler had relieved Kluge of his command. On the recommendation of General Jodl, he had appointed Hausser acting commander of Army Group B. By this time, he had narrowed the choice of the new OB West to Albert Kesselring or Walter Model. Jodl apparently recommended Hausser as a permanent appointment, but Hitler had always distrusted Hausser because of his beady eyes. The fact that he had lost one of them serving the Third Reich on the Eastern Front apparently did not count for much. Besides, he was not a "pure" SS man, having been a general staff officer who retired from the army as a lieutenant general, and he had once retreated against orders at Kharkov. Hitler finally decided on Model because he felt that*

*Kesselring could not be spared in Italy. Kluge was not yet informed of his relief. He was merely ordered not to go back into the pocket.*

If and when 7th Army ordered a quick withdrawal of the front on August 16, I do not remember now. The 5th Panzer Army was fighting at Falaise that day. On the left flank of the 7th Army, we lost La Ferte Maci. The front had to be pushed back approximately to the line of Le Crais–Nanes–Bouce.

During the night, I transferred my CP to the staff of the II SS Panzer Corps in Montabard, north of Argentan. Staff of the 7th Army shifted to Necy. The work of staff was disturbed by heavy artillery fire and air raids. The troops suffered hunger. Also, my staff had had no bread for two days.

### The Transfer of II SS Panzer Corps to Vimoutiers.

In the morning of August 17, the II SS Panzer Corps and the rocket launcher brigades received the order to proceed immediately to Lisieux as a reserve for the army group. The fuel necessary for this move had arrived at night. The front gaps on both sides of Argentan, which had just been filled, were thus opened again by the removal of the corps. I had nothing left with which to close them.

After a few hours, a new order arrived for the II SS Panzer Corps. The enemy had taken Falaise, and the corps had as soon as possible to go into battle positions near Vimoutiers and to march during daylight hours, despite casualties. As the 2nd SS Panzer Division had lost all of its big radio stations, it was difficult for Bittrich to transmit the new order to his divisions. At last he succeeded in doing it, and the corps was set to march to Vimoutiers. It suffered heavy losses from fighter-bombers on the way.

Late in the afternoon, when the whole corps was on the way and Bittrich alone was still present, a third order came: "Enemy has broken through southeast of Falaise, pushing on Trun. II SS Panzer Corps is to throw enemy back and hold Trun."

Could General Bittrich still reach his division commanders? The radio stations were dismantled, and it was difficult to drive on the utterly congested roads. Bittrich immediately set out personally in order to try to reach his division commanders. At the same time, the 116th Panzer Division reported that the enemy had overrun the weak security detachments which had replaced

the II SS Panzer Corps east of Argentan and had taken Le Bourg
St. Leonard. Chambois was impassable due to heavy enemy
artillery fire. The rumor was that Trun had been taken by British
troops.

The gap for the retreat of the army had been reduced to only
10 kilometers [6.21 miles]!

### Conference with Field Marshal Model (August 18).

At night, I received a wireless message stating that Field Marshal
Walter Model,[5] who had relieved Kluge, would like to meet the
commanding generals of both armies and me the next morning
at 9 A.M. at the headquarters of the 5th Panzer Army in Fontaine
L'Abbi. The distance was 75 kilometers [46.5 miles]. I needed
from 3 P.M. to 11 P.M. for the trip—first of all, because I got
caught in the movement of the II SS Panzer Corps. We saw griev-
ous pictures.

Bittrich's attempt to reach his divisions and to lead them
against Trun had failed.

Every day, I had, as often as possible, visited the divisions subordinate to me. I could therefore give Field Marshal Model a
true picture of the actual situation—strengths, supply, morale—
and did so.

Model's order was: "My intention is withdrawal behind the
Seine. For this purpose first we must stiffen the bottleneck at
Trun and Argentan with panzer divisions, in order to enable the
infantry divisions of the 7th Army to retreat." I was ordered to
lead the panzer corps to the bottleneck. In the course of our
conference, a report reached us that Trun was in the hands of
British troops, thereby practically completing the encirclement.

*Meanwhile, Model's own Army Group B headquarters was temporarily elimi-
nated from the battle. On the afternoon of Friday, August 18, an American
detachment reached the Seine, just across the river from La Roche-Guyon, and
began shelling it with mortars. There was considerable confusion as the staff evacuated the chateau and fled west to Margival, a town about five miles north of Sois-
sons and sixty miles west of Paris, where it resumed operations the next day. One of
the last to leave was Field Marshal von Kluge, who bade an emotional farewell to
his former staff. He was in no hurry to return to Germany, since he knew that the
Gestapo would soon be after him, if it was not on his trail already. He finally
headed back by car on August 19, but he was under no illusions as to what would*

*happen to him if he finished the journey. He ordered his driver to halt in a peaceful place near Metz, the site of some of his World War I battles. Here he spread a blanket and asked to be left alone. After his driver and aide returned to the car, Kluge quietly bit down on a cyanide capsule. He left a letter for Hitler, calling on him to end the war. The Fuehrer read it without comment, and then canceled the field marshal's state funeral, for which Rundstedt had been scheduled to deliver the eulogy. Kluge was buried quietly on the grounds of his estate, with military pallbearers, but without military honors. (His grave has since been destroyed.) The Propaganda Ministry announced that he had died of a cerebral hemorrhage.*

### Breaking Out of the Encirclement

*Preparation.*

Instead of SS General Hausser, the chief of staff of the 7th Army, Major General Rudolf-Christoph von Gersdorff,[6] was present at the conference with him (Field Marshal Model). We came to an agreement that I should immediately leave the staff of the II SS Panzer Corps near Meulles in order to lead the corps to the combat area near Trun. The distance to Meulles was 35 kilometers [21.2 miles]. I was, however, so often attacked by fighter-bombers and my car was pierced through by bullets that I did not arrive at the staff of II SS Panzer Corps until 10 P.M. There I was informed that the British and American troops had met southeast of Trun and thus completed the encirclement of the 7th Army.

At the same time, Bittrich reported that his corps was utterly torn asunder in consequence of the night marches and air attacks. Until now he could not contact any of his division staffs, but he knew that his troops had neither fuel, ammunition, food, nor signal equipment. He could not tell when the corps would again be ready for action.

I gave Bittrich the order to lead his corps as soon as possible to the combat zone on both sides of Vimoutiers and to be ready to attack the area southeast of Trun, in order to support the operations for breaking out of the encirclement. I then immediately proceeded at night to the staff of the 5th Panzer Army, in order to have my decision confirmed and to coordinate the attack of the corps with that of the 7th Army. I also wanted to secure from the 5th Panzer Army, as soon as possible, the necessary supplies for the II SS Panzer Corps.

My decision was confirmed. The attack of the II SS Panzer Corps had to begin on the night of August 19–20. The 7th Army was accordingly informed by me through wireless, as well as all the corps in the encirclement that I could reach by radio.

During the afternoon of August 19, I visited Bittrich again. He still had no fuel and had received very insufficient quantities of ammunition. Despite this, he expected to be ready for action in the evening. The fuel arrived only near daybreak. It took some hours before it was distributed and tanked. The army group made haste, and at about 10 A.M. on the twentieth, the divisions were ready to fall in. They were able to do so because bad weather hindered the actions of the enemy air forces.

### The Counterattack.

Both divisions together had only twenty tanks. One of the divisions possessed only one battalion of infantry, and the other only two. One road of advance was packed with burned-out vehicles to such an extent that the tanks had first to clear out an alley before passing.

As far as I can remember, one combat group of the division advanced along the route Vimoutier–Trun, the other along the road Cambert–St. Lambert.

At first, the advance made good progress. It came to a stop, however, in front of a range of hills (Hill 258 south of Les Champeaux, Hill 240 at Ecorches, and Hill 262 north of Coudehard). In the afternoon, the range of hills was taken. After that, the advance made practically no more progress. In spite of this, a gap was forced into the encirclement and the first 2,000 men joined the division, getting out of the pocket.

### The Results.

During the rest of the day, and throughout the night, soldiers with and without arms streamed out of the encirclement, as well as about fifty guns and twenty-five tanks.

The achievement of the units forcing the "breakthrough" was a big one. Nevertheless, as a troop, they could be used no more. The commander of the 7th Army, the commander of the 1st SS Panzer Division, and other generals were wounded.

*As Paul Hausser advanced down the road with a machine pistol around his neck, an American artillery shell exploded in front of him. A sizable piece of shrapnel struck him in the throat. Fortunately for him, it was partially spent, but he nevertheless was seriously wounded. Some men from the 1st SS Panzer Division witnessed the incident, performed first aid on the semiconscious SS general, and placed him on a tank. Eventually he reached safety, but he could not return to active duty for months and was temporarily replaced by Baron von Funck. The next day, August 20, SS Maj. Gen. Theodor Wisch, the commander of the 1st SS Panzer Division, was so seriously wounded that both of his legs had to be amputated.[7]*

A number of generals were killed in action and others were captured. Almost the whole armament of the army—tanks, guns, radio stations, motor vehicles, substantial parts of trains, and supplies—was lost. Even the number of rescued machine guns was insignificant.

The number of men who got out of the encirclement after it was closed can be estimated at about 20,000, although the Allied forces reported the number of prisoners taken at 50,000. It is very difficult to estimate the number of men killed in action. Having no actual data at hand. I would estimate their number for the period of August 10–22 at 20,000.

*Of the 100,000 men encircled in the pocket, 10,000 were killed and 40,000 to 50,000 were captured or missing. Fewer than 50,000 escaped, and a high percentage of these were supply and service troops. In material terms, the losses were devastating. Army Group B lost 220 tanks, 160 assault guns or other pieces of self-propelled artillery, 700 towed artillery pieces, 130 antitank guns, 130 half-tracks, 5,000 motorized vehicles and 200 wagons. At least 1,800 horses had been killed in the pocket, and the U.S. 90th Infantry Division alone captured 1,000. Between them, the ten panzer divisions that broke out of the pocket had lost 1,300 tanks. They now had only 62 tanks and 26 guns between them. The Panzer Lehr, 10th SS Panzer, and 9th Panzer Divisions had no "runners" left at all. The infantry divisions were in equally bad shape. Both the 5th Panzer and 7th Armies were smashed. Since D-Day, they had lost at least 50,000 men killed and more than 200,000 captured. As a result, the Germans' hold on Paris was doomed. Eberbach's task now was to get as much of his force back to the German border as he could—assuming he could get there himself.*

Rallying points for all the mauled divisions were fixed, where potato and meat supplies were kept ready. Bread could not be procured. These points, however, did not correspond with those assigned by the 7th Army, so nothing remained to be done but to establish new rallying points behind the Seine. At the Seine, points were established for guiding stragglers, issuing rations, making payments, and for the distribution of clothing.

By noon on the twenty-first, when the arrival of soldiers from the encirclement had stopped entirely and when the pressure of the American and British troops on the II SS Panzer Corps became stronger, I considered the task of the corps fulfilled.

The retreat to and over the Seine commenced. [See map on facing page.]

## Reasons for the German Defeat

### A. Hitler's Supreme Headquarters failed:

1) by denying the fact that, with the success of the American-British invasion (i.e., about four weeks after the start of the invasion), the war was lost and failed to draw the necessary conclusions from this;

2) by making a false estimate of the place of the invasion, resulting in incorrect dispositions of the reserves;

3) by discovering too late that only *one* landing place for the Allied troops in western France could be taken into account. Hence, an insufficient number of divisions were sent to the gravity point: Normandy;

4) by distrusting all of the army generals and making incessant changes in the leading command and staff positions;

5) by not giving the army groups and armies the necessary authority for independent actions. All decisions, despite clear reports from the front, were drawn up in the Supreme HQ and based on illusions, not on intimate knowledge of the situation, actual estimates of the condition and the efficiency of the German and American divisions, and of the situation in the air and of supplies;

6) by demanding too obstinate a defense instead of a flexible defense, which would have given more advantages to the defender;

7) by false estimate of the effect of superior enemy air forces, foremost of all on the rear services and on the displacements of units;

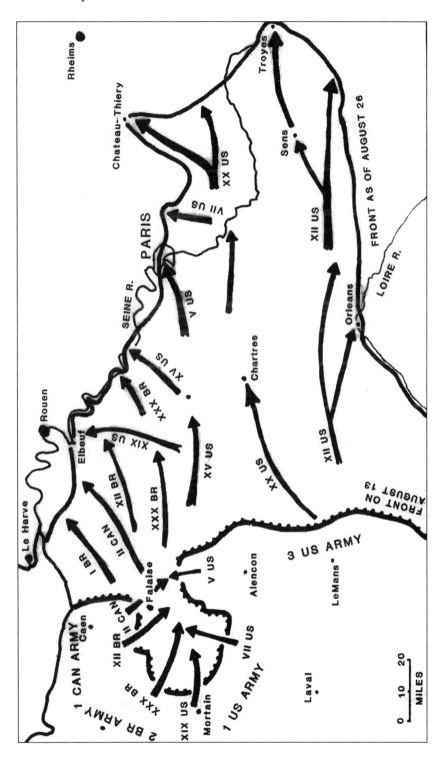

8) by making all decisions, especially the decisive one of drawing back to the Seine, too late;

9) by failing to subordinate the air forces and the navy to Army Group B, leaving very big reserves of men and motor vehicles in these branches which the army could not use;

10) by using up the panzer divisions at the front, instead of holding them for counterattacks, with the exception of Avranches.

### B. *The* Luftwaffe *Failed:*

1) because of poor production planning, an insufficient number of airplanes were manufactured;

2) by using poor tactics for commitment at the beginning of the invasion, resulting in the destruction of the German planes engaged;

3) because of a lack of fuel, the personnel of the air forces were so poorly trained that their quality fell below that of the Allied forces;

4) because the numerical supply of airplanes was absolutely insufficient.

### C. Neglect of the Western armies in 1941–44 in respect to composition of the army staffs and setting up stocks of supply goods.

We omitted to make good these faults before the beginning of the invasion, as well as to make the supply service depots mobile.

### D. Neglect of Supply Services.

Besides the enemy air forces, the failure of taking the necessary precautions, and the failure of the Supreme Command to place the trucks of the *Luftwaffe* and the navy at our disposal, the arrest of the very efficient chief supply officer of Army Group B, Colonel of General Staff Finckh, is added to the reasons for the German defeat. Finckh was arrested for having previous knowledge of the assassination attempt of July 20. [For further particulars, see the November 1945 report of Gersdorff.[8]]

## Effect of the Enemy's Arms

The chief merit of the successes of the Allied forces in Normandy has to be accorded to enemy air forces. Their successes were obtained through choking off the delivery of services in the communications zone (railroad stations, bridges, etc.) and in the combat area (making movements impossible during daylight hours). The losses of panzers from lack of gasoline were larger than those destroyed by all kinds of enemy armaments put together.

The enemy air forces made impossible any displacements of troops at daytime (except during periods of bad weather).

Bombers had a big effect on morale and materiel.

Commitment of close support airplanes (particularly rocket-firing Typhoons) against German combat elements had big material and morale effects, especially against panzer units.

American tank divisions met with great success through proper commitments, deep breakthroughs, quick and resolute actions, attacks into deep flanks and into the rear of the army. They were correctly organized and had a great number of tanks.

Tank personnel were well trained. The fine achievements of the American tanks must be especially appreciated because of the fact that the Sherman tank, considering its armaments and the armoring, is not quite equivalent to the German Tiger and Panther.

The American tank destroyers, owing to the rare attacks of the German panzers, were not in such evidence as to enable me to pass judgment on them.

The American infantry was master of its missions. It was well trained and brave. Being fully motorized, it was superior to the German infantry divisions.

The enemy's artillery's efficiency was due to his high expenditure of ammunition, his aerial observation, and his concentration of fire. The effects of the light artillery on the morale and materiel was less than that of the middle and heavy artillery.

I estimate the percentage of casualties to German soldiers due to enemy aircraft as 50 percent; due to enemy tanks, 20 percent; to artillery, 20 percent; and to infantry, 10 percent.

## NOTES

1. William B. Breuer, *Death of a Nazi Army* (New York: Stein and Day, 1985), 236–37.
2. Guenther Hans von Kluge was born in Posen, Prussia (now Poznan, Poland), in 1882. He attended various cadet schools and joined the Imperial Army in 1900. Commissioned in the 46th Field Artillery Regiment in 1901, he was sent to the War Academy to undergo general staff training in the early 1910s. After graduating, he was sent to war in 1914 as adjutant of the XXI Corps. He later led a battalion on the Western Front (November 1915–April 1916) before returning to General Staff assignments. He was seriously wounded at Verdun in 1918. After the war, he served in various staff and command assignments, and in 1930, he succeeded Baron Werner von Fritsch as commander of the 2nd Artillery Regiment. In 1931, he became artillery commander III (*Artilleriefuehrer III*) and deputy commander of the 3rd Infantry Division. In February 1933 he was promoted to major general and named inspector of signal troops. The following year, he was promoted to lieutenant general and became commander of the 6th Infantry Division in Muenster. Kluge continued his rapid advancement in 1934, when he was given command of *Wehrkreis VI*, also in Muenster. He was promoted to general of artillery in 1936. He was firmly on Fritsch's side during the crisis of 1938, and was on Hitler's list to be retired when the Fuehrer replaced Fritsch with Walter von Brauchitsch. Kluge was, however, brought out of retirement in October 1938, when it appeared that Nazi Germany was about to go to war with Czechoslovakia and its allies over the Sudetenland. This time, Kluge commanded Army Group 6, which headquartered in Hanover, and controlled *Wehrkreise IX, X,* and *XI* in northern Germany. In August 1939, just before World War II began, Army Group 6 became the 4th Army. Kluge led it very well in Poland, resulting in his promotion to colonel general on October 1, 1939. He also led this unit in the French and Russian campaigns, and Hitler promoted him to field marshal on July 19, 1940. When the German Army stalled before Moscow, Kluge was given command of Army Group Center on December 18, 1941. He led it until October 28, 1943, when he was seriously injured in an automobile accident in Russia. He did not return to active duty for eight months. Kluge was known throughout the Officers' Corps as "Clever Hans." He was on both sides of the anti-Hitler conspiracy, and after the July 20, 1944, assassination attempt failed, he was very frightened that Hitler and the Nazis would find out about it and was desperate not to appear disloyal to the Fuehrer, who was by now very suspicious of him.
3. Adolf Kuntzen was born in Magdeburg in 1889 and joined the 1st Hussars Regiment as an officer cadet in 1909. He fought in World War I, primary with the 7th Hussars (1914–17). He was transferred to the staff of the XXVI Reserve Corps in early 1917, took an abbreviated general staff course, and served on the general staffs of the military governor of Metz and the 10th Replacement Division in 1918. Selected for the *Reichswehr,* he spent the 1920s and early 1930s in general staff, cavalry, and Defense Ministry assignments. He was on the staff of the Army Personnel Office until Hitler purged it of anti- and non-Nazis in 1938. Kuntzen was then named commander of the 3rd Light Division. He led this unit in Poland and France, and oversaw its conversion into the 8th Panzer Division in the winter of 1939–40.

Kuntzen led the LVII Panzer Corps in Russia (1941–42) and took charge of the XXXII Corps Command in 1942. This headquarters was later upgraded to the LXXXI Corps. Relieved of his command on September 4, 1944, he was never reemployed. He had been promoted to general of panzer troops in 1941. He died in Hanover, Lower Saxony, in 1964.

4. Breuer, *Death of a Nazi Army*, 260–61.

5. Walter Model was perhaps the most capable of the Nazi generals. He was born in Genthin, near Magdeburg, on January 24, 1891, the son of a music teacher of very modest means. He joined the army in 1909 as a *Fahnen-junker*. He spent most of World War I in the infantry on the Western Front, where he was wounded several times. Late in the war, Model was appointed to the greater general staff in Berlin without ever having attended the War Academy—a rare distinction. He was selected for the *Reichsheer* in 1919 and established himself as an expert on technical matters and training. He was promoted to colonel in 1934 and was named chief of the Technical Department of the Army in 1935. Advanced to major general in 1938, he was chief of staff of the IV Corps during the Polish campaign and of the 16th Army during the French campaign of 1940. Promoted to lieutenant general in 1940, he led the 3rd Panzer Division in Russia until October 1941, when he became commander of the XXXXI Panzer Corps. An officer known for his courage and exceptional energy, he was promoted to general of panzer troops in late 1941. Then, on January 12, 1942, he was given command of the 9th Army, which was nearly surrounded just west of Moscow. Model saved 9th Army, and in the spring of 1943, he conducted a skillful withdrawal. In early 1944, he was given command of Army Group North. Later he commanded Army Groups South (later South Ukraine), North Ukraine, and Center, before being sent to the Western Front. Known as the "Fuehrer's fireman," he was promoted to field marshal on March 1, 1944.

6. Baron Rudolf-Christoph von Gersdorff was born in Lueben, Silesia, in 1905. He joined the army as an officer-cadet in 1923 and was commissioned second lieutenant in the 7th Cavalry Regiment in late 1926. He began his general staff training at the War Academy in 1938. An orderly officer with the 14th Army during the Polish campaign, he became I-c of the XII Corps (November 1, 1939), I-a of the 86th Infantry Division (May 6, 1940), I-c of Army Group Center (April 1, 1941), and chief of staff of the LXXXII Corps (February 1, 1944) and 7th Army (July 29, 1944). He was promoted to lieutenant colonel in 1942, colonel on January 1, 1943, and major general on January 30, 1945. He was a member of the anti-Hitler conspiracy and, after his wife died, even outfitted himself as a human bomb and pulled the timed detonator. But Hitler then suddenly left the room, and Gersdorff had to hurriedly find a restroom, where he defused the bomb and flushed part of it down the toilet. After the July 20, 1944, plot failed, Gersdorff was fortunate enough not to be identified by the Gestapo. He was, however, severely injured during the battle of the Falaise pocket, where he escaped hails of American artillery fire and attacks by fighter-bombers, only to be struck by lightning. He surrendered to the Americans on May 9, 1945, and remained in the POW camps until November 1947. On August 16, 1967, he was injured in a horse-riding accident and was paralyzed for life. He died in Munich on January 26, 1980.

7. Theodor "Teddi" Wisch was born in Wesselburenerkoof, near Wesselburen, Holstein, on December 13, 1907. He joined the SS in 1930 and was commissioned SS second lieutenant in 1933. He was a captain and company commander in the *Leibstandarte Adolf Hitler* (LAH) when the war began and remained in the unit (which evolved into the 1st SS Panzer Division "Leibstandarte Adolf Hitler") from 1930 to 1944, rising from SS private to SS major general (effective January 30, 1944). He commanded the 2nd SS Motorized Regiment "LAH" (later the 2nd SS Panzer Grenadier Regiment) from 1942 to 1943, when on October 22, he became commander of the division. After being wounded on August 20, 1944, he never returned to active duty. He eventually learned to walk without legs, using sticks, but only very slowly. Something of a recluse after the war, he died in Hamburg on January 11, 1995. His family reportedly auctioned off his medals and documents after his death.

8. Rudolf-Christoph von Gersdorff, "Avranches Counterattack, Seventh Army (29 Jul - 14 Aug 1944)," Foreign Military Studies MS #A-921, unpublished manuscript, Office of the Chief of Military History, 42–44.

# CHAPTER 5

# The 7th Army

## My Work as Commander in Chief of 7th Army

*Prefatory Note.*

Even less notes and data were available to me on this period than I had about my former duties in Normandy. I also have no maps of the territory between the Somme and the Seine. The happenings which took place during the period under review have not left as vivid an impression in my memory as the time prior to it. Hence I had to confine myself to recounting the deliberation of the 7th Army headquarters staff and the essentials of the few orders issued by my headquarters during that time. I have forgotten many details, particularly the designation of the divisions under the corps headquarters and the names of the commanders of such divisions.

*Assuming Command of the 7th Army.*

On August 22, 1944, after the close of the battle of Falaise, I was at the command post of the 5th Panzer Army in Cantelour, west of Rouen. All units south of the Seine were controlled by the 5th Panzer Army. On the arrival of Field Marshal Model, I reported to him, informing him that I had disbanded my small staff ("Panzer Group Eberbach") and requested his permission to apply to the Army Personnel Office for an assignment as commander of a panzer corps on the Eastern Front. Model replied that for the time being, I was to take command of the 7th Army as deputy for SS Colonel General Hausser, who had been wounded. The army staff itself required rehabilitation. So far, the only order the army had was to take up the remnants of nine infantry divisions that had escaped from the pocket north of the Seine and to rehabilitate them.

Major General von Gersdorff, 7th Army chief of staff, working together with the 5th Panzer Army and a few military administration headquarters, had already done good preliminary work in taking up the divisions that had escaped the pocket. Only a nucleus, some smaller and some larger, of each division had managed to escape. Around each of these cores, stragglers were collected. Each soldier crossing the Seine was stopped and given a slip with information as to where the division was assembling, how he was to reach that point, where he would receive food, pay, and clothing. Patrols were also sent out to pick up individual stragglers behind the lines and give them their directions. Some of the men had no rifles. Some of the men had even lost their uniform jackets in the course of their flight or in the numerous trucks that had been set on fire. However, all were perfectly willing and obeyed orders without a murmur. Thus units were quickly formed in the assembly areas, each such unit amounting to a division, ranging in numbers from 1,500 to 2,500 men.

The staffs to be made available to the 7th Army were LXXIV Corps (General Erich Straube), LXXXIV Corps (Lieutenant General Otto Elfeldt), and II Parachute Corps (General Eugen Meindl).[1] However, on the following day, orders arrived that II Parachute Corps was to proceed to Nancy with the remnants of its two divisions for the purpose of rehabilitation, and that Straube's headquarters was reassigned to 5th Panzer Army in order to take over a defense sector on the Seine. Of the remaining seven divisions, all combat-effective units of company strength and upward, and in particular all guns, were to be made available to Straube. Corresponding orders were issued by our headquarters immediately. The last remaining corps headquarters staff, however, namely Elfeldt's LXXXIV, had been annihilated in the Falaise pocket. Hence the 7th Army found itself compelled to execute its mission without corps staffs.

What was left of the divisions after detaching all combat-efficient units, ranging in each case from 1,500 to 2,500 men, was to be organized in such a manner that to begin with, a reinforced regiment could be formed from each division after reinforcements and weapons had been brought forward. What made things most difficult was the fact that the divisions commanded by us no longer had any wireless sets. Our sole means of communication with the divisions was the already overtaxed telephone network. Assembly areas for the divisions were situated in the region north of Lyons la Foret.

At the outset, my army staff was not quite satisfactory. It had been in France since 1940, and the four years of inactivity had not improved it. An additional drawback was that during that period all younger officers had been provisionally replaced by elderly officers between thirty-five and fifty-five years of age. Gersdorff, my chief of staff, had only been assigned to 7th Army at the end of July and, in the course of the heavy fighting, had not been able to freshen up the staff since then. He requested me to relieve a number of officers who had not proved suitable. In addition, we immediately released 20 officers and 150 enlisted men as surplus, for whom we required no replacements. Both of us were convinced that the staff would soon be in good order after this measure.

Our operations staff was first in Lyons la Foret. During the night of August 25–26, we transferred it to Metz-en-Conture.

### The Somme Line.

At that time, we heard little about the situation at the front, except so far as the 5th Panzer Army, whose headquarters either my chief of staff or I visited almost daily, was concerned. The whole of southern France seemed lost, and Army Group G (Blaskowitz) seemed to be in a difficult position. It appeared that the Americans were advancing without a stop east of Paris, one thrust aiming past the French capital at Laon. The Seine west of Paris was to be held at least until August 30, but the enemy already had established a number of bridgeheads across the river. To us it seemed doubtful that the Seine front could be held that long. The distance to the Somme was at least a three days' march for my infantry divisions. Therefore on August 27, sooner than would have been wise, we found ourselves compelled to force our tired divisions to march out of the area north of Lyons la Foret across the Somme, in order to avoid becoming involved in the withdrawal movement of the 5th Panzer Army.

Two infantry divisions were already behind the Somme and in the process of rehabilitation. They were hardly at 50 percent of their authorized strength. Together with the three strongest of our seven infantry divisions, they were to man the Somme line.

The remnants of the remaining four divisions were to be transported to Cambrai en route to the Reich by railroad for rehabilitation.

The withdrawal of the 5th Panzer Army from the Seine to the Somme was to be carried out in eight days. The intervening lines of resistance had been determined exactly on the map. Accordingly, it seemed that our 7th Army would have some time to establish itself on the Somme.

The panzer divisions were then to be pulled out through our lines and moved to the Verdun–Namur–Charleroi area for rehabilitation. At the same time they were to halt any further eastward advance by the Americans there. On reaching the Somme (approximately on September 7), the 5th Panzer Army was to relinquish command to the 7th Army, and all infantry divisions hitherto under 5th Panzer Army were to pass under my command on that date. These infantry divisions were not to remain on the Somme, but rather were to move on into another line of resistance at Arras for rehabilitation. My defense sector adjoined that of the 15th Army and extended from there to east of St. Quentin.

The Engineer Headquarters Staff Vierow (under General of Infantry Erwin Vierow), which controlled a number of engineer battalions and auxiliary forces, was subordinate to me.[2] Since recently it had been engaged in reinforcing the Somme position, Field Marshal Model hoped that the work on the positions had already made good progress.

The Somme would prove quite a considerable obstacle, provided we succeeded in getting it between ourselves and the enemy, and provided we managed to blast the bridges. I requested that at least one panzer division remain with my forces as an attack reserve. My request was refused.

On August 27, Gersdorff and I issued the necessary orders in writing. The division commanders were also summoned to a conference and everything was discussed verbally with them.

The reinforcement work on the Somme positions worried us. Contrary to Model's assumptions, nothing much had been done as yet. Instead of making preparations to blast the bridges as their first step, they had set up ineffectual antitank obstacles, which greatly impeded our own troops in the crossings, as they had been so arranged as to create bottlenecks. It was only with great difficulty that the necessary demolition charges for the bridges were obtained.

On the basis of experience gained in the Seine crossings, we had prepared a careful plan for the crossing of the Somme. Certain bridges had been assigned to each division and repair material piled up at required points. Ferry sites had been determined, the points of crossing fixed, and guides placed along the routes. Thus the crossing could have succeeded even in the face of Anglo-American air attacks against the bridges.

We had practically no artillery left. So far as I recollect, each of the two divisions that had been in position behind the Somme for some time had one artillery battalion, whereas the three battered divisions only had a gun or so each. Antitank guns were almost entirely lacking. Improvised mines were yet to be manufactured.

On August 28, I drove to the 15th Army Headquarters in Tourcoing, in order to consult there with Colonel General Salmuth and to request help.[3] However, Salmuth had meanwhile been relieved of his post as commander in chief and replaced by General of Infantry Gustav-Adolf von Zangen, who promised me the speedy dispatch of guns from the bunkers in Dieppe.[4]

## NOTES

1. The LXXXIV Corps had, in fact, been destroyed in the Falaise pocket and had ceased to exist. Elfeldt was a prisoner of war. Meindl had been wounded but escaped the pocket.

2. Erwin Vierow was born in Berlin in 1892. He joined the army as a *Fahnenjunker* in 1908 and was commissioned second lieutenant in the infantry in 1910. He served in World War I, was selected for the *Reichsheer*, and was chief of staff of *Wehrkreis XI* in 1937. Promoted to major general in 1938, lieutenant general in 1940, and general of infantry on January 1, 1941, he led the 96th Infantry Division (1939–40), the 9th Infantry Division (1940), the LV Corps (1941–43), and XX Corps (early 1943). He was then transferred from the Eastern Front to the west, where he became commander of northwest France. He was named leader of the Somme Command in June 1944 and was captured on September 1, the day after General Eberbach was taken prisoner. Released from the POW camps in 1947 or 1948, he settled in Bremen, where he died in 1982.

3. Hans von Salmuth was born in Metz, then a German garrison town, in 1888. He entered the service as an officer-cadet in 1907 and was commissioned in the 3rd Grenadier Guards Regiment in 1909. During World War I, he served as a battalion executive officer and then as a general staff officer. He served during the *Reichsheer* era and was chief of staff of Army Group North (later B) during the invasions of Poland and France. He was promoted to general of infantry in 1940 and commanded the XXX Corps (1941), 17th Army

(1942), 4th Army (1942), 2nd Army (1943–43), 4th Army again (1943), and 15th Army (1943–44). Promoted to colonel general on January 1, 1943, he was relieved of his command on August 25, 1944, when it was determined that he had been approached by the conspirators of July 20 and had not reported them. He was tried as a war criminal by the U.S. Military Tribunal at Nuremberg and was sentenced to twenty years' imprisonment in 1948, for assisting SS murder squads (*Einsatzgruppen*) in murdering Jews; however, he secured an early release in 1953. Salmuth retired to Wiesbaden and died in Heidelberg during the night of December 31, 1961–January 1, 1962.

4. Gustav-Adolf von Zangen was born in Darmstadt in 1892. He entered the Imperial Army as an officer-cadet in 1910 and was commissioned in the infantry. After World War I, he was discharged from the army, so he joined the police. Zangen reentered the army as a lieutenant colonel in 1935 and rose rapidly, commanding the 88th Infantry Regiment (1938–41), 17th Infantry Division (1941–43), LXXXIV Corps (1943), LXXXVII Corps (1943), Army Detachment von Zangen in northern Italy (1943–43), and 15th Army. Zangen was promoted to colonel (1938), major general (1942), lieutenant general (1943), and general of infantry (1943). A talented commander, he was nevertheless forced to surrender the 15th Army to the Americans at the end of the battle of the Ruhr pocket on April 18, 1945. He lived in Hanau/Main after the war and died there in 1964.

# CHAPTER 6

# The 5th Panzer Army: Second Tour

*Assuming Command over the 5th Panzer Army.*

What caused us the gravest concern was the developments in the situation at the front. The defense on the Seine had collapsed so much sooner than we had anticipated that the date for our assumption of command of the 5th Panzer Army's infantry divisions was moved up to September 3. Northward retirement of the front line was to take place in nightly laps of 15 kilometers [about 10 miles] each. However, once the German front had been deprived of the Seine obstacle, enemy tanks quickly succeeded in piercing the thinly held German lines and it proved impossible to hold the lines of resistance ordered. The date for the assumption of command was advanced to September 1. An immediate start was made, long before reaching the Somme, at pulling out the remnants of the panzer division. Thus the infantry divisions, which had lost the greater part of their anti-tank guns south of the Seine, were robbed of protection and exposed to annihilation. Everything depended upon whether the British would advance slowly and methodically or, in realization of our weakness, would seize their opportunity to effect a large-scale breakthrough. An enemy penetration began to take shape on the left flank of the 5th Panzer Army.

When I reached the command post of the 5th Panzer Army at noon on August 30, the commander of the center corps, General Kuntzen, was just giving a personal report to the effect that his corps (LXXXI) had been broken through about 45 kilometers [27.98 miles] southward on that morning and was retreating. Similar alarming reports also arrived from the corps on the left flank. No reserves were available to fill the gaps.

The situation was explained to Model when he arrived at the command post. Simultaneously, Sepp Dietrich requested that orders be given for his army headquarters to be pulled out on August 31, to enable him to retain control of his panzer divisions that had already been pulled out of the line.

The infantry elements in action for the days past had covered 15 to 30 kilometers [9.32 to 18.64 miles] each night for the sole purpose of being able to fight again during the daytime. The divisions earmarked for the defense of the Somme were to arrive in their respective defense areas on August 30. Everything these divisions needed was lacking. I had discussed all of this with Field Marshal Model. He was well aware of the situation and the possible consequences. The circumstances were stronger than we.

I offered no resistance to Dietrich's request that I assume command on August 31. After all, there was no difference whether I assumed command a day sooner or later. Model set noon, August 31, as the time for the command to change hands. I requested Model's approval for the transfer of my command post to north of the Somme, as it seemed too seriously menaced in its present position, He emphatically refused approval before September 1, however, giving the morale of the troops as his reason. In view of the fact that I had only ordered Gersdorff with a small operations staff forward from Metz-en-Conture, I did not press my point with Model.

Sepp Dietrich's chief of staff, Gause, briefed me on the situation. Pressure on our left flank had abated somewhat. The effects of the breakthrough in the central sector, on the front held by LXXXI Corps (Kuntzen), had not yet begun to make themselves felt. From captured enemy maps, it seemed that the enemy intended a thrust on Dieppe and Abbeville in order to envelop the forces of the 15th Army, in position between Le Havre and the mouth of the Somme. Such an intention seemed quite feasible and would have relieved the situation somewhat on our front. We had no reserves. The only panzers in the entire army zone were five Tiger tanks, the remnants of one battalion. The parachute division in action on the left flank was the sole motorized unit. Possibly a regiment could be taken from there as army reserve. I talked this possibility over with the general in command of the left sector, but in an enemy attack, one of his infantry divisions had been battered, and he had already committed those elements of the parachute division that were avail-

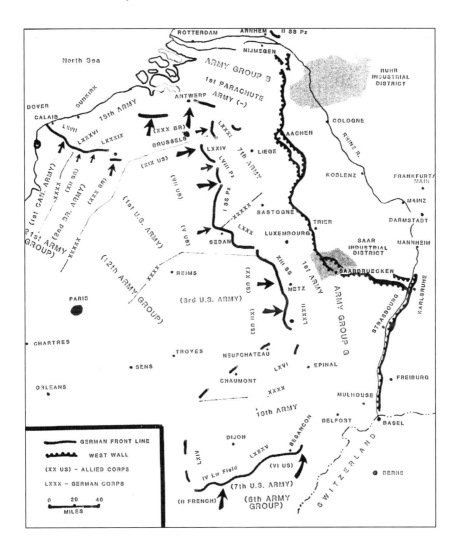

able in an effort to restore the situation. The only thing I was able to do was to arrange for Gause at least to order the transfer of the five Tiger tanks to Kuntzen's sector, in an attempt to halt the advance of the enemy tanks that had penetrated there.

*It is significant that the deterioration of the* Wehrmacht's *resources had reached the point that three German generals, including the commander-designate of a panzer army, were concerning themselves with the deployment of a mere five tanks. (The map above shows the situation on September 5 and clearly exhibits the disintegration of large parts of the German Army.)*

The afternoon reports on the situation in northeastern France, where the 5th Panzer Army was to take command, showed that the American forces were already approaching the Belgian border. Sepp Dietrich therefore requested me to assume command in the Somme sector at 6 A.M. on August 31, instead of at noon that day, so as to enable him to move at that time to his new sector with his staff. It was obvious that the situation in the Namur region called for the early arrival of an army staff to collect the divisions moved there for rehabilitation and provide united command for them. For this reason, I agreed to assume command at the earlier hour.

By evening, the British breakthrough had reached such a stage that their spearheads were already in the lines our troops were to have to retire into during the coming night. The Tiger tanks had not yet arrived at the positions they had been ordered to. It was hoped that they would succeed in halting the enemy spearhead. Hitherto, the British tanks, fortunately for us, had always halted their advance during the night. The distance to our headquarters was still roughly 30 kilometers [18.64 miles]. The enemy thrust still seemed to be directed towards Abbeville, but it was possible that it was intended for Amiens.

I telephoned General von Zangen, commander of the 15th Army, informing him of the grave situation of the army and of the quickened pace of the withdrawal that the enemy had forced upon us. He would have to speed up his withdrawal along the coast from Dieppe to keep pace. In view of the small number of forces at my command, I also requested him to take over the defense of the Somme to as far as the vicinity west of Amiens, and further requested support by the artillery forces of his army at Amiens. General von Zangen asked for time to consider, promising to inform me during the night. I further arranged for Gause to inform Lieutenant General Speidel, the chief of staff of Army Group B, as well as the subordinate corps.[1] I also arranged for orders to be sent to those divisions that were responsible for the bridges across the Somme, stressing that arrangements must be made to guarantee the demolition of the bridges in the event of a surprise attack by enemy tanks.

At about 9 P.M., my chief of staff arrived with a few other officers. Gause and I oriented them. No new reports arrived before 11 P.M., I asked to be called in the event any important messages arrived during the night. However, I was not disturbed.

*My Capture.*

I arose at about 5 A.M. on August 31. At 5:30 A.M., we [Eberbach and Gersdorff] had breakfast with Dietrich and Gause, who were ready to leave. After breakfast, I saw from the map that, according to a message received during the night, an enemy spearhead had advanced to within 15 kilometers [9.3 miles] south of us. I asked Gause about this. He confirmed that a message had been received during the night to that effect, but added that the person reporting had no doubt just been seeing ghosts. I inquired whether anything had been done—whether any reconnaissance had been undertaken. However, that had not been considered necessary.

I then accompanied Sepp Dietrich to his car. Before he had even entered the car, tank-gun fire and machine gun fire were suddenly heard in the immediate vicinity. Sepp Dietrich and his staff left. [Actually, Dietrich sped away, and the British—who obviously assumed (correctly) that there was someone important in the staff car—pursued him for some miles. It was, in fact, a race. Dietrich escaped only because his car was faster than the British reconnaissance vehicles.] The enemy had arrived. We immediately prepared for departure and sent off messages to army group and all corps headquarters that the enemy tanks had advanced to our immediate vicinity and that we were transferring to Metz-en-Conture and would then attempt to break out in some direction. On the way, I received a message from Amiens, which read: "In a surprise attack British tanks penetrated Amiens and continued northward."

Our attempts to escape were fruitless. At 7:30 A.M., we were captured. Only my chief of staff, Major General von Gersdorff, and my I-a (operations officer), Major Gemmerich, succeeded in escaping on foot.

*General Eberbach thus never actually assumed command of the 5th Panzer Army for the second time, because of the intervention of the enemy. He was attempting to escape in a Volkswagen when he was apprehended by members of the British 11th Armoured Division. Gersdorff and Gemmerich made good their escape and eventually joined Gen. of Panzer Troops Erich Brandenberger, who had been charged with the task of rebuilding the 7th Army. Sepp Dietrich remained in command of the 5th Panzer until September 12, when he was replaced by Gen. of Panzer Troops Baron Hasso von Manteuffel. Dietrich was given command of the 6th (later 6th SS) Panzer Army.*

*Reflections.*

Field Marshal Model's decision, taken immediately after his arrival on the Western Front, to retire Army Group B first to behind the Seine and from there in leaps to the Meuse was the right course to adopt. The fact was that this decision came too late, and it was not the fault of Model.

The 15th Army, which was still intact, should have been employed in time to establish and man covering positions along the Seine and the Somme. The construction troops in the Atlantic Wall should have been utilized for this purpose.

If the Seine front was not to be developed, then the 15th Army, which still had at its disposal all the weapons in the Atlantic bunkers, should have been concentrated along the Somme. Assignment of Engineer Headquarters Vierow for the purpose of developing the Somme positions was insufficient, even though it was good. Neither from the point of view of development nor the occupation could the Somme line be described as a position up to August 31.

On August 18, the 147th Infantry Division was moved from the Channel coast to St. Quentin to defend the Somme. This shows that the intentions were wise. However, one week later, this division was advanced to the northern outskirts of Paris, where its power was soon exhausted in battles that were not of such grave consequences as a determined stand on the Somme would have been. It is unknown to me who gave the orders for this commitment.

The intentions of the Armed Forces High Command (OKW) to pull out the panzer divisions, rehabilitate them, and send them into action against the American eastward thrust was right. On the other hand, however, it was obvious that in the event of the infantry divisions being left to their own devices during their withdrawal to the Somme, they would be crushed by the British armored wedges.

As this would perforce have led to a collapse, as it eventually did, one panzer division at least should have been left behind to halt the enemy armored spearheads and to cover the withdrawal in the center of gravity.

**NOTES**

1.  Dr. Hans Speidel did not remain chief of staff of Army Group B for long. Despite Field Marshal Model's efforts to protect him, Speidel was arrested on suspicion of being involved in the anti-Hitler conspiracy, but his guilt could not be conclusively proven, and the Court of Honor did not expel him from the army; he therefore could not be executed, but he did spend the rest of the war in prison. Freed by French troops in the spring of 1945, he became a university professor. He was chief military negotiator in the European Defense Community discussions of 1952–53. He joined the *Bundeswehr* (the West German Armed Forces) when it was founded in 1955 and became a lieutenant general (the equivalent of a three-star general in the U.S. Army under the new rank structure). He was promoted to full general in 1957. He was the first German to be commander of NATO's Allied Land Forces Central Europe, headquartered in Fontainebleau, France. Speidel retired on March 31, 1964, and died at Bad Honnef, a village on the Rhine, on November 28, 1984.

# CHAPTER 7

# The Last Years

Following his capture by British forces, Eberbach was sent to Trent Park, a VIP prison camp in the London area. Here one of his prison mates was his eldest son, Heinz, a naval lieutenant. Heinz Eugen Eberbach had joined the navy on August 15, 1939, as the international crisis over the Danzig corridor brought the world to the edge of war. He earned his commission, underwent submarine training, and by the fall of 1941 was a watch officer on a U-boat. He did eight patrols on *U-407* before being named commander of *U-230* in southern France in June 1944. *U-230* was the last U-boat operating in the Mediterranean when the massive Allied invasion of southern France began on August 15, 1944. On August 21, *Oberleutnant zur See* Eberbach attempted to attack the invasion fleet but was not able to break through its antisubmarine defenses. He was forced to run aground near St. Mandier, France, where he destroyed his vessel with explosives. He and his entire crew were captured shortly thereafter.[1]

Although the relationship between father and son remained cordial and loving, the twenty-three-year-old lieutenant was duped by Nazi propaganda and still held out hope that Hitler's "wonder weapons" might yet turn the tide in Germany's favor. His more experienced father, on the other hand, deemed the overall situation as "hopeless."[2]

While he was a prisoner of war, British intelligence collected a dossier on General

Eberbach. They noted that Heinz Guderian had praised him highly, noting in Eberbach's fitness report on March 1, 1944, that he was a "lively, open character brimming with confidence . . . proven in battle . . . gutsy, superior panzer leader able to handle the most difficult situations. One of our best." The British intelligence officer noted that he was a "strong character with clear-cut views. Has kept aloof from politics. Supported Nazis some years . . . Has realized that the Nazi government is a criminal body to whom he feels no longer bound by his oath . . . he was in agreement with the Generals' revolt."[3]

British intelligence bugged Eberbach's room and was able to learn that he had knowledge of the anti-Hitler conspiracy prior to July 20,

1944, but did not report it. He was, in fact, prepared to follow the orders of his commander, Field Marshal Rommel, even if they went against those of Adolf Hitler and OKW. As late as July 16, he discussed the anti-Hitler conspiracy with the Desert Fox, who declared that day that Hitler must be "*umlegen*"—a German euphemism for "killed."[4] In his confidential conversations, Eberbach praised Stauffenberg and his confederates for their idealism but criticized their coup as amateurish.

In early 1945, Eberbach lamented the effect that Nazi propaganda had on the German people. He expressed concern that his wife and fifteen-year-old son, who would believe Goebbels's lies and wreck their health laboring for the country and the Nazi war effort. Because of the possibility that his letters could fall into the hands of the Gestapo, Eberbach could only hint at the truth, even after he was captured by the British. (The Gestapo had uncovered the letters of Eberbach's friend and superior, Col. Gen. Rudolf Schmidt, the commander of the 2nd Panzer Army on the Eastern Front. In letters to his brother, Schmidt had made several derogatory remarks about the Nazis in general and Hitler in particular. The Gestapo discovered the letters upon arresting Schmidt's brother in 1943. Schmidt was promptly relieved of his command, expelled from the army, and thrown into a lunatic asylum.)

Eberbach did not seem too upset about the Holocaust when the Allied media initially broke the story. He did not particularly mind that the SS were killing Jewish men—who were often partisans—but was appalled that women and children were also being murdered. He was shocked and mortified, however, when he learned of the magnitude of the Holocaust and was one of the few generals to admit personal responsibility for it, even though he was in no way involved in the murders. "There is not one of us who is not to blame for this human tragedy," he wrote to his wife in July 1945. He also noted that while at Trent Park, he went on what might be described as a voyage of self-discovery. "This time for thought which I have enjoyed here was very necessary for me," he wrote to his wife. "The Bible, Sophocles, Goethe, Shakespeare, they all helped. And nature, too."[5]

After the war ended, Eberbach was transferred to a number of different POW locations in the United Kingdom. In December 1945, he was sent to Aurich as a witness for SS *Oberfuehrer* Kurt "Panzer" Meyer. Although the two men held radically different political views, they were nevertheless friends, and Eberbach would later write the foreword for Meyer's book, *Grenadiers*—even after Meyer had learned that Eberbach was peripherally involved in the anti-Hitler conspiracy and told the general to his face that had he known this in July 1944, he would personally have shot Eberbach from across the table.[6]

During the return flight from Aurich, Eberbach suffered "a serious failure of his health."[7] Sometime in the summer of 1946, he underwent an operation that appears to have corrected whatever was wrong with him. After he recovered, he was transferred to Island Number 11 POW Camp in Wales.

In the fall of 1947, Eberbach was transferred to the American prison at Neustadt/Hesse in Germany. He was released from here on January 6, 1948, and was obliged to undergo a six-month confinement in a hospital. Upon his recovery, the general was in refugee care under the evangelical special care group at Ravensburg.

From the summer of 1950 to the summer of 1962, he acted as assistant director in the Evangelical Academy in Bad Boll, from 1956 on specifically working with soldiers. The entire 2nd Soldiers Convention, held in the year 1950, was his doing.

With the 12th French Cuirassiers, with whom his regiment had engaged in the first armored battle of 1940, and which was lately stationed at Tubingen, the general formed a genuine bond of friendship.

On November 24, 1965, in the sleepy little village of Notzingen, close to Kircheim in Teck a band of the *Bundeswehr* played the Fanfare from the "Old Comrades March." In the entrance to the hotel stood three men wearing Knight's Crosses about their necks. Their guest of honor, General der Panzertruppen a.D. Heinrich Eberbach, was on this day seventy years old. His stride was loose and comfortable. Of medium size, with compelling eyes, this was the man about whom Stauffenberg wrote in 1989, "As a soldier he was so dreaded that the British searched twice as hard for him behind the front near Amiens in August 1944, as a man he was so respected that friends and former foes alike today are pleased to be together with him, to render him honor for no one at any time could ever regard him as anything but an upright and honest soldier."[8]

The greetings of the burgomeister were followed by the speech of Lieutenant Colonel Woehl, the commander of the Darmstadt Panzer Battalion of the *Bundeswehr*, which carried on the tradition of Eberbach's 35th Panzer Regiment.

More especially heartfelt, though, was the reception of the peacetime commander of the 35th Panzer Regiment in Bamberg. It was held by Lieutenant Colonel Tilson, the commander of the American 35th Armored Battalion, at this time stationed at that very same garrison town of Bamberg. In addition to Eberbach, retired colonel Hans Christern was also there; he had been the last commander of the Bamberg regiment. As a major and commander of the 2nd Battalion of the 31st Panzer Regiment, he had been awarded the Knights' Cross. Both soldiers had known each other well for thirty years. Maj. Arthur Wollschlaeger had also come. As a young lieutenant, he had commanded the 2nd Company of the regiment under Eberbach and was awarded the Knight's Cross on January 23, 1942, for his conduct of operations in the battles of the Russian winter.

The American 4th Armored Division had designated Eberbach, the former commander of the 4th Panzer Division and their antagonist on the invasion front, an honorary armored soldier of their division. Thus they recognized Eberbach as a person of incontestable rectitude and integrity.

General Eberbach reportedly spent his last months in a retirement home. He died on July 13, 1992, at ninety-six years old.

## NOTES

1. Sonke Neitzel *Tapping Hitler's Generals: Transcripts of Secret Conversations, 1942–45*, Geoffrey Brooks, trans. (Barnsley, United Kingdom: Pen and Sword Ltd., 2007), 289. Heinz Eugen Eberbach was released from the POW camps in February 1946. He resumed his career with the West German Army in late 1956 and eventually retired as a full commander. He died on November 20, 1982.
2. Ibid.
3. Ibid.
4. Ibid., 57. Rommel was critically wounded by an Allied fighter-bomber the next day.
5. Ibid., 52. Initially, Eberbach did not seem to believe that even a million Jews had been murdered. He was appalled when he learned the true magnitude of the Holocaust.
6. Tony Foster, *Meeting of the Generals* (Toronto: Methuen, 1986)
7. Stauffenberg Papers.
8. Ibid.

# APPENDIX A

# Table of Comparative Ranks

| U.S. Army | German Army |
|---|---|
| General of the army | Field marshal (*Generalfeldmarschall*) |
| General | Colonel general (*Generaloberst*) |
| Lieutenant general | General of Infantry, Panzer Troops, etc. |
| Major general | Lieutenant general (*Generalleutnant*) |
| Brigadier general* | Major general (*Generalmajor*) |
| Colonel | Colonel (*Oberst*) |
| Lieutenant colonel | Lieutenant Colonel (*Oberstleutnant*) |
| Major | Major (*Major*) |
| Captain | Captain (*Hauptmann*) |
| First lieutenant | First lieutenant (*Oberleutnant*) |
| Second lieutenant | Second lieutenant (*Leutnant*) |
| None | Senior officer cadet or ensign (*Faehnrich*) |
| Officer candidate | Officer-cadet (*Fahnenjunker*) |

* Brigadier in British Army

# APPENDIX B

# German Staff Positions

Chief of staff (not present below the corps level)

I-a.  Chief of operations

I-b.  Quartermaster (chief supply officer)

I-c.  Staff officer, intelligence (subordinate to I-a)

I-d.  Chief training officer (not always present)

II-a.  Chief personnel officer (adjutant)

II-b.  Second personnel officer (subordinate to II-a)

III.  Chief judge advocate (subordinate to II-a)

IV-a.  Chief administrative officer (subordinate to I-b)

IV-b.  Chief medical officer (subordinate to I-b)

IV-c.  Chief veterinary officer (subordinate to I-b)

IV-d.  Chaplain (subordinate to II-a)

V.  Motor transport officer (subordinate to I-b)

National Socialist guidance officer (added 1944)

Special staff officers (chief of artillery, chief of projectors [rocket launchers], etc.)

# Characteristics of Selected German and Allied Tanks of World War II

| Model | Weight (in tons) | Speed (mph) | Range (miles) | Main Armament | Crew |
|---|---|---|---|---|---|
| **BRITISH** | | | | | |
| Mark IV "Churchill" | 43.1 | 15 | 120 | 16–pounder | 5 |
| Mark VI "Crusader" | 22.1 | 27 | 200 | 12–pounder | 5 |
| Mark VIII "Cromwell" | 30.8 | 38 | 174 | 175mm | 5 |
| **AMERICAN*** | | | | | |
| M3A1 "Stuart" | 14.3 | 36 | 60 | 137mm | 4 |
| M4A3 "Sherman" | 37.1 | 30 | 120 | 176mm | 5 |
| **GERMAN** | | | | | |
| PzKw II | 9.3 | 25 | 118 | 120mm | 3 |
| PzKw III | 24.5 | 25 | 160 | 150mm | 5 |
| PzKw IV | 19.7 | 26 | 125 | 175mm | 5 |
| PzKw V "Panther" | 49.3 | 25 | 125 | 175mm | 5 |
| PzKw VI "Tiger" | 62.0 | 23 | 73 | 188mm | 5 |
| **RUSSIAN** | | | | | |
| T34/Model 76 | 29.7 | 32 | 250 | 176mm | 4 |
| T34/Model 85 | 34.4 | 32 | 250 | 185mm | 5 |
| KV 1 | 52 | 25 | 208 | 176.2mm | 5 |
| JSII "Joseph Stalin" | 45.5 | 23 | 150 | 122mm | 4 |

* All American tanks were also in the British inventory. The British "Sherman" was sometimes outfitted with a heavier main battle gun and was called a "Firefly."

# Bibliography

**BOOKS, MANUSCRIPTS, AND JOURNAL ARTICLES**

Absolon, Rudolf, comp. *Rangliste der Generale der deutschen Luftwaffe nach dem Stand vom 20. April 1945.* Friedberg, Germany: Podzun-Pallas-Verlag, 1984.

Barnett, Correlli, ed. *Hitler's Generals.* London: Weidenfeld and Nicolson, 1989.

Blumenson, Martin. *Breakout and Pursuit.* Washington, DC: Office of the Chief of Military History, Department of the Army, 1961.

———. "Recovery of France." In Vincent J. Esposito, ed., *A Concise History of World War II.* New York: Praeger, 1964.

Blumentritt, Guenther. *Von Rundstedt: The Soldier and the Man.* London: Odhams Press, 1952.

Breuer, William B. *Death of a Nazi Army.* New York: Stein and Day, 1985.

———. *Hitler's Fortress Cherbourg.* New York: Stein and Day, 1984.

Carell, Paul. *Invasion: They're Coming!* New York: Dutton, 1963.

Chandler, David G., and James Lawton Collins, Jr., eds. *The D-Day Encyclopedia.* New York: Simon & Schuster, 1994.

Choltitz, Dietrich von. *Soldat unter Soldaten.* Konstanz, Germany: Europa Verlag, 1951.

Cooper, Matthew. *The German Army, 1933–1945.* London: Macdonald and Jane's, 1978.

D'Este, Carlo. *Decision in Normandy.* New York: Dutton, 1983.

Dierich, Wolfgang. *Die Verbaende der Luftwaffe, 1935–1945.* Stuttgart, Germany: Motorbuch-Verlag, 1976.

Eberbach, Hans. "Pz Group Eberbach at Alencon and its break through the Encirclement of Falaise." Foreign Military Studies MS #A-922. Unpublished manuscript, Historical Division, Headquarters, U.S. Forces, European Theater, 1946.

———. "Report on the Fighting of Panzergruppe West (Fifth Pz Army) from July 3–9 August 1944." Foreign Military Studies MS #B-840. Unpublished manuscript, Office of the Chief of Military History.

Ellis, L. F. *Victory in the West.* Vol. I. *The Battle of Normandy.* London: Her Majesty's Stationery Office, 1968.

Essame, H. "Normandy Revisited." *Military Review* 43, no. 12 (December 1963): 76–77.

Florentin, Eddy. *The Battle of Falaise Gap.* Meryvn Savill, trans. London: Elek Books, 1965.

Forman, James. *Code Name Valkyrie: Count von Stauffenberg and the Plot to Kill Hitler.* New York: S. G. Phillips, 1975.

Foster, Tony. *Meeting of the Generals.* Toronto: Methuen, 1986.

Fuerbringer, Herbert. *9.SS-Panzer-Division.* Heimdal, Germany: Editions Heimdal, 1984.

Gavin, James M. *On to Berlin.* New York: Viking Press, 1978.

Gersdorff, Rudolf-Christoph von. "Avranches Counterattack, Seventh Army (29 Jul-14 Aug 1944)," Foreign Military Studies MS #A-921. Unpublished manuscript, Office of the Chief of Military History.

Geyr von Schweppenburg, Baron Leo. "Panzer Group West (mid-1943–15 July 1944)." Foreign Military Studies MS #B-258 and MS #B-466. Unpublished manuscript, Office of the Chief of Military History.

———. "Panzer Tactics in Normandy." U.S. Army ETHINT 3, an interrogation conducted at Irschenhausen, Germany, December 11, 1947. On file, U.S. National Archives.

Goralski, Robert. *World War II Almanac, 1931–1945.* New York: Putnam, 1981.

Graber, Gerry S. *Stauffenberg.* New York: Ballantine Books, 1973.

Greenfield, Kent R., ed. *Command Decisions.* Washington, DC: Office of the Chief of Military History, Department of the Army, 1960.

Guderian, Heinz. *Panzer Leader.* London: M. Joseph, 1952.

Harrison, Gordon A. *Cross-Channel Attack.* Washington, DC: Office of the Chief of Military History, Department of the Army, 1951.

Hastings, Max. *Das Reich.* London: M. Joseph, 1981.

Haupt, Werner. *Das Buch der Panzertruppe, 1916–1945.* Friedberg, Germany: Podzun-Pallas, 1989.

———. *Rueckzug im Westen, 1944.* Stuttgart, Germany: Motorbuch-Verlag, 1978.

Hayn, Friedrich. *Die Invasion von Cotentin bis Falaise.* Heidelberg, Germany: K. Vowinckel, 1954.

Hildebrand, Karl-Friedrich. *Die Generale der Luftwaffe.* 3 vols. Osnabrueck, Germany: Biblio, 1990–92.

Hildebrand, Hans H., and Ernst Henriot. *Deutschlands Admirale, 1849–1945.* 4 vols. Osnabrueck, Germany: Biblio, 1988–96.

Hoehne, Heinz. *Canaris.* J. Maxwell Brownjohn, trans. Garden City, NY: Doubleday, 1979.

Hoffman, Peter. *The History of the German Resistance, 1933–1945.* London: Macdonald and Jane's, 1977.

Irving, David. *Hitler's War.* New York: Viking Press, 1977.

———. *The Trail of the Fox.* New York: Dutton, 1977.

Jacobsen, Hans A., and J. Rohwer, eds., *Decisive Battles of World War II: The German View.* New York: Putnam, 1965.

Keilig, Wolf. *Die Generale des Heeres.* Friedberg, Germany: Podzun-Pallas-Verlag, 1983.

Kluge, Guenther von, Personnel Record. Air University Archives, Maxwell Air Force Base, Alabama.

Kraetschmer, Ernst-Guenther. *Die Ritterkreuztraeger der Waffen-SS.* 3rd ed. Preussisch Oldendorf, Germany: K. W. Schuetz-Verlag, 1982.

*Kriegstagebuch des Oberkommando des Wehrmacht (Fuehrungsstab).* 4 vols. Frankfurt am Main, Germany: Bernard & Graefe, 1961–65.

Kurowski, Franz. *Das Tor zur Festung Europa.* Neckargemuend, Germany: Vowinckel, 1966.

Liddell Hart, Basil H. *History of the Second World War.* 2 vols. New York: Putnam, 1970.

———. *The Other Side of the Hill.* London: Cassell, 1948.

Luettwitz, Heinrich von. "Avranches." Foreign Military Studies MS #A-904. Unpublished manuscript, Office of the Chief of Military History.

Luther, Craig W. H. *Blood and Honor: The History of the 12th SS Panzer Division "Hitler Youth," 1943–1945.* San Jose, CA: James Bender, 1987.

MacDonald, Charles, and Martin Blumenson. "Recovery of France." In Vincent J. Esposito, ed. *A Concise History of World War II.* New York: Praeger, 1964.

Mason, David. *Breakout: Drive to the Seine.* New York: Ballantine Books, 1969.

McKee, Alexander. *Last Round against Rommel.* New York: New American Library, 1966.

Mehner, Kurt, ed. *Die Geheimen Tagesberichte der deutschen Wehrmachtfuehrung im Zweiten Weltkrieg, 1939–1945.* 12 vols. Osnabrueck, Germany: Biblio, 1984–95.

Mellenthin, Friedrich Wilhelm von. *Panzer Battles: A Study in the Employment of Armor in the Second World War.* Norman, OK: University of Oklahoma Press, 1956.

Messenger, Charles. *The Last Prussian: A Biography of Field Marshal Gerd von Rundstedt, 1875–1953.* Washington, DC: Brassey's, 1991.

Miller, Robert A. *August 1944.* Novato, CA: Presidio, 1988.

Mitcham, Samuel W., Jr. *Men of the Luftwaffe.* Novato, CA: Presidio, 1988.

———. *Rommel's Desert Commanders.* Westport, CT: Praeger, 2007.

Montgomery, Bernard Law, the Viscount of Alamein. *Normandy to the Baltic.* Boston: Houghton Mifflin, 1948.

Neitzel, Sonke. *Tapping Hitler's Generals: Transcripts of Secret Conversations, 1942–45.* Trans. Geoffrey Brooks. Barnsley, United Kingdom: Pen and Sword Ltd., 2007.

Perger, Mark C. *SS-Oberst-Gruppenfuehrer und Generaloberst der Waffen-SS Paul Hausser.* Winnipeg, Canada: J. J. Fedorowicz Publishers, 1986.

Perrett, Bryan. *Knights of the Black Cross.* New York: St. Martin's Press, 1986.

Preradovich, Nikolaus von. *Die Generale der Waffen-SS.* Berg am See, Germany: Vowinckel-Verlag, 1985.

Ritgen, Helmut. *Die Geschichte der Panzer-Lehr-Division im Westen, 1944–1945.* Stuttgart, Germany: Motorbuch-Verlag, 1979.

Rommel, Erwin. *The Rommel Papers.* B. H. Liddell Hart, ed. New York: Harcourt, Brace, 1953.

Ruge, Friedrich. "The Invasion of Normandy" in H. A. Jacobsen and J. Rohwer, eds., *Decisive Battles of World War II: The German View.* New York: Putnam, 1965.

———. *Rommel in Normandy.* Ursula R. Moessner, trans. San Rafael, CA: Presidio Press, 1979.

Ryan, Cornelius. *The Longest Day.* New York: Simon & Schuster, 1959.

Scheibert, Horst. *Die Traeger des Deutschen Kreuzes in Gold: das Heer.* Friedberg, Germany: Podzun-Pallas-Verlag, 1983.

Schneider, Jost W. *Verleihung Genehmigt!* Ed. and trans. Winder McConnell. San Jose, CA: R. James Bender Publishing, 1977.

Seaton, Albert. *The Battle for Moscow.* New York: Stein and Day, 1971.

————. *The Fall of Fortress Europe, 1943–1945.* New York: Holmes & Meier Publishers, 1981.

————. *The Russo-German War, 1941–45.* New York: Praeger, 1960.

Shulman, Milton. *Defeat in the West.* Westport, CT: Greenwood Press, 1971.

Speidel, Hans. *Invasion 1944.* Chicago: Regnery, 1950.

Stacey, C. P. *Official History of the Canadian Army in the Second World War.* Vol. 3. *The Victory Campaign (The Operations in North-West Europe, 1944–1945).* Ottawa, Canada: E. Cloutier, 1960.

Stauffenberg, Friedrich von. "Panzer Commanders of the Western Front." Unpublished manuscript in possession of the author.

————. Papers. Unpublished papers in possession of the author.

Stoves, Rolf. *Die Gepanzerten und Motorisierten deutschen Grossverbaende: Divisionen und selbstaendige Brigaden, 1935–1945.* Friedberg, Germany: Podzun-Pallas-Verlag, 1986.

Stumpf, Richard. *Die Wehrmacht-Elite: Rang- und Herkunftsstruktur der deutschen Generale und Admirale, 1933–1945.* Boppard am Rhein, Germany: H. Boldt, 1982.

Tessin, Georg. *Verbaende und Truppen der deutschen Wehrmacht und Waffen-SS im Zweiten Weltkrieg, 1939–1945.* 16 vols. Osnabrueck, Germany: Biblio-Verlag, 1979–86.

Thomas, Franz. *Die Eichenlaubtraeger.* 2 vols. Osnabrueck, Germany: Biblio, 1997–98.

Tippelskirch, Kurt von. *Geschichte des Zweiten Weltkrieges.* Bonn, Germany: Athenaeum-Verlag, 1951.

Warlimont, Walter. *Inside Hitler's Headquarters.* Trans. R. H. Barry. Novato, CA: Presidio, 1964.

Wilmot, Chester. *The Struggle for Europe.* New York: Harper, 1952.

Winterstein, Ernst Martin, and Hans Jacobs. *General Meindl und seine Fallschirmjaeger: Vom Sturmregiment zum II. Fallschirmjaegerkorps, 1940–1945.* Braunschweig, Germany: Suchdienst des Bundes Deutscher Fallschirmjaeger, 1976.

Yerger, Mark C. *Waffen-SS Commanders.* 2 vols. Atglen, PA: Schiffer, 1997–99.

Ziemke, Earl F. *Stalingrad to Berlin: The German Defeat in the East.* Washington, DC: Office of the Chief of Military History, U.S. Army, 1968.

Zimmermann, Bodo. "OB West: Command Relationships." Foreign Military Studies MS #308. Unpublished manuscript, Office of the Chief of Military History.

**INTERNET SOURCES**

www.forum.axishistory.com. Accessed 2005 and 2006.

www.islandfarm.fsnet.co.uk. Accessed 2006.

# Index of Military Units

## British

2nd Armoured Division, 42, 90
2nd Army, 61
2nd Tactical Air Force, 88
4th Army, 35
VIII Corps, 42
11th Armoured Division, 177
21st Army Group, 98
49th Infantry Division, 42
50th Infantry Division, 42
51st Highland Division, 100
Guards Armoured Division, 93

## Canadian

1st Army, 90, 98
II Corps, 98, 100
2nd Infantry Division, 100
3rd Infantry Division, 100
4th Armoured Division, 100

## French

2nd Armored Division, 97

## German

1st Army, 33, 34, 42
1st Infantry Division, 16
I SS Panzer Corps, 33, 66, 70, 81, 84, 96
1st SS Panzer Division, 33, 34, 55, 66, 70, 76, 78, 79, 80, 81, 86, 90, 91, 95, 96, 97, 99, 144, 150, 151–52, 158, 159
2nd Panzer Army, 182
2nd Panzer Division, 4, 33, 34, 55, 67, 80, 82, 86, 87, 89, 90, 97, 144, 150, 151, 152
2nd Panzer Group, 8
II Parachute Corps, 61, 93, 168
II SS Panzer Corps, 42, 66, 67, 70, 71, 74, 75, 76, 82, 84, 93, 94, 95, 147, 151, 153, 155, 156, 157, 160
2nd SS Panzer Division, 33, 58, 86, 88, 89, 97, 144, 147, 155
3rd Air Fleet, 62
III Flak Corps, 37, 55–56, 61–62, 65
3rd Panzer Division, 6, 16
IV Infantry Corps, 17
4th Panzer Division, vii, 4, 5, 6, 7, 8, 10, 11, 184
5th Panzer Army, vii, 32, 83, 84, 86, 89, 90, 95, 98, 143, 146, 147, 149, 155, 157, 159, 167, 168, 169, 170, 173, 176, 177
5th Parachute Division, 89
6th Panzer Army, 177
6th SS Panzer Army, 177
7th Army, 33, 34, 39, 42, 53, 55, 58, 86, 87, 88, 89, 90, 91, 93, 95, 96, 98, 102, 143, 146, 147, 149, 151, 153, 155, 156, 158, 159, 160, 167, 168, 169, 170
9th Panzer Division, 33, 86, 97, 98, 146, 147, 148, 150, 151, 159
9th SS Panzer Division, 42, 55, 66, 84, 86, 90, 94, 98, 146, 147
10th Army, 5
10th SS Panzer Division, 55, 66, 71, 73, 75, 86, 90, 94, 98, 146, 159
11th Panzer Division, 33
12th SS Panzer Division, 33, 34, 37, 42, 55, 66, 68, 70, 76, 79, 81, 86, 96, 98, 100, 101
13th Panzer Division, 17
15th Army, 33, 34, 39, 58, 60, 86, 170, 171
16th Luftwaffe Field Division, 66, 67–69, 77, 81, 82, 83

# General Index

# Stackpole Military History Series

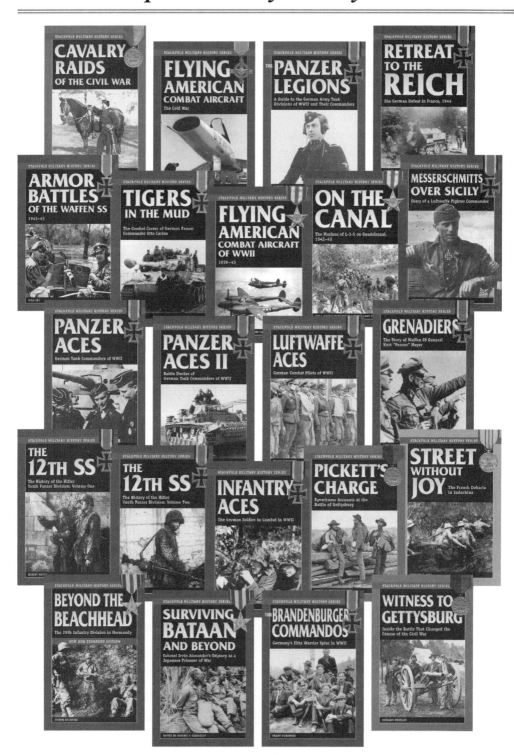

# Real battles. Real soldiers. Real stories.

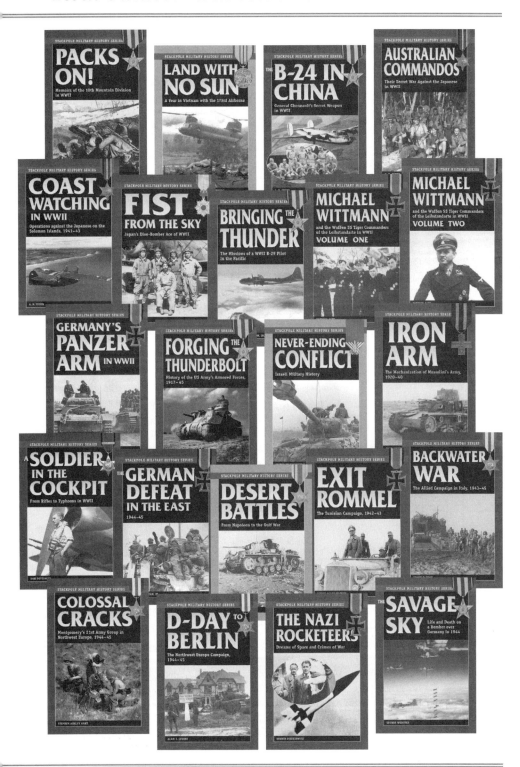

# *Stackpole Military History Series*

# *Real battles. Real soldiers. Real stories.*

# Stackpole Military History Series

# Real battles. Real soldiers. Real stories.

**GOODWOOD**
STACKPOLE MILITARY HISTORY SERIES
The British Offensive in Normandy, July 1944
IAN DAGLISH

**DESTINATION NORMANDY**
STACKPOLE MILITARY HISTORY SERIES
Three American Regiments on D-Day

**EXPENDABLE WARRIORS**
STACKPOLE MILITARY HISTORY SERIES
The Battle of Khe Sanh and the Vietnam War
BRUCE B. G. CLARKE

**D-DAY DECEPTION**
STACKPOLE MILITARY HISTORY SERIES
Operation Fortitude and the Normandy Invasion

**RED STAR UNDER THE BALTIC**
STACKPOLE MILITARY HISTORY SERIES
A Soviet Submariner in WWII

NEW for Spring 2009

**HITLER'S NEMESIS**
STACKPOLE MILITARY HISTORY SERIES
The Red Army, 1930–45
WALTER S. DUNN, JR., WITH A FOREWORD BY DAVID GLANTZ

**PENALTY STRIKE**
STACKPOLE MILITARY HISTORY SERIES
The Memoirs of a Red Army Penal Company Commander, 1943–45
ALEXANDER V. PYL'CYN

# Stackpole Military History Series

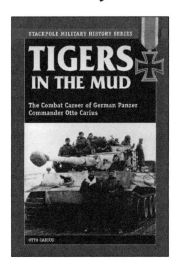

# TIGERS IN THE MUD

## THE COMBAT CAREER OF GERMAN PANZER COMMANDER OTTO CARIUS

*Otto Carius,*
*translated by Robert J. Edwards*

World War II began with a metallic roar as the
German Blitzkrieg raced across Europe, spearheaded
by the most dreadful weapon of the twentieth century:
the Panzer. Tank commander Otto Carius thrusts the
reader into the thick of battle, replete with the
blood, smoke, mud, and gunpowder so common
to the elite German fighting units.

*$19.95 • Paperback • 6 x 9 • 368 pages*
*51 photos • 48 illustrations • 3 maps*

## WWW.STACKPOLEBOOKS.COM
## 1-800-732-3669

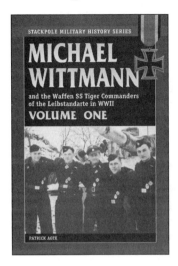
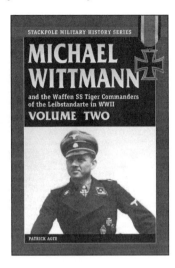

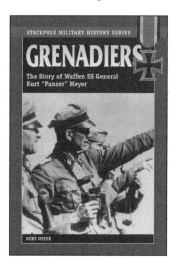

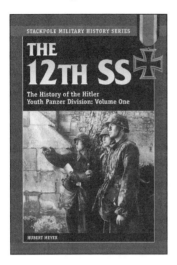 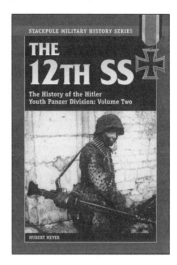

# Stackpole Military History Series

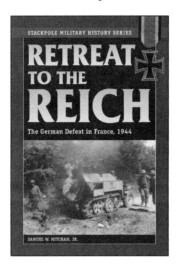

# RETREAT TO THE REICH
## THE GERMAN DEFEAT IN FRANCE, 1944
*Samuel W. Mitcham, Jr.*

The Allied landings on D-Day, June 6, 1944, marked the beginning of the German defeat in the West in World War II. From the experiences of soldiers in the field to decision-making at high command, military historian Samuel Mitcham vividly recaptures the desperation of the Wehrmacht as it collapsed amidst the brutal hedgerow fighting in Normandy, losing its four-year grip on France as it was forced to retreat back to the German border. While German forces managed to temporarily halt the Allied juggernaut there, this brief success only delayed the fate that had been sealed with the defeat in France.

*$17.95 • Paperback • 6 x 9 • 304 pages • 26 photos, 12 maps*

## WWW.STACKPOLEBOOKS.COM
## 1-800-732-3669

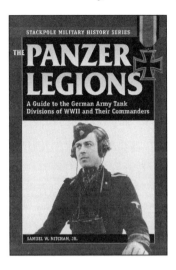

# Stackpole Military History Series

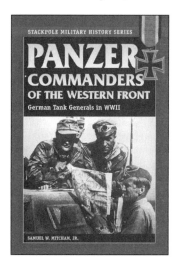

# PANZER COMMANDERS
# OF THE WESTERN FRONT
## GERMAN TANK GENERALS IN WWII
*Samuel W. Mitcham, Jr.*

Generals like Heinz Guderian have received most of the credit
for devising and executing the German blitzkrieg, but without
the field commanders who led armored corps, divisions, and
regiments, the lightning offensive that overtook France in
1940 could not have triumphed. Nor could the Germans have
lasted as long as they did against the Allied onslaught in
northwest Europe in 1944–45. Mitcham profiles five of these
panzer leaders, from the fall of France to Normandy, the
Battle of the Bulge, and the final struggle for Germany.

*$17.95 • Paperback • 6 x 9 • 272 pages • 37 b/w photos, 19 maps*

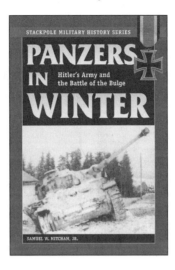

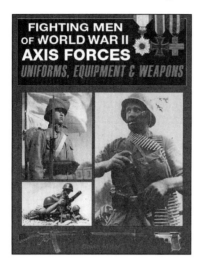 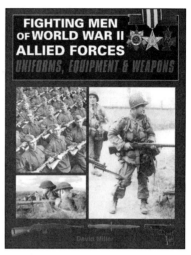